D1605904

A Process Philosophy of Signs

A Process Philosophy of Signs

James Williams

EDINBURGH
University Press

© James Williams, 2016

Edinburgh University Press Ltd
The Tun – Holyrood Road,
12(2f) Jackson's Entry,
Edinburgh EH8 8PJ
www.euppublishing.com

Typeset in 11/13 Adobe Sabon by
IDSUK (DataConnection) Ltd, and
printed and bound in the United States of America

A CIP record for this book is available from the British Library

ISBN 978 0 7486 9500 3 (hardback)
ISBN 978 0 7486 9502 7 (webready PDF)
ISBN 978 0 7486 9501 0 (paperback)
ISBN 978 0 7486 9503 4 (epub)

The right of James Williams to be identified as the author of this work has been asserted
in accordance with the Copyright, Designs and Patents Act 1988, and the Copyright and
Related Rights Regulations 2003 (SI No. 2498).

Contents

Acknowledgements

Research for this book was supported by the Carnegie Trust for the Universities Scotland and the Alfred Deakin Research Institute for Citizenship and Globalisation. I benefited greatly from generous questions and remarks by audiences on papers preparing for the book at the following seminars and conferences: 'Lyotard et le langage' Paris 1, Panthéon-Sorbonne; UCL Institute of Education Research Seminar; the Australian Society for Continental Philosophy Annual Conference, Melbourne 2014; Department of Management and Marketing, University of Melbourne; Philosophy, Metaphor and Violence conference, Deakin University; Politics of Signs and Practices of Transformation workshop, Wollongong University; Collectives in French Thought conference, Deakin University; Society for Phenomenology and Existential Philosophy annual conference, New Orleans; A Thousand Plateaus and Philosophy workshop, New Orleans; Erasmus Mundus postgraduate students seminar, Université de Toulouse 2; SEP-FEP joint conference, Utrecht University; Deleuze's Cultural Encounters with the New Humanities conference, Shue Yan University, Hong Kong; and Séminaire machines et imaginations, Université Paris 7. I learned much from my students at Dundee University and as professeur invité at Université Paris 8. I would like to thank my colleagues at Dundee, Dominic Smith, Todd Mei, Ashley Woodward and Nicholas Davey, and at Deakin, Jack Reynolds and Sean Bowden, as well as John Protevi, Jeffrey Bell, Anne Sauvagnargues, Michael Wheeler, Nardina Kaur, Rosi Braidotti, Andrew McDonald, Pierre Cassou-Noguès and Dan Smith for their valuable critical insights and even more valuable support. Jon Roffe very kindly shared his research on signs and markets with me. This taught me much and allowed me to see new fields for the

process philosophy of signs. Carol Macdonald, Tim Clark, James Dale and Rebecca Mackenzie at Edinburgh University Press gave me editorial and artwork support that were essential for bringing this project to fruition. As ever, this book could not have been written without the love of Claire, Rebecca, Nathan and Alice.
{for, R, N, A, C, O, R}

Introduction: The Process Sign

So you turn around and there it is: a cross of dripping white paint on the door. Your home has been marked with a sign. What does it mean?

The question is an understandable reaction, steeped in the history not only of signs singling out people, but also of ways of defining signs. Signs have meaning. They are about an indication and a sense. Maybe the cross is like the yellow jack flying over a ship. With its black and yellow quadrants the flag signifies disease and quarantine. Maybe the drips and hasty brush strokes lead back to hateful crowds. The meaning is then not only in the direct indication of a scapegoat but also in the irrational fears and violent impulses of an ignorant mass and perhaps the plans of more cynical leaders.

The question of meaning and indication is the wrong one though. Or rather it is the wrong question to begin with, if you want to understand the real workings and power of the sign, if you want to define signs in the right way. The sign is not a fixed relation between an indicator and a meaning, where the yellow and black checked flag simply means quarantine. It is not a mark that signifies reliably; for example when a hasty demarcation of a vulnerable subgroup signifies the threat of a pogrom. The sign has a meaning, but it is never fixed. The sign is a mark, but it is not reliable. Why?

The main argument of this process philosophy of signs is that the sign is neither static nor dependable because the sign is many different processes. The sign is not a fixed relation over any period of time; it is changing and it changes other things. The paint on your door is drying and the colour is fading; the meaning of the cross varies with its surroundings. The effect of the sign changes you. The day started out well. Children were playing upstairs; a pot was brewing fresh tea. Now, the young have been marked out and a threat hangs over them. Your tea will taste bitter behind drawn curtains. The sign is doing this. How should we think of it to account for all these changes?

The preliminary task of the process philosophy is to define the different processes at work in the sign. It will be argued that they are interdependent and they set conditions for one another. First, the sign is a selection. In order to appear as a sign the threatening message painted on your home had to bring together a set of elements; for instance, the sign is yourself, your door, your thoughts about a message, your feelings, white paint and the shape of a cross. There is a selection of a set, the condition for the appearance of any sign, before there can be meaning.

A cup of tea as a sign could be the set made up of tea, breakfast, Britishness and tradition, but it could also be tea, tea leaves and the hills of Sri Lanka, the history of plantation life, the exploitation of young women and its many modern guises. The pictures on boxes of tea on my breakfast tables sometimes took the sign one way, reflecting an early cool and good humour of British family life back on those supposedly living it; sometimes they went another, showing distant hills and happy pickers, in images dishonestly shorn of the struggles of plantation labour.

One of the main aims of this book is to give a formal definition of the process sign. The effectiveness of structuralism as a science of signs and of semiology as the practical interpretation of signs has rested on generally applicable formal models. This process philosophy seeks to renew the fading success of those disciplines. The variety and complexity of signs requires an incisive mode of explanation and analysis. Formal definitions allow for economical and yet profound presentations of the sign stemming from the logical extension of graphic representation. The formal model combines direct presentation with rigorous and far-reaching consequences. However, one of the more persistent criticisms of formalism is its inability to grasp its subject accurately. The form is not adequate to the thing, in the same way as the general definition of a species falls short of individuals belonging to it. The formal definition might not be adequate to real signs. To respond to this critical point the argument here is dialectical: the suggested model for the sign is to be constructed in debate with opposed positions and cases. So, although I am about to give an initial presentation of the sign free of wider debate, in the following chapters each definition will arise out of a critical discussion with alternatives.

Formally, the process philosophy defines the sign as the selection of a set. This selection is {a, b, c} where the elements a, b and c stand for any combination of elements a, b, c, and so on. Importantly, anything can be an element. A sign is identified through a selected set. 'Why do you look so troubled?' your partner asks you. The answer could be this sign: {us, our door, fresh white paint, dripping cross, threat, disquiet about the future}.

The challenge of this speculative process philosophy is in the claim that every sign is a selected set {a, b, c}. This implies that signs have two names: the usual proper name 'the dripping cross', and the selected set. A consequent claim is then that any familiar sign can be given as a selected set; for instance {red, stop} and {green, go} for very simple indicators of halt and proceed. This capacity to be rendered as a set holds for more complex signs; for example {sun, clouds, alternating, today, 12 hours from 9 a.m.} for the sign of a day of variable weather.

How can a set be a process? The nature of sets seems to run opposite to movement and change. As a group of elements a set is a fixed relation. It is a belonging and not a becoming. But this is a misunderstanding of how the set works for the process sign. I have used the terms 'select a set', 'identified by a selected set' and 'grouping together' to describe the set as selection. The sign is not sufficiently determined by the set alone. It works through the selection of a set, and this is a process.

No set is independent of the event of its selection. The elements of the set and those not included in it are determined by the event of selection such that they cannot be considered satisfactorily as independent of the event connecting and disconnecting the elements. When you buy a second-hand item, or when a friend tries to convince you to let go of a bad experience, there is an attempt to break with an earlier state and to constitute a new set. Nonetheless, wider associations linger after the supposed break and the new remains in the grip of the old. *One careful owner, 'perfectly maintained', the marketplace advert said ... You've got to get over him... She's no good for you...*

Selection is a drawing out and a bringing together. The elements of the set are taken out of a background consisting of all other elements. They are also brought together and united in the set. Two processes then: extraction and collection. You did this – or rather a selection happened to you – when the cross on your door was drawn out of the background of many things: wear and tear on the step, clouds hovering slightly lower over your roof, neighbours' curtains swishing back and forth in observant suspicion. In order for the sign to appear as sign it had to collect some elements by drawing away from others.

There is a trick of perspective in the idea of drawing out. We focus on the elements isolated by the extraction; when a lassoed calf is separated from the herd, the director's camera and our attention are attracted to the single beast about to be branded by the hot iron. The rest of the herd are affected too, though, as they trample with fear and apprehension. So we could reverse our attention away from the elements isolated by extraction and return to the open set of all other things. To draw out is to alter two groups of things in different ways. The selected elements are brought together and extracted. The remaining elements are shorn away from and relegated.

In the next chapter, I will introduce a new term to explain this two-way process. It is linked to the idea of a background to the sign: all the elements the set selects from. The term 'background' overemphasises that which comes to the fore. It connects too readily to ideas of a still figure and a less distinct ground such as we encounter, for instance, in crude descriptions of figure-based paintings. So instead I will speak of the substratum to the set. The substratum is everything left out of the selected set and yet transformed in detailed and precise ways by the extraction. The set and its substratum are in ongoing and open-ended transformation. The singeing of the calf's hide resounds back through the herd while this wider panic increases its terror.

Signs operate on their substratum. The selection changes values in activities such as attention and concern in the case of animals, or activities and states for other living and material things. You were going to inspect a leaking drain as you turned back to the house, but the selection by the paint sign devalued your attention to the leak and your concern for its effects. The smell of burning puts forest animals on alert and turns their attention to flight. As a process sign, an electric current activates a cell and changes its action potential in relation to a broader environment of other processes. A switch can be activated by the sign of an electric current or human input to change the state of a system, thereby altering its many connections to other physical and biological systems. *Don't flick the switch until I am down the ladder!*

Now you should be suspicious. Thinking of signs as operating for human animals according to states of consciousness such as attention is understandable. Why, though, speak of signs for other animals and for biological and physical systems? There is no need for the idea of the sign when we have better explanations provided by the sciences. Moreover, the ideas of selection and substratum are ill-suited to such systems when compared to descriptions simply in terms of potential or states, with clear accounts of what the system is changing between – for instance, on or off states with different effects for a switch.

You might have noted a passing qualifier for the method of this process philosophy: speculative process philosophy. Why is the philosophy described as speculative? Doesn't this add to the weakness implied by the extension of signs into domains to which they are not suited? My answers to these lines of sceptical questioning are connected. The process philosophy of signs is speculative in so far as it suggests – speculates about – definitions of the sign in order to construct a philosophy aiming neither to base itself on the sciences, nor to offer a complete and consistent alternative to them. Instead, the point is to design a process philosophy of the sign working in critical debate with other ways of thinking about signs, meaning and the wider systems signs operate in.

In Chapters 2 to 7 I will return to the difference between speculative philosophy and other philosophies of the sign in order to defend a definition of the sign independent of the sciences and in contrast with other definitions from philosophy and structuralism. I will keep returning to the critical and creative roles of signs and to their capacity to introduce alarm and novelty into a system.

The first process suggested for the definition of the sign as process is selection. The relation between the selected set and its substratum leads to a second process around changing values in the sign and background. Every sign is a change in values of relations. When a ship in port raises the flag of quarantine, we have not only the selection of ship, flag, meaning and location. There is also an effect on the surrounding ships (greater watchfulness, more curiosity about the nature of the disease, and increased desire to leave the port quickly) and on those ashore (rising disappointment about a delay in seeing loved ones, fear of the spread of illness, worry about not receiving an important shipment).

The emphasis in the definition of this second process in the sign is on changing relations. Any sign is defined by differences in values for relations between the elements of the sign and its background. This change is not the same as the physical effects of a sign, for instance, when a flag of quarantine leads to other ships leaving the port. The difference comes before acts and effects and prepares for them. For the sign and its substratum, this process philosophy defines these differences in values as changes of intensity in the relations between elements: greater watchfulness, more curiosity, increased desire and rising disappointment.

This means that any selected sign is accompanied by a network of changes in intensity around relations in the sign and its substratum. These networks are represented by diagrams. We do not have a full grasp of the sign without them. So instead of the usual binary relations given for signs, for instance between a signifier and a signified, such as a smile signifying happiness, we should describe the sign through a set and a number of diagrams which express the changes in intensity that accompany the sign as multiplicity: not two, but many.

Formally, I define any sign as a selected set {a, b, c} and at least one diagram of the changes in intensities of relations in and around the set S{a b, c}. For example, the selected images on tea boxes are accompanied by changes in the intensity of relations. One way the British represented their zany cool to themselves over tea was to replace humans by chimpanzees in supposedly humorous scenarios on tea boxes and television adverts. The sign selected the primates, but in doing so it altered intensities around many other elements: the tendency to anthropocentrism, ideas about the nature of chimpanzees, and the relation between animals and humans. The tea box picture as sign should therefore be given as a selected set and a diagram of those changing relations.

When Brooke Bond used on its packaging idealised images of a contented woman picking tea they decreased the intensity of ideas around the exploitation of tea pickers and about their conditions and the effect of large single-crop plantations on their environment. These changes in intensity are in the relations around the elements. They occur in different directions, such as greater fear, and around particular beings, such as the devaluing of this or that person or group of people, or in relation to ideas, such as the diminishing of ideas of colonial exploitation. Anything that could have been included in the sign and everything on the substratum of the sign can in principle be mapped according to these changes in intensity brought about by the sign.

The diagram accompanying a selected set is a picture of increasing and decreasing intensities of relations around things and in different directions. You could think of it as the sketch you draw for your family of all the potential effects and implications of the painted sign on your door. Or you could explain it as the diagrams we draw of the many directions of social and political change that come with a new sign such as a novel technology or idea. Or you could use the diagrams to map the intended and unintended directions of change in values brought about by a particular use of signs in political campaigns and in the presentation of political figures. *Please do not wear the purple tie.*

The idea of mapping potential through diagrams is essential to understanding why signs are a matter of intensities or relations. I have insisted on the way process in signs comes before the actual effects occurring around the sign. In a rage you paint over the cross marking out your family, or you crush the box carrying the offensive distortions of adverts made to blunt our senses. The main question for the process philosophy is how did the sign work to prepare for this act? The speculative move is to suppose there must be change in and around the sign and this change can be represented in terms of rising and falling intensities around the multiple relations between the sign and its background.

Why refer to a series of intensive diagrams? Why will there be more than one? The speculative and hence experimental nature of this process philosophy extends beyond its method for defining signs. It also applies to the diagrams for signs themselves. They are defined to prioritise their capacity to raise critical questions and alarm around ideas and things in the world. In order to do this, signs are detached from established ways of representing the world in two ways. First, signs are unconditioned selections. Anything can be selected into a sign and there are no laws or rules for this selection. This is a controversial claim and it will be returned to in depth over Chapters 5 to 7.

Second, the drawing of a diagram for a sign is not determined by any particular philosophical method or science. Each diagram is itself a speculative representation of changes in the intensities of relations around elements associated with the selection of a sign. As experimental, it can take inspiration from sciences, arts, or philosophical ideas about the nature of the world and particular methods. However, the diagram remains philosophically speculative and independent, so none are necessary reference points according to the definition of the sign. Diagrams are suggested and there will be critical debates around implied and underlying interpretations. This means that diagrams are not unique. Each sign is by definition open to many different diagrams that challenge and transform one another.

The sign is therefore a selected set and a series of conflicting diagrams which represent rising and falling intensities of relations. As mathematical forms they can be given as vectors with directions, intensities and singular points they direct flows around. A diagram does not have to involve a representation by vectors. You might be bad at drawing and write all the intensities of the sign as a list, or you might act it out with gestures and words. The main point is that the sign must be seen not only as a process of selection but also as a process of multiple changes in intensity represented by way of diagrams.

Defined speculatively, signs operate alongside other processes, such as causal chains or ranges of probabilities described by the sciences. But they cannot be reduced to these other processes; rather, they introduce alternatives to them. The sign is therefore a moment of uncertainty providing the opportunity of thinking and acting differently. Where some processes can be described as necessary or extremely likely, for the sign there is a moment of hesitation and openness which provides a gap for things to be otherwise, not only as critical alarm but also as creative difference.

Ideas of hesitation and alarm raise the question of whether signs are only adapted to kinds of beings capable of these behaviours. Signs would then be restricted to humans and some other kinds of animal. They would be deemed irrelevant to things explicable strictly in causal or probabilistic terms. There would be no need for signs in electrical circuits or plants. Indeed, if we could think of humans simply in terms of physical processes, then signs would also be redundant for them.

This objection will be raised frequently through the book. A simple answer turns on the idea that signs and systems are not independent and do not allow for well-determined internal or external boundaries. So while a system might be explained locally in a satisfactory manner without signs, when its background is extended or when its internal states are shown to be touched by apparently quite distant phenomena, the idea of the sign regains traction along with hesitation, uncertainty and creative models.

Due to the speculative nature of the process philosophy, distance is taken from the idea of an objective representation of signs. In addition, the process definition of signs implies that they do not allow for an objective stance with respect to the world. This is not to say that the philosophy is opposed to such representations in principle. It is rather to position the sign at a critical distance from them and to situate the sign at transition points between stable ways of seeing the world. The sign seen as process is a creative and critical approach designed to allow for shifts between established pictures. In Chapter 8 it will be argued that the sign is therefore always political in a broad sense of the term.

The idea of a suite of diagrams for each sign is given the formal definition S{a, b, c}/Vs, where Vs indicates a series of revaluations of an initial diagram S. In the example of the white cross on the door the sign might be the selection {us, our door, fresh white paint, dripping cross, threat, disquiet about the future}, a diagram S{us, our door, fresh white paint, dripping cross, threat, disquiet about the future}, and a series of further diagrams opposed to the first S{us, our door, fresh white paint, dripping cross, threat, disquiet about the future}/Vs. When your partner sits you down and reminds you of the annoying but benign local tradition of door splattering, the diagram for the sign is revalued away from threatening directions.

The selected set and diagrams are the sufficient formal definitions of process signs. They are not satisfactory definitions of the wider critical context for the sign. The sign has been defined as resistant to overarching laws and codes for the representation of its diagrams and as unconditioned in terms of the selection of its set. Alternative ways of defining the sign which offer such codes and laws therefore provide a wider critical context for the process sign. For example, when neuroscience explains how perceptions of signs lead to types of actions, the idea of intensive diagrams for signs is challenged.

Any sign defined as a selection and as a series of diagrams will run counter to other positions on the elements and processes described by the sign. The sign is placed in a critical context of opposition to and dialogue with other ways of accounting for its relations. If these can be included in the series of diagrams as a new suggestion, then they will be consistent with the process definition. Some of them, though, will make general claims incompatible with the process account, for instance when they involve propositions contradicting the undetermined nature of selection or the intensive properties of relations.

This critical context for signs is described as stipulations over the sign. They should be considered as part of the sign in the sense that each sign will have stipulations over it providing a basis for counterclaims and dialogue around the sign. The process philosophy is therefore not universal, as if it allowed for a comprehensive account of all phenomena through a theory of the sign. Process signs are always part of a wider and mixed environment of ideas and ways of explaining the world. That's why they can also take on critical and creative roles in relation to this broad environment of competing claims. The process philosophy is ontologically modest: it does not claim validity over all phenomena. It is dialogically engaged: signs are the basis for critical debates with opposed positions about the nature of signs and what they apply to.

To close this introduction I want to draw attention to another objection. Most of my examples have been about visual signs. This could be symptomatic of a wrong approach to signs. It could be claimed that my definition of process involves an aesthetic bias because it does not give priority to the real nature of signs as linguistic. A sign, even an aesthetic one, should be defined in linguistic terms because signs are about meaning, sense and signification. The set and diagram definition therefore involves a fundamental mistake about the nature of the sign.

There are two features of the process sign allowing for an answer to this objection. First, since process signs can include anything, meanings, referents, significations and sense can be included in the sign. It is fine to have sets that just include sense and designation, or signifier and signified. Linguistic signs are not excluded from process signs. Second, since the background or substratum to the sign in principle involves relations across all things, meanings and other linguistic entities cannot be excluded from the sign. The process view shifts the problem to questions of degree rather than exclusion.

The intensity of linguistic relations might be at a very low degree for a given set and as described by a given diagram, but different selections and different diagrams can challenge this. The main difference is then not about whether signs are linguistic, it is about whether they are exclusively so. As defined here, the process sign can never be restricted to a linguistic realm or even to a binary relation between this realm and another non-linguistic one. It cannot be restricted to any limited number of relations. The sign is always an open multiplicity of intensive relations. It is therefore always more than language and more than a binary relation between terms. Questions of language and structure are considered in depth in Chapters 5, 6 and 7.

Different diagrams can assign higher or lower intensities to relations in the set for a sign and in its diagram. For example, in the picture on a tea box, one diagram might draw all relations to a strong meaning, perhaps around exclusion, while another might do so around a sensation, taste for instance. There is no final objective way in the sign to resolve these differences, though there can be arguments as to which diagrams are better or worse representations of the sign and of the intensity of the relations determined by the selection of its set.

This is a critical philosophy of signs rather than a process metaphysics claiming dominion over all phenomena. Signs are events on the threshold of actions and effects, but they must not be confused with them. Actions and effects can be included in signs, but then only as intensive relations. The definition of the process sign allows for layers of process by including signs within others, for example when the sign {tea, taste, good health} is included in another sign {exploitation, {tea, taste, good health}}. The main threat to this process definition comes from boundaries imposed on the sign as process, where the sign is given as static or limited. The paradigm of such limitation, as the imposition of false borders on signs, will be taken from Wittgenstein.

The Independent Life of Signs

DIAMONDS ARE NOT FOREVER

How do signs go wrong and wear out? Why do they stop working? What can we learn from their changes? And should we see these modifications as negative? This process philosophy of signs suggests a model explaining failure, erosion and renewal internally, from their formal definition and independent of external interpretation and reception of the signs. The model is radical in its pursuit of internal change in the sign. Its contention is that signs are never at rest, never removed from failure and from degradation. This also means that they are always close to renewal and reinvention. Internally, signs are processes rather than fixed relations that can only change due to external factors.

When your lover has departed and you toy with the diamond on your finger the sign works through a series of unstable intensities that interact with each other. You note them because they induce reactions through their variations: the striking sharpness on your cheek; the coldness on your tongue; the gradual appearance of a heart shape on the mirror as the jewel engraves it around your reflected image; its destruction when you add a second diagonal and turn cupid's arrow into a cross.

Is no sign fixed? Stability appears when processes vary in relation to one another. A slower process can appear fixed in relation to faster ones, just as a diamond can seem to last forever when flowers and chocolates rot and decay around it. That's only a matter of angle, though. If we begin with the falling rose petals, the diamond appears to increase in its hardness and reliability. If we add other signs and values, love as fragility for example, then as the flower droops it comes closer to love and makes the diamond fade. To borrow from the process philosophy of biology studied in Chapter 4, signs are multiplicities and they acquire determinacy through processes of stabilisation and destabilisation, rather than from externally imposed identities.

When we receive a value from a sign we perceive or posit as stable, we are really in a variation of speeds. You might think nothing is changing in the serenity of the face opposite you as the sun sets behind it. The calmness is changing, though, and its alteration is a process bringing together every speed of variation around it: light, wind, mood, thoughts, dying and new born cells – no movement can be rightfully excluded.

The illusion of fixity isn't necessary, as if speeds have to be frozen to be measured and communicated, or as if signs have to be given a settled meaning, if only for a short time. All we need is a differential of speeds and directions. The illusion is only enforced by a mode of thinking through identities, or it is stipulated by kinds of rules, with moral and political presuppositions and consequences. We shall see later, in Chapters 5 and 6, that it is also encouraged by a difficulty of representation. It seems that we have to depict a sign formally as having fixed components.

What is process in these differential speeds? It is related change. In this philosophy of signs, speed is relative change rather than a comparison against an external measure. It is not about travelling across space in a given time, but about changing in relation to another change. The exact time it takes a shadow to cross a face is not process. The changes in respective warmth and light are. Isn't the shadow crossing a face external to it? Isn't the face a stable sign which alters according to different perspectives and interpretations? The externality is illusory. Interpretations and perspectives on signs are responses to ongoing processes in the sign rather than independent judgements about their identity.

The argument for free interpretation of a stable sign, based on the different ways we can take a sign, does not demonstrate the fixity of the sign. According to the process philosophy of signs, the open set of interpretations rests on the multiplicity of the sign as process, rather than on freedom of interpretation. There is a variety of receptions of signs and values because they are multiple processes. As sign, the face is many ways of becoming, inviting many forms of interpretation.

The distinction between the inside and outside of signs is therefore only a temporary move to stall the idea that movement and significance in the sign come from the outside. Process is relational such that it allows no boundaries between inside and outside. All such borders are artificial. The sign is in an unbounded relation with other signs and a wider world. This raises two difficulties for a process philosophy. First, what kind of world or environment is determined by a sign? Is it all of existence, such that everything is signifying process? Or is the sign a partial aspect of existence? If so, how does this aspect relate to others?

Second, how many worlds are determined by signs? Is it one world or many? If it is many, are they independent or do they communicate? If they are independent, does this leave us with an atomised and isolated view of existence? If they communicate, how does this happen? If it happens through further signs, doesn't that lead to an infinite regress of worlds and signs?

These questions will be addressed in later sections on the idea of many worlds and on the limitations of signs. Prior to that, though, I will respond to one of the most powerful arguments for the sign as dependent on the outside. This is Wittgenstein's contention that the sign is dead until we breathe life into it. If Wittgenstein is right, then this process philosophy is at best pointless, at worst some kind of mystical necrophilia.

IS THE SIGN DEAD UNTIL WE BREATHE LIFE INTO IT?

> 432. Every sign *by itself* seems dead. *What* gives it life? – In use it is *alive*. Is life breathed into it there – Or is the *use* its life?
>   432. Jedes Zeichen Scheint *allein* tot. *Was* gibt ihm Leben? – Im Gebrauch *lebt* es. Hat es da den lebenden Atem in sich? – Oder is der *Gebrauch* sein Atem?[1]

Against Wittgenstein, my guiding claim is that signs as process are alive prior to use. Signs are always alive because they are ongoing multiple processes independent of use. Interpretation responds to this movement and multiplicity. Use is an interaction with already living signs and not the gift of life to dead ones.[2]

Wittgenstein's aphorism 432 from *Philosophical Investigations* is more than a simple proposition on how signs come to life.[3] It is a puzzle set by a chain of remarks and questions. Each link is important for an understanding of the strength of the challenge to process philosophy. First, the sign *appears* dead when it is alone. The emphasis is on the isolation of the sign as implying its deathly appearance.

This is the beginning of the puzzle because it is hard to think of a sign that appears alone. A sign always appears against a background. This means that it appears alongside other things. Even if we imagine a secluded sign, perhaps in some kind of vacuum, it is still as a product of the apparatus designed to create the vacuum. Can a sign ever appear alone, or is Wittgenstein making a different point?

The isolation of the sign is of a special kind for Wittgenstein. The sign appears isolated *without us*, without a world of users. Even when it is against a background of other things, it is alone if we are not using it. This too is a distortion. Independent of whether it is in use, when a sign is in an environment it is changing in its relation to other living and inanimate things in that environment. Against Wittgenstein, my contention is that this living change precedes and predetermines the use. Use is haunted by a prior life of signs.

Set a blood-soaked parchment, 'the Rizzio testament', with a colony of ants in a sealed box.[4] We cannot use the sign, but it is alive according to my definition because it is changing in its slow destruction by the insects. The sign is in a living relation to the ants. The use we can make of the parchment differs while we watch the countdown to its disappearance as the ants do their work. The sign is alive before the use and the use is conditional on the pre-existing life of the sign. Why then claim that all signs are dead before they enter into use? Perhaps Wittgenstein means something very strange when he says life?

Wittgenstein's second remark responds to this challenge. His emphasis shifts to life as something given. As we shall see shortly, life-giving power is a potent metaphor steeped in myth, but the most important aspect of the shift is to life as something that has particular qualities. When the sign is in use it can take on different roles and grow with them. Use shapes the sign as something that lives through its manipulation.[5] Like a mysterious stone inscribed with squiggles landing among inquisitive onlookers, the sign's life seems to come from their actions, from the way they go on to exchange and decipher it.

The puzzle is not exhausted for all that. The sign *seemed* dead or *appeared* as dead when it was isolated (*Scheint allein*). Was this only an appearance? If it was, then the use ignites or reveals a life already contained in the sign. The English translation misses this point and loses the sense of the shift to Wittgenstein's last question. It drops the German '*in sich*', 'in itself', and thereby puts too much weight on 'there' (*da*). There, use is enough to explain life; it is the life of the sign as used. Wittgenstein sees the deeper problem, though, because this latter life does not necessarily imply that the sign is not alive beforehand or 'in itself'.

We would not say we gave life to a horse by hitching it to a wagon. The strange beast in the wild might have no ready meanings and might seem blankly available for inscription in our most fanciful tales or greedy plans, but that does not mean it has no life. When a paint-laden brush moves across parchment and a sign appears, should we say that the spreading wet stains, splashes, coloured swoops and swirls are dead until we appear on the shoulder of the artist and suggest specific uses? The opposite claim is more puzzling. How can use ever be enough to explain the life of something, to give life fully to something, when it does not first appear as dead but as full of a life of its own?

So Wittgenstein asks a final question: 'Or is the *use* its life?' This time, use is stressed. Again, the translation is important, since the question picks up on living breath (*lebenden Atem*) from the previous sentence as opposed to the more simple use of 'life' in the opening sentences of the aphorism. In the English version 'life' is given for 'breath'. The elision of the metaphor of living breath is noteworthy because, by splitting the sign into inert matter and living breath, Wittgenstein is responding to the problem about the life that signs already have in themselves. It is not a full life; it is inert. Use gives the breath of life to the inert matter of signs. This gives signs a special status among living things.

Life is different for signs because they are dual: they have a material form and they have meaning in use. This duality is crucial for signs as defined by Wittgenstein, not only because it allows us to distinguish between different kinds of life for signs, before and after use, but also because the dual nature of signs allows us to distinguish them from other things. A sign is different from a mere material thing because the sign can be brought to life when it is put to use.

Against this duality, my claim is that for a process philosophy signs are distinct from other things because they are special kinds of process which bring things into relation. Signs are selections and variations in the intensities of relations, but neither selection nor variation depends on use or indeed on any human intervention. The 'life' of the sign is a matter of changing intensities in multiplicities of relations, rather than a straight distinction between inert and alive.

However, without the dual nature of the sign, or some other reason for a sign and world distinction, it will be difficult to avoid fusing signs with the ways in which we explain change in mere things, for instance by appealing to causes or laws. In Chapters 3 and 4 this problem will be addressed around differences between biological philosophies of signs, process philosophies of biology and the process philosophy of signs.

Wittgenstein's final point is that without meaning the form is dead. Since without use there is no meaning, signs as material forms are dead unless they are in use. A horse is certainly alive, whether we take control of it or not, but as a sign the horse only acquires meaning when it is in use, for instance when we begin to use horses as currency, or power, or a symbol for the unconscious. This is the strongest criticism to be made against the process philosophy of signs. Though signs may well be processes before they are in use, only when they are put to use does their proper process appear: as meaningful signs.

MULTIPLICITY OR DUALITY OF THE SIGN?

My response to Wittgenstein is based on the multiplicity of processes in signs and on the inseparability of these processes. It denies the priority of the distinction between inert form and living meaning, and the importance accorded to use as determinant of meaning. These points can be conveyed partly through a study of the work done by the metaphors of breath, life and death used by Wittgenstein to underpin the form and meaning distinction, but the main argument is about the formal definition of the sign.

The difference is between a dual form of inert matter and meaningful sign in use, and a multiple and continuous form where meaning is replaced by multiple changes in intensity across relations. A sign might appear dead, but it is just running at low intensity for selected relations or even running at high intensity but in a way we are not conscious of. Continuous processes cannot be disentangled and reassigned into clear categories of inert form and living use according to dualist distinctions.

Wittgenstein's argument draws rhetorical force from the imagery and historical precedents of the metaphor of life-giving breath. In order to give a purer version of the argument I will study antecedents to the passages in *Philosophical Investigations* from *The Blue Book*. The earlier manuscript has many background notes for the remarks on signs in the later work. It would be wrong to say that they fully explain Wittgenstein's questions and statements. They do however provide simpler versions of the later puzzles.

Here is the proposition about use and life from *The Blue Book*: 'But if we had to name anything which is the life of the sign, we have to say that it is its use.' The conditional 'if we had to' indicates a reluctance to fully invest in the image of life. Life is a preliminary metaphor for Wittgenstein; something more is going on in the distinction drawn between life and death. What matters is the lack of meaning when signs are not in use, as he says for propositions:

> Without a sense, or without the thought, a proposition would be an utterly dead and trivial thing. And further it seems clear that no adding of inorganic signs can make the proposition live. And the conclusion which one draws from this is that what must be added to the dead signs in order to make a live proposition is something immaterial, with properties different from all mere signs.[6]

The reference to use, meaning and thought is quite loose at this stage of his analysis because the focus is on the contrast with inorganic signs and the test presented by different kinds of addition. A senseless proposition is dead and we cannot remedy this by adding other senseless material signs.

The references to 'something immaterial' and to 'thought' are stages in Wittgenstein's argument. They will be dismissed in favour of use when he turns away from the idea that there might be something mystical giving life to signs, or something unattainably private in thought. This is important for the argument around signs because it makes clear that the dualism at stake in Wittgenstein's definition of the sign is not Cartesian mind-body dualism or the dualism of extended matter and ethereal ideas.

The life of signs does not rely on some mystical agent, or on some private inner life for thoughts.[7] It depends on use. So, if Wittgenstein's account does not fit easily into traditional metaphysical dualism, what is the basis for my charge about the dualism of the sign? First, it rests on the metaphorical distinction between life and death. Second, this metaphor leads to an essential formal definition in Wittgenstein's work. Use is alive and belongs to a form of life, in the sense of being shaped by living activity. Without this activity matter and signs are dead. The dualism of the sign is therefore between its inertness and its life when in active use.

This dualism invites a two-pronged counter. First, signs are multiple processes that cannot be separated into 'dead' and 'live' sides without consequence where meaning is concerned. Second, the addition of material signs changes and constitutes meaning. To support these claims, I replace meaning by changes in intensities of relations.

The shift from meaning to intensity can be understood, in an initial way, as a transition from the idea of meaning to the ideas of significance and signification. I will discuss the first here and leave the second to Chapter 6.

Meaning involves linguistic understanding; significance can involve that but more broadly it involves an increase or decrease in interest, attention, response, preparedness or other factors which indicate a change in the intensity of something – for instance, an increase in attention or a decrease in responsiveness. So though we might not say a cold winter means something to a herd of deer, it does have significance for them. The change in cold is a significant value. Though we might not say an underlying spring has meaning for a rock face, the pressure value building along deep fault lines is significant.

An underlying motivation behind this modification is resistance to an anthropocentric foundation for meaning. I want to handle signs formally such that they can operate with significance between non-humans, including animals and inanimate processes such as plants, machines and natural formations such as landscapes. The idea of changes in value as changes in degrees of intensity, for instance of attention, is designed to capture the moment where a deer halts to listen, or where the morning sun hits a leaf, or where the threads of a rope begin to respond to a heavy load. Something is changing; it can be taken as a sign.[8]

Wittgenstein's dualism and its reliance on human use imply a restriction of signs to human or perhaps near-human activity and forms of life. Importantly, this does not rely on any prior definition of the nature of the human. This emerges in different forms of life and can vary with them such that the use determines what the human can be rather than the other way round. It could therefore perhaps be objected that there is no anthropocentrism in his account of signs.

I believe this objection is wrong for three reasons: Wittgenstein's account of the use of signs is restricted to human use; the dualism of the sign follows from the distinction between human meanings and the non-human as inert; and the denial of the addition of non-human or inert signs as constituting meaning and life reinforces the anthropocentric foundation for Wittgenstein's philosophy of signs. Though the meaning of the human is open, the essential role played by it in assigning meaning remains in place.

Counter to this constitutive dualism I argue that meaning is a change of intensity within signs, so we have meaning when there is an alteration in signs rather than in their use. Merely adding a material sign to another is sufficient for a change in significance, because the addition introduces intensity-based change in the signs. For instance, when a series of signs becomes longer this is accompanied by a change in values along the series independent of any human observer as a precondition for any potential observation. The sign is always alive, in the sense of always in process. The external role of meaning is denied, since meaning is made by process and not by 'immaterial' use. Finally, that use can itself be redefined as one of the processes of the sign.

Formally, the difference between the two positions therefore turns around the hard line drawn between inert material and meaningful life for the sign in use, where a clear distinction can be made between them, and the view that any sign is many inseparable connected processes. The strong claim is that the distinction between inert material and living use makes a contingent and distorting cut into the manifold of processes.

DUST AND THE GOLEM

I will illustrate my claims for process and against the inertness of the sign by returning to Wittgenstein's metaphors. Though it is not made explicit in *Philosophical Investigations*, there are at least two religious sources for the image of life-giving breath.[9] They share the same root. The first is from the Bible; the second from the Kabbalah.[10] They share content and implications.

In Genesis 2:7 God gives man his living soul: 'And the Lord God formed man of the dust of the ground, and breathed into his nostrils the breath of life; and man became a living soul.'[11] In the Elberfelder German version of the verse, *Atem* and *Lebens/lebende* as used by Wittgenstein come out clearly: 'der HERR, den Menschen, aus Staub vom Erdboden und hauchte in seine Nase Atem des Lebens; so wurde der Mensch eine lebende Seele'.[12] Wittgenstein's division of material and immaterial, death and life, is represented in the dust and soul. The distinction becomes operational with the shared image of life-giving breath, where one realm and a particular power assume greater importance. Wittgenstein and Genesis part over the agent of change. Life is either given by God or by human use.[13]

Though they are clues for the overall interpretation of Wittgenstein and for the question of dualism considered earlier, my interest here is not in the differences in agent or substance. I am concerned with the gift of life to 'dust' or to inert material signs and with the external and independent situation of meaning and soul, irrespective of whether this appeals to a Godly realm, or to immaterial meaning, or to use.

My opening point is prosaic and aimed at the work of conceal-ment done by the metaphor. As gardeners, farmers and biologists know well, a portion of soil or dust is a microcosm of living pro-cesses, of decay and birth, of animal and microbial life. Other things live on and around dust. They interact with it, breathing it in, stand-ing on it, feeding off it, allowing it to alter their conscious and physi-cal states, dying after ingesting it. Dust is alive before God or humans get to it. Weeds do not cease to grow when we snooze on a warm afternoon.[14]

More formally, if like dust the sign is already teeming with life, the distinction between supposedly lifeless matter and the living breath afforded by use requires an extraction of life from signs. This act recalls a false legal declaration of terra nullius, where land is stated to be free of original sovereign claim, lifeless as it were, when in fact it is inhabited and subject to a form of ownership; for instance in the Mabo case in Australia, where a declaration of terra nullius was reversed to do justice to original peoples.[15]

Could the declaration of inertness in the sign be a violent expro-priation? My claim is that the life of signs, away from use, is of essential importance even to later use. This life gives us reason for an extension of the critique of declarations of terra nullius beyond human occupants and to all living and even immaterial forms capa-ble of emitting signs and participating in their intensive values.

The dualist distinction between lifeless sign and sign in use is an abstraction operating on signs which do not fit the dualist represen-tation. It is a fiction designed to facilitate the reduction of meaning to use, but it does not reflect the life of signs. The doctrine of life-giving breath from the Kabbalah demonstrates this artifice in the stories of the Golem, given life through breath and words.

Here is Bruce Chatwin's version of one of the most famous instances of Golem tales, centred around Rabbi Loew from Prague, in Chatwin's minimalist masterpiece Utz:

All golem legends derived from an Ancient Jewish belief that any righteous man could create the World by repeating, in an order prescribed by the Cabbala, the letters of the secret name of god. 'Golem' meant 'unformed' or 'uncreated' in Hebrew. Father Adam himself had been 'golem' – an inert mass of clay so vast as to cover the ends of Earth: that is, until Yahweh shrank him to the human scale and breathed into his mouth the power of speech.[16]

The myth of the Golem is close to Wittgenstein's work on signs because it plays on speech and on language alongside the idea of breath. The Golem is given speech and, in some versions, this gift requires a set of signs added to breath.

As in Genesis, for the myth of the gift of life to function the Golem must be defined as 'an inert mass of clay'. Yahweh, or at times humans, can then give meaning to this dead matter by breathing and reciting life into it, as use can in Wittgenstein's account of the sign. This donation of life and language is the basis for the dualist account of existence. It can be seen operating in the myth of the Golem in the distinction between ordinary humans and the Golem. In its dual nature as inert clay then active automaton, the Golem is brought into existence as an exceptional non-human creature to defend the Jews of Prague.

The alternative to Wittgenstein's model is to replace the division in the metaphor of life and death, and the split of the sign into inert and in use, with a continuity of living processes across all states of the sign. Formally, it is to claim that signs are always networks of continuous intensive processes that cannot be separated from one another without giving a false representation of how value and significance work in signs. This means that distinctions such as living and dead, or inert and in use, are false if they are taken to imply absolute lifelessness or inertness in a state of a sign. It also means we should give up stark distinctions between those said to be devoid of life, like the Golem, and those claiming to be closer to God, or to meaning.

AN OBJECTION: WHERE MEANING IS CONCERNED WE CAN DISCOUNT SOME KINDS OF LIFE

There is a two-part objection that could be made to my rejection of Wittgenstein's account of the sign. First, it could be conceded signs have some kind of life independent of meaning, but this life matters not one bit when we turn to signs as meaningful. Signs might well alter when we are not there to observe and use them, but it is only when we do so that they are meaningful.

Second, returning to Wittgenstein's challenge that adding inert signs to others cannot give life or meaning to them, it could be claimed that even if signs alter when others are set alongside them, this never amounts to life but rather to some kind of mechanical process that still needs to be put to use before it comes to life.

These objections can be exemplified by another of Wittgenstein's points, about Frege and signs in mathematics.[17] The metaphor of death also plays an important role here:

> Frege ridiculed the formalist conception of mathematics by saying that the formalists confused the unimportant thing, the sign, with the important, the meaning. Surely, one wishes to say, mathematics does not treat of dashes on a bit of paper. Frege's idea could be expressed thus: the propositions of mathematics, if they were just complexes of dashes, would be dead and utterly uninteresting, whereas they obviously have a kind of life.[18]

Wittgenstein is prescient in his discussion of signs and addition in *The Blue Book* and *Philosophical Investigations*, since his remark about the addition of signs to signs, and later discussions of number series, prepare the way for a response to the possibility of life in a digitally generated series of signs, for example in a digital simulation of life. Such a series could be taken to be a kind of life, a process in my version of signs. For Wittgenstein this would still be confusion about life and about importance.[19]

Wittgenstein's examples of mechanical processes contrast them with a different and genuine kind of life. This is the life of signs in language games around the use of words:

> I give someone the order: 'fetch me six apples from the grocer', and I will describe a way of making use of such an order: The words 'six apples' are written on a bit of paper, the paper is handed to the grocer, the grocer compares the word 'apple' with labels on different shelves. He finds it to agree with one of the labels, counts from one to the number written on the slip of paper, and for every number counted takes a fruit off the shelf and puts an apple in the bag. – And here you have a case of the use of words. I shall in future again and again draw your attention to what I shall call language games.[20]

These mechanical examples entail a degree of risk for Wittgenstein's argument about the death of signs, since they invite the remark that formally generated chains of signs produced by a machine are just like his example of the apples. What if each part of the apple exchange is played by robots? What if the order is a code run on a machine? Is that not use and a language game? Why would a computer simulation not be a life?

He is caught in this bind because his examples of language and games are designed to counter the idea that there is something special and mysterious about meaning. Wittgenstein does not want a mystical explanation for the source and importance of meaning, that it is an expression of some secret inner life, for instance. That is not the case because meaning emerges from and can be brought back to language games. If that's right, though, then what is wrong with defining games as mechanical and therefore saying that the meaning is generated by an inert mechanism and not human use? The answer is that meaning must not be identified with the mechanical rule following, but rather with the act of using the mechanism and the rule.

The grocer is therefore essential to the example. He 'compares', 'finds', 'counts' and 'takes'. He uses the sign and the rules. When he does so, meaning emerges. It could well develop differently with different interpretations of the rules, with a different interpretation of the language game. Life does not amount to a mechanical generation of signs, but rather to the use of such a mechanism in broader forms of life. The life of mathematical signs is in their use and not in chains of symbols, even if those chains are set in motion and move according to complex mechanical or digital processes.

My answer to the point about the irrelevance of any purported life of signs prior to use is two-fold. First, I deny the clean border between those two lives of the sign. Where do you draw the line between life before and after use and can you do so cleanly? My definition insists on the continuity of process against the legitimacy of a clean cut between inert and living sign. The processes before and after use connect and interact, so the division of the sign into dead and alive, or inert and in use, is a misrepresentation of use and the process of the sign.

For example, as you trek along an unstable ice and snow front, you hear the soft but growing crunching sound of deer leaping above and to the side of you. They are hungry and panicked. The cliff is melting and unstable. So you begin to compute the grim possibilities around the impending avalanche, listening to the hoof impacts. Where is the border between the dead sign and the live ones? Is it at the point where you once studied about deer coming lower down the mountain due to starvation, or when you first unconsciously registered their leaps as a presentiment of bad things about to happen? Or is it where you begin to act? Or where the deer first suffer from the effects of the harsh winter? Or simply where you begin some kind of linguistic analysis of the languages of avalanche, survival techniques and animal movements? According to my claim, any cut or definitive answer at the point of use is an abstraction from continuous processes because the cut will draw an artificial line between connected processes. These connections can be revealed when we show linked values, for instance between action and earlier learning or between later use and much earlier unconscious events.

The distinction between inert and in use is false because it draws a line between multiple connections that cross the divide. It does not matter whether we draw the line at action or interpretation, at the limits of a programme or rules of a game, at the limits of an axiomatic, or at the beginning and end of an algorithm. Each time we do so the limit will prove to be porous. Explanation of differences and of significance in the use, of processes and value in my definition of the sign, crosses the boundaries designed to limit the process to a proper realm.

It could be countered that, even though the cut is an abstraction, it is a necessary one since otherwise we have to deal with a limitless chaos of signs and values. My reply is that it is true that we have to make selections when interacting with signs, giving priority of some things over others. Part of my definition of a sign is as an unconditioned selection of a set. However, the selection is not only made by use. There is a prior selection for there to be any sign at all, including ones judged to be inert in Wittgenstein's account.

The point about the necessity of selection has far-reaching consequences because it turns on the difference between a well-grounded selection and one that must carry its artificiality and contingency with it, as aspects of its motivations, reasons and exercise. Can selection rest easy on secure grounds such as forms of life and language games, or should it retain constant attentiveness and doubt about its imposition of false boundaries?

If any selection is a product of necessity but not of legitimacy, then awareness of its exclusions matters for practical reasons. We might have made the wrong selections. It matters for ethical reasons. We might have made a selection where negative values accompany sets of distinctions around others. This is why I study the process sign as necessarily political in Chapter 8.

Given my definition of signs as processes at different speeds, any abstraction or selection of processes involves a relative slowing down and speeding up between them, and not a full cut. The selection draws some processes into closer proximity and temporarily distances others, decreasing the intensity of their hold on each other. For instance, when we focus on the movement of the deer rather than their hunger, we speed one up and slow another down.

It might appear that a process can be simply cut away and discounted, but that is not the case. It is rather that a relative slowness can remain undetected. It can rapidly increase again, for example as you spot a bale of hay dropped by helicopter above you on the snow field – the deer smelt it long ago. Your predicament is at the moment very slow and distant for the well-meaning ecologists who dropped the feed. It might speed up when their helicopter ferries your frozen and broken body off the mountain after a failed rescue attempt.[21]

THE SUBSTRATUM

Use and interpretation of the sign exist against a substratum of processes extending back to all the earlier processes of significance in the sign, such that any cut based on their independence is false even when we consider use in abstraction from the so-called dead sign. We might call this unseen connection the unconscious or subconscious, but I do not want to attach it strictly to the play of different levels of consciousness.

The concept of substratum is also used by Wittgenstein in *Philosophical Investigations* in relation to the substratum of an experience and the 'mastery of a technique'.[22] But this is a different and opposite use of the term to mine, since the substratum is intensive for me, whereas it is a form of conceptual knowledge for Wittgenstein. For the process sign, the substratum is the potential for undoing conceptual knowledge and mastery through intensive relations which stretch the practice and knowledge away from the spheres they are practised in.

In Chapter 5, where I give the full formal definition of the sign, the substratum will be defined as the changing intensities of relations between the sign as the selection of a restricted set and all the things not included in that set. The substratum is given by a suite of intensive diagrams which must accompany any given sign as defined by a selected set. The sign is therefore a selection accompanied by changes in intensities that in principle include all relations to all things, though many of these will be at very low degrees. The sign is hence an intensive continuum determined by a restricted selection.

This definition of the sign implies that signs include other signs, since signs can be selected into others. Given the continuum within the sign, this means that such signs are never independent. Two further objections applicable to the current discussion will be responded to in Chapters 5 and 6: first, that selection depends on a human subject, since this would confirm the importance of use; second, that this definition of the sign is esoteric and does not correspond to many, let alone all signs. In this chapter, I will continue with the informal discussion of the sign in relation to a substratum of various processes. Formally, though, the sign includes these in relation to its determining selected set.

Wittgenstein fails in his attempt to keep the sign metaphysically pure, as it were, due to the introduction of a new kind of dualism around the sign and its inertness and life. However, I do not want to defend the project of a position free of metaphysical speculation, but rather one where the basic metaphysical claim is made overtly and with as few presuppositions as possible, as a speculative claim, with an attempt to be as true to the sign in its relation to worlds as I can. The definition of the sign as process and as selection is that attempt – some of its pitfalls are already apparent in the as yet loose ideas of 'true' and 'can' in the previous sentence.

So the necessity of selection accompanied by an attentiveness and doubt about any given selection applies to the very philosophy giving rise to it. A speculative philosophy is itself an essay in certain selections and a critical exercise in their presuppositions, repercussions and critical positions. To speculate is to create new signs. That's why it is important to test a speculative position against other choices, such as Wittgenstein's. It is also why we need to test its design and values, such as commitment to the avoidance of limits, the value associated with minimal metaphysical presuppositions, and the selection of the process philosophy of signs as a valuable approach to problems.

A sense of what 'as true to the sign as I can be' means here can be garnered from my answers to the two earlier objections. In insisting on the continuity and multiplicity of the sign, and on the impossibility of cutting into processes, I combine a speculative definition and a critical angle on other claims about the real state of things. The argument is that the sign is process and that we should think it is as such because we encounter difficulties if we base it on a dualist cut and abrupt distinctions between types of process.

Does this mean I have a well-defined notion of reality to fall back on? No. It is a hotchpotch of remarks and observations from a wide range of fields. Is this a problem? Yes, if there is a definition of the real which applies reliably to signs and does not encounter difficulties in individual cases, or make metaphysical commitments less preferable to those made by the process definition of signs. That's why the speculative approach attempts definitions of the sign and tests them on reality against critical readings of other claims about the sign.

The speculative approach brings together definitions and principles. In the process philosophy of signs given here, the substratum for the sign as selected set is all the changes in intensities of relations around all things as implied by the selection. This relation of the sign to the substratum is governed by principles. There is no legitimate limit for any treatment of the sign tracking back through the life of signs and their multiple processes. Any way of following on from a sign is a selection in its substratum. Selection requires an assessment of its commitments in contrast to other selections and stipulations over the sign.

For example, it is illegitimate to claim that there is a full disconnect between signs as used by animals and signs used by rational entities. When we select the rational use of language as the domain of signs we do so against a substratum that includes animal signs. The rational selection should be open to a critical evaluation of what it commits to, for instance, in excluding animal cries. From this philosophy, it might be interesting or wise to treat our use of logic, say, as an independent sphere with no animal attributes or connections, but it would never be legitimate, in the sense of finally and unquestionably justified. There could well be something of the warning cry or sexual display or the call of the pack in a logical demonstration.

The sign is always open to an ongoing evaluation back through the different lines of processes relating to it. There is no limit, in principle, to the significance of different values in those processes. Any abstract cut is therefore a breach of this principle. This violation matters not only as damaging behaviour towards the sign. It also matters as self-damaging behaviour, as the imposition of a limit which hinders the critical use and creative interpretation of the sign.

For example, in the case of rule following, Wittgenstein's apples and grocer are overly simple because they take place in a kind of emotional and historical vacuum. Imagine a child sent by a violent and impoverished parent with a note and not quite enough money to a kindly grocer. The language game is fluid, difficult and rapidly evolving. It takes place against a complex background of processes: a partially hidden and continuous substratum. The grocer needs to project back beyond the paper, past the child's stuttering and bruised arm and beyond the shaky scrawl on the paper. She needs to calculate how generous she can be, but also how much generosity might be taken as insulting and thereby trigger a vengeful attack. She needs to study and wrestle with her own feelings, perhaps extending back to her own childhood, while she works through emotions, affects, values and reactions in all that she does. There is an art to this act which is not only an art of language games and sense, but a creative art wrestling with sensed and as yet unfelt background processes, a life of signs beyond the explicit life of use and action.

Maybe she needs to weigh up the irreversible decision to invite the child into her home and call for help. Throughout all of this, signs do not come alive as they are considered. They are already alive and have a hold on us prior to consciousness and prior to action. Any process is ongoing and multiple. To rewrite Wittgenstein's metaphor: signs catch their breath up close to us. They breathe down our necks. They give life to us before we breathe back on them.

So to the objection that my more elaborate example for the grocer does nothing to escape the priority of use in the interpretation of signs, I respond that there is a difference in extent and type of field for the two grocers. The field of use is not satisfactorily determined by a social practice giving life to signs. Instead, any use occurs in the middle of ongoing changes in signs with multiple pressure points in practice, such as a faintly remembered childhood, the shock of a bruise on a child's forehead, and differences between kinds of measurement and number when they become a matter for existential and ethical concern. The effect of these signs begins before any defined practice and operates in excess of them, as for instance when they communicate through the unconscious and the body.[23]

Signs are continuous processes unfolding at different speeds in many tangled lines and according to different diagrams. The decision to break with abuse or to try and manage it is a struggle with accelerations in violence and thresholds in behaviour with long histories and individual trails. Each sign is a continuous and multiple process of shifting values, never a mere cypher in a game of rule following.

It is important to insist on the pragmatic and immersive nature of selection at this point. It is not the case that Wittgenstein's asceticism, his distaste for the metaphysical and the mystical, are necessarily bad selections. It might be valuable to withdraw from a deeply tainted world and begin anew with a different model of its truths and functions. Purification, renewal and forgetting are powerful yet dangerous tools.

The mistake lies in the justification of this selection on the grounds of a distinction about the sign. Why is it a mistake, though, since it could be a practical selection? Interpreters will claim Wittgenstein's work on the life of signs has an exemplary or even ironic practical role, rather than breaking a paradoxical new ground. It is not another metaphysical commitment but rather an ironic questioning of such commitments and an exceptionally fruitful suggestion of how to proceed in their absence.[24]

But there is no such absence. Any set of definitions, principles, rules and distinctions has background metaphysical commitments, as a connection to a metaphysical system of signs and processes. My concern is with those clashing with the definition of signs in relation to a process philosophy of signs. Whether cast in irony or not, Wittgenstein's remarks on the sign lead to commitments. Irony is itself such a commitment, as can be felt in the hollowness that gradually seeps into the ironist and audience, to the point where they might easily surrender to a new succour, in a new escape to eternal metaphysical forms, or a return to commonplace conservative values.

The connection between these commitments and the accompanying practice of the sign frames my use of the term 'mistake'. It is a mistake when a practical move with positive values such as 'to have done with the mysticism of the sign' and 'to bring the sign into its life world as use' ends up prey to more distant and yet powerful effects such as an abstraction from processes that continue to work in the background. For instance, from the point of view of a speculative process philosophy, there is such a practical mistake in the denial of a process which can be shown to work in the act of denial itself. I discuss these aspects of process philosophy as a critical speculative philosophy in Chapter 7.

Like the Bible and the Kabbalah, Wittgenstein cuts signs into two unequal and asymmetrical sides according to when they are touched by breath or by use. There is an inequality of value in the ascription of inertness to one side. There is also an asymmetry of process, since the living process is set on the side of use, against the presence of movement on the inert side, for instance in the automatic addition of signs according to a programme or in the unconscious development of pressures, which are dismissed as lifeless because their continuity with other processes of life is denied.

According to the process philosophy of signs this unequal and asymmetrical separation is a false move. Signs are never dead. They are self-generating and self-dividing zombies, the living dead from a substratum we cannot escape. They bring a dynamic and oozing inhabitation and haunting to all subsequent lives and uses. Like dreams, they work away when we sleep and when we wakefully seek to shake them off. It is mistake to think we can ignore this work and only tackle signs as they appear in use and forms of life, as if their past trysts are only in our current records, rather than ongoing transformations on a substratum experimenting inventively on us.

ZOMBIE POSTCARD GAMES

The life of signs is continuous and multiple. Signs do not live and die at our whim. They regenerate and connect with one another at ever changing speeds and in multiple interconnecting lines. When we are not looking, when we think they are asleep – when we are – their changing relations are altering our lives. Indeed, for the speculative search to be true to signs, these images are unfortunate, since we are still within the ambit of human relations to signs. For this process philosophy, signs and all beings are zombies for each other, if by this we understand that inertness is always an illusion and distance offers no safety from rapid increases and decreases in number, intensity and place, for any type of existence, human, animal or rock. Signs are never dead, only dormant.

This does not mean we should not be interested in the human. There is nothing wrong in selecting a type of existence out of interest, passion, care or worry. It is however essential to be aware that it is a selection rather than a necessity; the set of elements we choose for any sign and the values we associate with the sign in relation to its background cannot be given an ultimate necessity. There is perhaps something right in selecting the human, though it drags a terrible track record with it, if we visit abattoirs and battlefields, or chart the rapid and violent decline of species at the hands of the human.

One of the principles of this process philosophy is that it is a mistake to take a limited type of sign as the basis for a fundamental or overarching thesis about the nature of signs. It is a mistake to ascribe necessity or naturalness to selected boundaries, qualities and attributes allowing us to define a type and a set of categories for signs. In Chapter 7, I will show how this can happen even within other philosophies of process, including work by Deleuze and Whitehead.

These difficulties are persistent and sometimes hard to track. They can appear in distilled yet potent forms in apparently very pure language and situations, for instance, in a new form of dualism in the definition of the sign, or in a determination of process based around a particular type of mechanism, such as combustion, or physical process, such as entropy, or biological processes, such as symbiosis, or apparently human-based processes such as interpretation or action, or very pure processes such as logic or mathematics.

To understand the continuity of intensive relations across signs and their backgrounds, I like the game of buying a postcard at random. Almost at random: I am in this tourist shop, in this town, now. I then cut a shape in the card carefully folded in half down a line from edge to edge. The card is now a window to be placed on the world, a picture around a window on a sign. In fact, even this picture is in a picture, as it is now.

If you believe me, my current card has a photograph of a gargoyle on it from the upper reaches of the Basilica of St Denis, near Paris. French kings are buried within. There appear to be gunshot marks on the extended neck of a fantasy beast, part eagle and part snake, holding an unfortunate screaming gnome-like figure in its claws. The figure is also mixed: half-lamb, half-human. The centre of the image is now missing, cut out according to a ragged rectangle.

The point of the game is to place the card over a support such that two different worlds are juxtaposed. The challenge is to trace as many significant relations running across the two worlds as you can. These work as an unseen background, forming a substratum to the world around us. We might think a world operates within well-defined boundaries and limits, of closeness and relevance for instance, but the premise of the process philosophy of signs is that there is no boundary resistant to blurring and multiple crossings, no two worlds of signs operating away from one another. There is no world that is not a zombie world for any other, ready to rise from the tomb and become a matter of urgent critical demands and creative openings through the medium of signs.

When I angle the card at the sky the idea of erosion through acid rain comes to the fore, but so too do the internal design of the gargoyle and the traces of centuries of rain running through it and projected away from the gothic building. I can place the card over the eye or hand of the new breed of reactionary demonstrator now occupying Paris, over a bloodshot eye haunted by the dead kings and saints of decaying cathedrals, and by the torturing claws of their mythical beasts or entrancing bones from their spiritual crypts. Or I can connect the stone of the gargoyle to the sand of a beach, or the simulated stone of a plastic kitchen top.

Is there a punctured card and support that cannot be connected, that can resist our ingenuity at detecting distant interactions? To play the game successfully the trace must be of relations and of related value shifts, that is, a change in one image must be traced to the other: the swish of the guillotine haunting the modern-day zealot; the polluted air above London carrying toxic droplets destined to fall on St Denis, *perfide albion*; the decrease in authenticity of the plastic top when even a soggy picture of sandstone reveals the absence of genuine patina.

Formally, the challenge the game puts to philosophy is for it to demonstrate that in some defined cases, or in principle, there can be no connections made between two worlds; that somehow when I take the card from its origin or far from its theme, then sufficient distance, or sufficient strangeness, or otherworldliness, or formal differences, or difference in content, will be enough to ward off unexpected zombie effects. Another way of thinking about the challenge is as a boast by art or literature to philosophy: any division you draw as absolute I will cross and erase, thereby raising a critical and creative potential in signs.

This challenge is not about meaning but about significance, that is, it is not whether the meanings of two signs can be said to be contradictory or impossibly distant, but whether the components of the signs can be traced to one another in some kind of intense relation. Is it possible to debar any connection of increases and decreases in speed and distance around two elements such that they can be said to be independent with no connection of changing values for one another? Is it possible to take two worlds and claim no relations can alter between them allowing subsequent language games to be haunted by those relations?

It is easy to cheat, of course, in these kinds of games. I enjoyed placing the card over images of the British royal family in one of our many magazines selling the rich to the poor and disenfranchised. The royals' efforts at ordinariness, while depending on the remnants of divine right to justify their unearned wealth, can be traced to the reposing beheaded figures from St Denis, from the miraculous saint who carried his head all the way from Paris, the kings who lost theirs, and future princes who might suffer similar uncrowning.

Why, though, would it be called cheating? It is that as an intellectual game we can trace narratives from one sign to another with apparent ease and according to fanciful connections, but the objection remains that those narratives aren't real. The lines we can trace between signs are fictional in some sense, where fiction indicates kinds of invention removed from how things really are. A fiction makes a difference but it is rarely anchored in real causal relations. A successful move in the game, one that draws a convincing possibility, does not have to rest on a real connection. This objection will become important in Chapter 4 where I discuss naturalism and process in the philosophy of biology.

Remarks on fictional lines of signs and on their disconnection from some kinds of reality are important because they raise deep problems for this philosophy of signs. They seem to indicate a set of restrictions for any process philosophy of signs speculating on the ubiquity and unbound connectedness of signs. First, the claim that everything is a sign does not seem to hold. There are signs and then there is the real world they relate to in some way. They can be about that world, but they can also not be about it.

Second, if signs relate to the world, is there something in that relation that holds as a condition for the nature of signs? If the world is made of distinct unchanging atoms, then the claim that signs are processes will fail as a way to allow signs to connect to the real world. So though it is possible to give an account of signs as a speculative model, the model must itself accord with conditions set by the real, if it is to make claims for a satisfactory relation to it.

Third, in reverse to the conditions the world sets for signs, a speculative philosophy of signs also sets speculative conditions for the world. I have made the claim that there are no legitimate cuts or abstractions in networks of signs as processes. If these signs are supposed to correspond in some way to a real world, then the claim about processes becomes a claim about the world. The process philosophy of signs becomes a wider claim about process as universal.

Fourth, I wrote earlier about different kinds of reality. Could it be that signs are different from other things such that we must either distinguish between the nature of real things and the nature of fictional signs, or such that we can speak of real signs and real things while drawing a firm distinction in reality, for instance that signs are always ideal or intellectual in some way whereas reality is concrete?

To answer these critical questions about the relation of the sign to some kind of external reality, the following chapters will take alternate approaches. Chapters 3 and 4 consider work on signs and process in biology and some philosophies of the sign, where process is introduced in the sign and as a metaphysical principle. The aim is to refine and clarify the design of the sign as process begun here, but in critical discussion with attempts to introduce process and sign into philosophy and biology.

With a formal definition of the process sign, in the context of other philosophies of the sign, Chapters 5 and 6 explain how the sign can follow from an unconditioned selection, giving rise to accusations of fictional content, and yet retain a critical role in relation to attempts to stipulate the proper content for a sign. Picking up the arguments from those chapters, Chapter 7 returns to the roots of this philosophy of the sign, found most strongly in the philosophy of Gilles Deleuze. It explains how the sign can be defined independently of external requirements such as typologies of signs, the need for a referent and a meaning, and logical limits for the consistency and validity of relations in signs.

Biology and the Design of Signs

SIGNS AND CRITICAL ALARM

At the end of the last chapter I raised a set of questions around the nature of the relation of signs to reality. If the sign is process, what does this imply for its relation to other entities? Are signs and other things different kinds of real entities? Would this imply a distinction between signs and nature? Could all things be signs and process?

There are many ways in which we might approach these problems, for instance from a prior philosophical definition of reality or according the latest dominant science – physics for our era. I will take neither of these paths. Instead, the speculative track of this process philosophy of signs is to test and refine definitions of the sign in relation to a set of critical cases. Formally, the sign has been defined as a selected set accompanied by a substratum consisting of a multiplicity of changing relations as mapped by a series of diagrams. This does not mean that the relations are between the elements as terms, but rather that the relations change the environment for those elements.

Metaphorically, the sign is like the wave of disruption crossing a crowded room when a strange event occurs in it. A rumour changes the faces, attitudes and interactions of a crowd as if its members bathed in an unstable medium of half-formed facts and feelings, like the supporters of a team hanging onto news from another match on which the survival of their team depends. Heist movies are good witnesses to process signs as intensively differential. They track the changing relations among a group of protagonists brought together during the raid, which itself becomes an overall sign for a kind of existential and social disruption. In a different register, condensed dramas of forced cohabitation for ill-matched characters, where external events and unexpected revelations are relayed unreliably into the space, also show process signs at work – in prison scenes, submarine pieces, or desperate journeys.

I have shown how this process sign contrasts with Wittgenstein's distinction between inert and live signs. In the case of heist films this comes out in the way a film can develop existential and material trails traced way back before the hold-up but operating on it in unexpected and unconscious ways – back from the dead, as it were. History works on the person through signs prior to their use.

In this chapter, I will work through a more precise account of the sign in the history of biology. This raises contrasts between philosophies of process and of the sign and allows me to refine my definition of the process sign. It enables me to distinguish definitions of process which make direct claims on the nature of reality and a process definition maintaining a critical distance between speculative definitions and ontological science-based ones. For a process definition of the sign I want to say that the real might accord with the sign, rather than that the sign is real.

The reference to past work in biology raises a background objection around philosophical naturalism, understood here in the loose sense of assigning priority to current sciences in determining the nature of the real. Why refer to historical cases when these have been superseded by current scientific theories? If the process philosophy is to be true in relation to some kind of reality, shouldn't that reality be defined by the latest and most secure scientific accounts? Would it not be absurd to test philosophical definitions against theories we knew to be outdated or flatly wrong?

There are two reasons for taking a wide view of the cases of signs and process. First, my concern is not directly with the nature of reality but with the problem of designing a process philosophy of signs. As such, though consistency with what we currently assume to be the correct theory is important, it is less so than the way in which past and current theories can teach us more about the right way to design the philosophy. If the appeal to the present is about current accuracy, the appeal to the past is about the robustness of future construction.

Second, a process account of signs must maintain a degree of independence from any given scientific theory if it is to remain robust as a philosophy of signs capable of making speculative claims about different time periods, fields and modes of significance to those of contemporary sciences. The definition of the sign developed here is an attempt to allow for such speculative critical claims. It therefore allows for a distance between the sign and any claim to truth.

I develop this idea of speculative reach further in Chapter 7 in my discussion of Whitehead.

The appeal to different periods indicates that claims to correctness and error are not the same for the speculative process philosophy and the sciences. The philosophy must be able to make a claim for correctness over different and inconsistent periods of scientific enquiry in order to be able to at least speculate about correctness were the current period to shift. Process philosophy is also philosophy of history, of the cuts, breaks, evolutions, wrong turns, felicitous accidents and cruel victories of historical unfolding. This historicity includes the sciences and their current states. They cannot be arbiters of their own historical place without overextending their proper domains or resting on claims to universality, in the sense of transcendence to time as change, or generality, in the sense of applying to any possible phenomenon at a given time.

Though he is known as a mathematician and as a philosopher of science, one of the secrets of Whitehead's process philosophy, as a speculative philosophy of experimental categories, lies in his historical awareness, where history is characterised by an ebb and flow of claims to pre-eminence and import, something we shall return to in a later chapter on signs as process in the philosophy of history. Process philosophy must worry about the problem of why any scientific period is one of shift and incompletion, as shown for instance in the debate around monistic and pluralistic views of science, to be covered in Chapter 4 in a study of John Dupré's recent work.

Given that we have undergone scientific revolutions and paradigm shifts, it is important for philosophy to maintain a distance from the latest claims of science, if only to produce non-scientific perspectives on the problems of such claims and on potential alternatives to them. Part of the interest in the speculative process philosophy then stems from the fact that claims are couched in signs and make assumptions about them, thereby providing a critical potential for speculative signs.

The reference to different fields draws out the speculative aim to have domains of application and flexibility between them such that fields of very different type and scale can be touched upon with as much sensitivity as possible and yet within an overarching philosophical frame, that is, with definitions of properly philosophical terms and relations, rather than ones adopted from a given science. Historical shifts justify scepticism towards the *latest* science. Differences in scale, for instance between populations and individuals, and differences in concern, for instance between a moral sign operating for an active intellect and a biological sign operating in a system, justify scepticism towards the *reach* of scientific theories when they lay claim to valid application across fields. This scepticism comes into play when, for example, a particular type of explanation is applied far from its core research field, as in the case of reductive explanations of complex forms of behaviour in terms of genetic codes or the evolution of populations.

None of this implies that a process philosophy of signs should be able to disprove sciences on their own terms. The appeal to modes of significance is meant to raise a different kind of interaction between historical and contemporary sciences and a speculative philosophy. This interaction is creative and critical rather than about the internal correctness of one or the other. 'Critical' indicates a prompt for reflection about the ways in which a philosophy or a scientific theory extend significantly into areas of concern far removed from their internal methods and criteria, as for example when a science has deep moral implications or when a philosophy makes broad claims about the nature of reality as mapped by the sciences.

'Creative' indicates the potential to generate new concepts and ideas out of step with current orthodoxies. The aim of the process philosophy of the sign is to foster critique and creativity by allowing the sign to roam free from dominant stipulations, for instance about the nature of the real. The sign must be able to generate counterfactuals, in order to allow for alternative worlds and ideas to work critically alongside current orthodoxy. This is why the process sign is defined in critical dialogue with a series of stipulations over the sign. Each sign is a node where multiple processes and a more limited number of stipulations over them meet and enter into dialogue and competition.

On the one hand, the critical and creative power of any sign lies in the way it can inform and provide a site for a debate between general claims about the sign and creative expressions of the intensive processes in the sign which resist these claims. On the other hand, a sign can also include a stipulation within it and thereby show how apparently independent claims of different orders meet in more complex genetic relations in the sign. Inclusion in a sign can help to show how a general theory has grown in relation to others, how it works with them now, and how it might fade in future.

The main point here is a distinction between error, which is determinant, and alarm, which is advisory. If a method has been misapplied or a criterion for experimentation misunderstood, we can frequently take the error as a basis for straight rejection. If a claim gives rise to alarm, we are not justified in discarding it, but we would be advised to embark on a critical reflection around the apparent disconnect between different systems of values, criteria and methods. In this usage, alarm should not only be seen as a reason for distress but also as an opportunity. It can be a pointer to novel developments as well as current threats.

An experimental error, perhaps the contamination of a sample or a statistical mistake, can rightfully lead to a quick rebuff. The triggering of a change in values is different. Distant discomfort, enthusiasm, intimations of adventure, crises, discordant findings, abnormal results, new discoveries, rapid or subtle warning signs, and disengagement or violent reactions are reasons to consider critical re-evaluation. For example, if a science leads to conclusions that are morally repugnant we cannot reject it on scientific grounds, but we can open a critical debate between different scientific theories, philosophical concepts and principles, and competing moral positions. This critical reflection cannot be fully scientific because the competing claims exceed the domain of any consistent set of sciences over time and at any given time.

NATURAL SIGNS AND MECHANISMS

Jakob von Uexküll's work on signs in biology is an important test for a process philosophy of signs. He was one of the first philosophers of biology to take the role of the sign as central to the discipline. In addition, he positions his turn to the sign against certain kinds of mechanistic reduction. This fits into the problem of the relation of process philosophy and science because the reaction to mechanistic models can be seen as an argument for kinds of value and process that exceed scientific accounts when they are based on crude determinism. Uexküll's critique of explanations in terms of cause and effect in mechanisms introduces special kinds of process requiring signs as instigators in a signal, perception, action and response process. This leads to cycles akin to dance steps exchanged between partners, where a signal such as a leading movement is perceived and then acted upon, thereby feeding back to the instigator of the initial movement and prompting a further change.

For Uexküll, animals are situated in environments of shared signs, perceptions and actions resonating with one another to form cycles: 'Since every action begins with the production of a perception mark and ends with the impression of an effect mark on the same carrier of meaning, one can speak of a functional cycle, which connects the carrier of meaning with the subject.'[1] When many such cycles work in counterpoint to one another, they come together to form symphonies. This symphonic view of nature and life, combining biological and aesthetic qualities, explains some of Uexküll's contemporary interest as a bridging figure between the arts and the sciences thanks to his holistic and non-reductive view of the natural world.

Early on in *A Foray into the Worlds of Animals and Humans*, his influential overview of a very wide series of sign-based processes in biology, published in 1934, Uexküll poses the main critical question of his work: 'We ask a simple question: Is the tick a machine or a machine operator? Is it a mere object or a subject?'[2] I want to stress the simple formal aspects of this question and distinguish them from their specific content. Uexküll wants to draw a distinction between something 'mere' and something more than 'mere'. This is both a value and a functional distinction. The mechanical is functionally different and in some ways inferior to that which is not merely a matter of mechanics.

As far as the design of a process philosophy of signs is concerned, I will question any absolute distinction drawn between different operations, such as those that are 'mere' or simply mechanical and those that are rich and endowed with life in some way. I am therefore interested in the way Uexküll uses signs to define a restricted yet rich domain and I will be critical of how this characterises the operation of signs and their proper domain. Finally, I wish to distance myself from a special kind of foundation for the operation of signs, one that depends on a transcendent pattern, plan or ideal determining which signs operate and how they do so. This is because the definition of the sign as an unconditioned selection and intensive multiplicity of relations must remain free from either transcendent conditions on the selection or transcendent stipulations over the internal relations of the sign. Uexküll's philosophy of biology includes both.

The contrast is between the claim that signs are everywhere but operating at different degrees dependent on selections and perspectives and the claim that signs operate in a special field, leaving others for different kinds of operation and values. It is also between the claim that signs operate in a specific way because they depend on other entities, such as subjects and ideals, and the claim that signs should be defined on an independent basis as multiple processes accompanied by variations in values, irrespective of which entities are then identified as dependent on the operation of signs. I want to avoid statements of the following sort: Where mechanisms are concerned there are no signs, because signs depend on special kinds of subjects whose operations on signs are pre-set according to an ideal encoded in the subject.

Once the formal distinction has been made between 'mere' and 'non-mere', the particular content given by Uexküll justifies the difference between the mechanical and non-mechanical through ideas of subject, meaning and plan. A subject-based activity is at work and its actions in response to meaning and according to a plan determine what's special and non-mechanistic about biological processes. The dependence on subjective action shows why I was concerned to raise the objection about the absurdity of an anachronistic philosophy of process. It cannot be right to go back to an outdated biology loosely based around a Kantian notion of the subject to develop a correct process philosophy of biology if contemporary biological research demonstrates the redundancy of such an appeal. If there is no evidence for transcendent plans and if they play no necessary role in explanation, then we should discount them. Why then refer to Uexküll's work on the sign in this study? I want to be critical of the appeal to the subject and to other Kantian and post-Kantian ideas while drawing lessons from the formal structures of Uexküll's account of signs and process for the design of a new process philosophy of signs.

Here is Uexküll's famous and influential explanation of why the world of the tick, and by extension any animal world, is more than a mechanism:

> Of all the effects emanating from the mammal's body, only three become stimuli, and then only in a certain sequence. From the enormous world surrounding the tick, three stimuli glow like signal lights in the darkness and serve as directional signs that lead the tick surely to its target. In order to make this possible, the tick has been given, beyond its body's receptors and effectors, three perception signs, which it can use as features, the progression of the tick's actions is so strictly prescribed that the tick can only produce very determinate effect marks.[3]

At first glance it is not at all obvious why this is not a description of a mechanism. This is the precise version of what happens to the tick according to Uexküll:

> The odor of butyric acid, which is given off by the skin glands of all mammals, gives the tick the signal to leave its watch post and leap off. If it then falls onto something warm – which its

fine sense of temperature will tell it – then it has reached its prey, the warm-blooded animal, and needs only use its sense of touch to find a spot as free of hair as possible in order to bore past its own head into the skin tissue of the prey. Now, the tick pumps a stream of warm blood slowly into itself.[4]

If we render this as a causal chain (acid causes leap, warmth causes hair-density search, low hair density causes boring, boring causes blood pumping) it seems that this is exactly the same as a causal account of a mechanism. It could apply to a pump system, such as a simplified hydraulic brake (foot on brake causes pressure increase in master chamber, transfer of pressure through liquids in brake lines causes increased pressure in piston behind callipers, this causes callipers to bite on disc, car slows down). There is no subject in this system to respond to the pressure on the pedal, so why assume that there is any subject in the tick? Furthermore, the sign also seems redundant once we rid ourselves of the subject. There is nothing to interpret and respond to as a meaningful sign in a brake cylinder. The increased pressure is not a meaning for the callipers, so there is no need to add signs to the causal chain. Is it not the same for the tick?

For the tick the process is different because the signs do not operate in the same way as mechanisms. First, like any other animal, the tick works on the world around it through a selection: 'only three stimuli'. This selection is made thanks to signs, because it is signs that determine a specific subsection of the world: 'from the enormous world surrounding the tick'. Second, once this selection has been made, the signs then determine the interaction of the animal with that subsection in terms of a strict order of point and counterpoint of signs, perceptions and actions according to a plan: 'the progression of the tick's actions is so strictly prescribed'. The plan determines the order of instantiation of perception organs and effect organs in the animal, and effectors and receptors in an object of the environment (which can also be another animal or animals). The sign triggers a perception organ and this then effects a change, for instance when the tick perceives the smell of the acid and drops from the branch.

So what exactly is the difference with a mechanism? The mechanism does not select within the world in the same way as an animal. Uexküll's point is that a wide range of causes can be satisfactory for a mechanism so long as they satisfy a particular requirement, for instance the pressure required to extend the callipers. A mechanism is not restricted in the same way as an animal or indeed a plant in relation to its signs. It could just as well be an emergency secondary brake circuit activating the callipers. Whereas for the tick it is an intimate and specialised relation to the acid and no other sign or cause. It has to be butyric acid presented in a specific way.

In a mechanism, the order of relation between causes and effects is not seamless and closed. Within quite broad limits, we can cut into and expand hydraulic and electrical circuits without harm to their overall operation. For the tick the time order and spatial coordinates of signs have to be exactly right. This synthesis of space and time as a condition for the synthesis of the world of the tick can be described as post-Kantian in so far as it is indebted to the a priori synthesis of space and time presented in the *Critique of Pure Reason*.[5] The debt is loose and complicated, though. The synthesis is not a priori for Uexküll since the tick is the product of evolution. The synthesis is necessary for the tick and allows for the description of a transcendent plan for ticks. Were the height of the tree to increase or the hair matting on the back of the animal to thicken, the tick and its environment would separate and the tick would die. Holistic ecological ideas about environments can therefore be mapped onto Uexküll's distinction between mechanisms and sign-based environments because the latter are seen as fragile, intimate and interdependent relations.

Selection thanks to signs creates closed and delicate relations, in the sense that only some signs will do for the living being in a specific series of operations. This sealed and fragile series differs from the causal world of the machine and its indifference to what instigates a necessary cause and its openness to extensions and changes, for instance when we add or remove components. The animal has an intimate environment (an *Umwelt* in Uexküll's original) whereas the machine has an extendable and indifferent physical world.

Uexküll's commitment to the closed and intimate nature of the animal and environment cycle is at the heart of his understanding of how signs work. Some of the evidence for this closeness comes from his reading of experiments that attempt to graft different parts between animals. Grafts fail because organs designed to respond to particular signs are included in cycles that are not adapted to them:

> In normal development, the originally homogeneous cell material arranges itself in buds that receive their meaning orders according to the primal layout – for the organism is composed of utilizers of meaning. Only then does the specific

melody of the buds begin to sound and build up the form of the utilizers of meaning. If one exchanges the buds of different animal species, each bud receives in its new place a meaning order which matches that place in the layout: 'Become a mouth, eye, ear, etc.'[6]

The maladaptation leads to unviable individuals. This lack of viability elicits strong reactions from Uexküll:

> The transplanted bud will follow the meaning command of the host, even if it had been located at a different spot in its maternal organism and had received accordingly another meaning order. But it then follows the maternal form development melody. It becomes a mouth, not a triton mouth, but rather, a tadpole mouth. The final result is a malformation, for a carnivore with a vegetarian's mouth is an abomination.[7]

Cycles of signs, perceptions and actions are sealed such that when they are broken up and recombined we are left with unviable animals. This is unlike the way different components can be swapped in engines or computers. However, we shall see later when we study Bapteste and Dupré's work on process in biology that we can have such biological cross-combinations. They are common at the microbial level. Another counterexample is stem cells since, even if they follow some kind of plan, it is one that allows for many different organs. This is in direct opposition to Uexküll's account of single melodies for each cell.

The interdependence of sign, meaning, subject and plan is central to Uexküll's argument, because signs require a subjective change responding to something meaningful in accordance with a wider plan. He contrasts the shape of clouds blown by different winds and the flight of seeds. This seems to be a bad example, since there appears to be little difference between the elongated trail from a smokestack and the scatter of seeds on a breeze. However, Uexküll's point is that the scatter is adapted to the wind. It has taken advantage of the wind as part of the purpose to scatter seed. This scattering is itself part of a precise plan for the reproduction of the plant:

> A completely different image appears to us if we follow the flight of the graceful parachutes of the dandelion in the wind or the corkscrew motion of the maple key or of the light fruit

of the linden. In this case, the wind is not a cause of the development of form, as with the clouds, but rather, the forms are adjusted to the meaning factor 'wind,' which they utilize in different ways for scattering seed. Nonetheless, there are those who want to speak of the wind as the causal agent of these forms because it has affected the object 'plant' for millions of years. Yet the wind has affected the clouds for a far longer time without shaping any lasting form. The meaningful form that lasts is always the product of a subject and never – no matter for how long – of a planlessly worked-on object.[8]

The key concepts here are 'cause', 'development', 'form', 'adjustment' and 'utilize'. The wind and the flight are in a meaningful relation, where the gust is the sign for the seeds to spin and drift in a certain way according to a developed form. This form is the plan for the dandelion, maple or linden. The seeds are adjusted to the wind which therefore becomes a sign for them. For Uexküll, cause and sign are different because, unlike mechanisms altering directly in relation to a cause, sign systems involve a third term, the plan, in the way they work with the sign.

The plume from the smokestack would only be equivalent to the flights of seeds if we had built the stack at a certain height to lift the vapour away from the ground. Then the parallel would work, because we could take the direction of the smoke as meaningful according to the plan to avoid ground-level pollution. In both cases, we move beyond simple cause and effect and into meaning because signs have been selected as meaningful for a specific process according to a pre-set plan. The plan defines the signs as interpretable according to it and as distinct from other features in the world. The wind is a meaningful sign for the seeds, not because they can reflect upon it or understand it, but because the wind makes sense in the plan for reproduction of the plant in a selected environment.

The intimate and specialist nature of the relation to an environment also implies that we cannot treat plant and animal structures in the same way as mechanisms, for instance when we seek to transform mechanisms through exploitation and maximisation of particular aspects. Each mechanistic move, such as the expansion or restriction of a particular part, can be assessed simply in terms of whether it increases or decreases a desired outcome, for example when we seek to extend a hydraulic system but have to weigh that against risks of leaks or decreases in pressure. This piecemeal and substitution-based approach is not possible for sign systems because the plan sets the relation of signs and process in closed cycles which fail when broken into or tampered with.

Intervention in the process of animal signs puts the whole environment and animal relation at risk much more quickly and with more devastating effects because of a 'complete dependency' of animal and environment:

> Each environment forms a self-enclosed unit, which is governed in all its parts by its meaning for the subject. According to its meaning for the animal, the life stage includes a greater or smaller space, in which the places are completely dependent in number and size upon the capacity of the sense organs of respective subjects to draw distinctions.[9]

The animal's senses pick up on signs in a precise and carefully laid out manner, thereby marking a deep difference with the flexibility of mechanical systems.

SIGNS, SUBJECTS AND PLANS

The closeness of living thing and environment leads to Uexküll's influential ideas about animals, signs and relations. Unlike a mechanism, the animal dwells in an intimate way in a selected and restricted environment. This selection is made by defining closed cycles of signs, perceptions and actions which relate animal to environment. The animal has a subjective time and space according to signs determined according to an ideal plan or design. Much of Uexküll's work in *A Foray into the World of Animals and Humans* and the later *Theory of Meaning* consists in beautiful descriptions of these times, spaces and preformed signifying patterns. This preformation is not absolute for Uexküll, since it follows from evolution over time. It is this idea of preformation that draws his account of synthesis of time and space according to cycles of signs away from the strict sense of a priori synthesis for the subject in Kant.

The reason why this intimacy of animal and environment must be thought of in terms of signs is that strict orders of time and space are set out by a counterpoint of animal and environment. This counterpoint works through the cycle of perception, action and response to signs. The points countering each other in complex networks are perception mark carriers, perception organs, effect organs and effect mark carriers. The reason Uexküll uses the term counter is that between the perception organ and effect organ a different process begins, for instance in the tick a smell is countered by a release from the branch.

This countering also takes place between the effect mark carrier and perception mark carrier, for instance when a trapped fly's movements turn it into a sign for the spider. The wings are an effect-organ. The effect mark is the vibration of the web. The counterpoint perception mark carrier is the perception of the movement by the spider and the countering effect-organ is the movement towards the fly: 'There is therefore a primal score for the fly as there is one for the spider. And I now assert that the primal score of the fly (which one can also designate its primal image) affects the primal score of the spider in such a way that the web spun by the latter can be called "fly-like".'[10] This description is given by Uexküll when he considers the accusation made against him by mechanists or determinists that the idea of plan is an illegitimate metaphysical import into biology. His response is that the plan is a necessary explanation for the counterpoint fit of signs across animals and environments.

The plan is the reason the animal to environment relation is meaningful. Signs determine the type of meaning as series of counterpoints in specific spaces and times. Environments and animals belong together because they mean something either to a form of minimal consciousness allowing for recognition of belonging – the marks an animal places around its territory – or through meaningfulness in relation to a deep inborn plan – the selection proper to a species. In both cases, the meaning is then given shape according to which signs operate in counterpoint with one another.

Belonging, intimacy and dwelling are central to Uexküll's argument. We do not live in homogeneous and general sets of things, but in a set of bubbles which can include one another but cannot be reduced to an indifferent collection of things: 'We must therefore imagine all the animals that animate Nature around us, be they beetles, butterflies, gnats, or dragon flies who populate a meadow, as having a soap bubble around them, closed on all sides, which closes off their visual space and in which everything visible for the subject is also enclosed.'[11] These bubbles allow us to define territories when we order the signs in them according to particular patterns of perception and action: 'Among all the many rocks and trees of the surroundings, there are a few that, placed one after the other, distinguish themselves as path markers from all the other rocks and trees, even though no sign makes this known to anyone not familiar with the path.'[12] The private path through a wood or the marks on a territory mean something to the humans and animals because they are a system of signs which creates a bubble or subjective sphere.

The environment of animals as defined by signs does not allow for the division of animals or of environments and the substitution of parts within them. Signs are subjective in the sense that they determine the belonging of animals as a relation of subjective meaning right down to interactions at the most apparently automatic level such as muscle movements: 'The muscle behaves like a living subject that transforms all external effects into the same stimulus, which causes its activity.'[13] Just as the environment of the tick means something for its specific design, the muscle does not simply react to a cause but rather defines a world of signs which it then reacts to. This is more like a conditioned reflex, requiring subjective input in accordance with a plan before it becomes automatic, than a simple law-driven relation of cause and effect.

Subjective meaning is the right word here because there is no universal substitutability or access through division and exchange, which would allow a wide range of objective causes to work so long as they satisfied certain conditions for certain effects. However, it is the wrong term if we understand it as meaning for an individual subject. It is rather meaning according to a plan which determines orders and relations of signs in time and space. The sign is tailored to the perception and action cycles of the animal. The environment means different things thanks to signs that cannot be applied in the same way by different species or individuals because their plans differ:

> These tones correspond to the peeping sound of the bat, which is the main enemy of the moth. Only the sounds emitted by their specific enemy are picked up by the moths. Otherwise, the world is silent to them. In the bats' environment, the peeping serves as a sign of recognition in the darkness. The same sound strikes the ear of a bat at one time and the ear of a moth at another. Both times, the peeping bat appears as a carrier of meaning – one time as friend, the next as enemy – depending on the meaning utilizer with which it is confronted.[14]

The main argument here is that the same cause has different effects for different subjects and their differing plans. These effects must be set in a perception and action cycle dependent on counterpoint set by the plan for there to be a successful combination of environment and animal. It is this specialisation determined by perception and action that allows for interpretation in terms of meaning rather than in terms of mere cause and effect.

Instead of identifying subjects with individual perceivers and actors, which might limit the concept to humans and near humans, the subject and sign are united by plans and designs. These vary in their scale of application from individuals to species. The design can be connected to individual actions, for instance when territories are determined by an individual human or animal, but they can also apply to species:

> Since the bat's perception-sign palette is large, the higher tone it hears remains one among many. The perception-sign palette of the moth is very limited, and there is only one sound in its world – an enemy sound. The peep is a simple product of the bat, and the spider's web is a very artful product. But both have one thing in common: Neither of them is only meant for one, physically present subject, but for all animals of the same structure.[15]

The plan sets the structure of perception capacities which in turn sets the range of signs from the environment. Meaning is therefore not restricted to kinds of individual reflection on signs. Signs need not have an independent linguistic meaning or sense. Instead, the signs, perceptions, actions and effects on the environment form a meaningful structure reflected in the design of different kinds of subject. A certain environment of signs means something for the subject moth or spider because of their specific designs. On an individual level, a certain trail of deposited signs means something for an animal or human in its territory. The subject therefore varies very widely in terms of scale from one to any member of a given species, 'for all animals of the same structure'.

To draw out the lessons of this use of signs in biology for the design of the process sign it is helpful to consider two opposing ways of reacting to Uexküll's philosophy of nature. We can see it positively as the basis for an argument for a musical and connected account of nature: an artistic and ecological philosophy. This tack is taken by Elizabeth Grosz in *Chaos, Territory, Art: Deleuze and the Framing of the Earth*, where she traces the influence of Uexküll on Deleuze and Guattari and then shows the artistic potential of his philosophy of biology:

For Uexküll, the music of nature is not composed by living organisms, a kind of anthropomorphic projection onto animals of a uniquely human form of creativity; rather it is the *Umwelten*, highly specifically divided up milieu fragments that play the organism. The organism is equipped by its organs to play precisely the tune its milieu has composed for it, like an instrument playing in a larger orchestra.[16]

Grosz underscores the new sense of subject at work in Uexküll's philosophy by insisting on its resistance to anthropomorphic models for action and creativity. This explains why she reverses the relation of subject to environment such that the latter plays the former. However, she removes the role of the plan by saying that a milieu composes for an organism. For Uexküll, the composition is in the plan because otherwise there would be no reason for specific relations of organism and milieu. The plan explains why a particular relation emerges rather than any other.

The problem with Grosz's musical and holistic account of nature is therefore that it underestimates the presuppositions and implications of the theory of the sign and the account of process devised by Uexküll. This theory arrives at the musical account on the basis of the counterpoint combination of environments or bubbles, signs, perceptions and actions in accordance with plans which also determine the nature of meanings and subjects. These presuppositions involve far-reaching philosophical commitments which are underplayed by Grosz, and by Deleuze and Guattari.[17]

In distinguishing Heidegger and Uexküll's accounts of space and in discussing Heidegger's 1929 reading of Uexküll, Jeff Malpas draws out some of these commitments and identifies their negative aspects.[18] There are strong affinities in the ecological tone and some of the terms shared by Heidegger and Uexküll. However, Malpas shows that these mask deep differences. First, he notes the 'subjectivist' character of Uexküll's definition of environment (*Umwelt*):

The character of any particular *Umwelt* (and von Uexküll does not restrict the applicability of the concept, taking humans, as well as animals, to have an *Umwelt* of their own) is always relativized to the creature whose *Umwelt* it is, constituting a sphere of sense and action that encloses the creature, and that is essentially its own.[19]

Second, he identifies a 'functionally-oriented' character to environments:

> In their functionally oriented character, von Uexküll's *Umwelten* thus appear in a way that suggests obvious affinities with the equipmentality-ordered structure of world as developed in *Being and Time*. It is perhaps no surprise then that Heidegger was so concerned to distinguish his account of world from the sort of account evident in von Uexküll.[20]

For Heidegger, a world is neither subjectively determined nor reducible to a set of functions because it 'emerges *as world*' with the being of the human, with what the human is rather than what individual human subjects do.[21]

This being is therefore neither subjective nor functional in its world-forming. The world emerges with the being of humans in ways that are not open to animals, for instance through world-forming with language, where language is essential to what the human is rather than something used or created by humans. Malpas argues that this allows Heidegger to maintain a difference between humans and animals, as defined by Uexküll, around their relations to worlds. For Uexküll, the worlds are subjective and functional. For Heidegger, they are ontological and world-forming.

My critical stance with respect to Uexküll is close to Malpas's but does not go quite as far. First, I think Malpas is at some distance from Uexküll in his description of subjectivist character. His use of 'relativized to creatures' and 'essentially its own' underplays the two-way and counterpoint nature of the animal and signs relation. As we have seen, the animal and environment emerge together in cycles such that it is not the case that the world is relativised to the animal, since we could just as well claim the exact opposite.

Grosz's focus on the musical and counterpoint aspects is much more accurate. So if we understand 'subjectivist' as indicating an orientation to an individual subject, as shown in the expression 'its own', then Uexküll's philosophy is explicitly not subjectivist since he has a flexible account which involves different kinds of subject, based on plans that unite them to their environments. This does not indicate subjective ownership of a territory but rather an intimate fit of animal and environment according to a subjective plan.

Second, Malpas's focus on function underestimates the importance of signs and meaning in Uexküll and therefore misses his critique of mechanisms. Uexküll certainly uses the language of function and it can seem that the relation of animal to environment is functional in its cycle of signs, perceptions, actions and responses. However, the important argument is that this cycle is itself the result of a selection of the environment according to a plan and that the cycle forms a delicate and closed meaningful relation. Though each part of the cycle can resemble a function, the cycle itself emerges with the environment and animal in a manner that cannot be reduced to function defined mechanistically.

Heidegger's ontological account of world-forming and the sense of the emergence of the world with the being of humans are consistent with Uexküll's understanding of the evolution for species and creation of territories for individuals. The distinction between them around the special ontological status of the human does not hold if it is to be based around function and subjectivist character. On the contrary, Uexküll's account of different kinds of subject within bubbles that enter into musical relations offers a counter-argument to Heidegger's human-animal distinction.

Grosz's description of the artistic and creative character of animal and human life shows how Uexküll far exceeds functional and equipment-based accounts of a relation to the world. The sign is never limited to function in Uexküll because the sign must always be understood as meaningful in relation to a plan, rather than determined by that plan. Nonetheless, the innovative definitions given by Uexküll do raise the concerns about thinking of the world as relative to something that underpin Malpas's critique. It is not a problem of subjectivism or functional determinism but rather a problem of the isolation of signs in particular cycles and according to specific plans. This difference around kinds of selection leads to my critical stance.

SIGNS ARE NOT PROPER

Uexküll's argument is vulnerable to developments in biology around general processes, the successful exchange of components across species, and cross-species evolution. If we can explain the relation of animals to environments through general genetic building blocks and laws, or through substitutions and evolution across species, then the claim for meaningful bubbles proper to species and individuals will be open to a critique in terms of alternative substitutions, divisions and syntheses. His philosophy runs counter to a homogeneous theory of nature that does not require plans proper to species and counterpoint between meaningful signs in cycles. These alternative accounts might well still appeal to the idea of signs, for instance in relation to codes, but they will not depend on subjects, counterpoint and plans.

Uexküll's biological definition of sign is bound to an era of biological research and to the scientific theories that accompany it. His wider explanations are also committed to the more philosophical ideas of subject, plan and meaning. The close attachment to science is to be avoided in this process philosophy of signs by avoiding dependence on the role of signs in nature. Signs, as defined here, are not natural if this means scientific explanations of natural processes should determine what signs are. Instead, natural elements can be included in the definition of signs but without claiming that they must conform to natural laws and processes.

I want to draw attention to the following features of Uexküll's definition of the sign in relation to animals and their environments:

1. For each animal there is a limited number of signs that operate in the environment.
2. Signs form chains and closed circuits that must follow specific orders.
3. These chains lead to closed times and spaces for animals and species.
4. The animal can only perceive and act on the sign in particular ways.
5. The operation and meaning of signs depends on transcendent plans.

These features allow Uexküll to define bubbles for animals because each bubble is characterised by the number, type and operation of its signs, for instance the tick bubble with its three signs. The features also underpin his claims for the special nature of animals and environments as meaningful and as different from mechanical systems. A bubble is an enclosed space-time whose processes involve meaningful signs.

My concern is that instead of a continuous multiplicity of signs that are differentiated through relative selections and different degrees of intensity in these relations, the sign is presented in individuated form in four ways. First, particular orders in time and places in space define signs in relation to spatial boundaries and limited times. Second, this means signs relate to limited environments and their operation is restricted to narrow cycles within them. Third, when signs are governed by a transcendent plan they are given boundaries of viability and properness by the plan. Fourth, these restrictions lead to an account of selection in signs which divides the world and defines the proper boundaries of this partition.

There is a possible answer to this critique around restriction since Uexküll allows for the connection of bubbles and closed signs through the sharing of signs between circuits. For him, shared signs can be taken up in different ways in different bubbles. These cannot be reduced to one another and instead connect in the symphonic vision of resonant environments invoked in the finals lines of *A Theory of Meaning*. If we think of individual instruments and voices and the melodies they play as analogous to individual animals and their sign bubbles, we can see how separate entities can come together in harmony and counterpoint to make a bigger whole yet without losing individual identity. As we have seen in the work of Grosz, this symphonic vision is attractive to later thinkers such as Ruyer, and Deleuze and Guattari:

> There are not only the manifolds of space and time in which things can be spread out. There is also the manifold of environments, in which things repeat themselves in always new forms. All these countless environments provide, in the third manifold, the clavier on which Nature plays her symphony of meaning beyond time and space.[22]

So though a sign is restricted to a closed cycle for a given animal in its particular space and time, this space and time forms a manifold with others that take up its signs and objects in different ways so 'things repeat themselves in always new forms'. The animal environment only works as a sign process in a restricted form, but this form extends into 'countless environments' taking up parts of each other in different ways, as for instance when bacteria are transmitted through ticks (in Lyme disease, say) and blood becomes a different kind of sign for the tick and for bacterium in their different cycles.

Uexküll takes this extension to the level of plans and meaning 'beyond time and space' where the structures for all things come together: 'We now know that our sun in our sky, along with the garden which is filled with plants, animals, and people, are only symbols in an all-encompassing natural composition, which orders everything according to rank and meaning.'[23] The ordering according to rank points towards an ethical and political problem in the appeal to transcendent plans. If signs must follow such plans they become conditions for judgements about proper use and boundaries, already apparent in Uexküll's abhorrence for cross-species mutations.

Meaning determined according to the right plan then becomes the basis for these judgements. Though it could be argued that these are natural rather than moral judgements, I want to oppose such a defence. Were they correct about nature – which they aren't in relation to current science – they would still invite critical alarm and pressing questions about the ethical and political implications of rank and organisation according to proper meaning.[24] So when I advocate a separation of the natural and sign realms, I do not want to exclude critique between the two. That's not to say Uexküll has crude ideas of rank or meaning which necessarily lead to violent exclusions, but rather that any prior ordering according to meaning implies fixed boundaries and judgements around them which may be detrimental to things lying beyond or across such boundaries.

Later interpreters of Uexküll could respond to this criticism by adopting some aspects of his philosophy, its musical tropes, for instance, while discarding his ideas of rank and absolute boundaries. This has the great merit of releasing new potential in concepts while breaking earlier and unnecessary historical attachments. However, despite the release of new potential through a discerning interpretation, a lot depends on whether the transformed concepts still carry risks within them despite innovative contexts and connections.

Anne Sauvagnargues has shown these risks in the work of Raymond Ruyer, a French philosopher of biology and technology whose work owes a debt to Uexküll. She coins two useful concepts to explain the problem. First, Ruyer's philosophy 'hardens' real individuality: 'Ruyer's unitary conception of form forces him to harden true individuality by polarising any form between its pole as actual agent and its ideal virtual pole.'[25] This means the real form is dependent on its plan or ideal so the animal is fixed or hardened as subject or agent in relation to its ideal identity.

So, second, the philosophy is 'locked down' twice. This is because agents are locked into an actual form and locked according to virtual ideals as transcendent and eternal identities: 'Ruyer's system is thus locked down twice: first around the granular individuality of true forms that actualize essences that they overfly mnemonically, and a second time around virtual ideals thus actualized but also preexisting in an antecedent eternity.'[26] The granular identity corresponds to the bubbles in interrelated environments in Uexküll. They form a coarse-grained universe where actual beings recall from memory, 'mnemonically', the essences they correspond to, without being direct copies of them.

According to Ruyer, real agents are in 'overflight' or skim over essences. I have taken this term from the French *survol* as translated by Ronald Bogue in a chapter on Deleuze and Ruyer, where Bogue is more sympathetic to the idea of a non-transcendent reading of Ruyer than Sauvagnargues:

> We should avoid seeing in Ruyer's developmental melody a version of preformationism. The developmental melody is not like the perforated paper roll of a player piano that mechanically generates the piano's performance of the actual organism. Rather the developmental melody is best thought of as a musical theme in the process of forming itself as a variation of that theme.[27]

The crux here is whether forming a theme, in a musical sense that draws an avowed link to Uexküll, amounts to freedom from the hardening and locking down identified by Sauvagnargues. I do not think it does because when we inspect the detail of Ruyer and Uexküll's processes we see effects that correspond directly to hardening, as the fixing of identity through boundaries for process, and locking down, as the settling of explanation of change through transcendent entities such as the proper theme, plan and essence for any given actor or subject.

Ruyer allows actual things in overflight to retain some independence and individuality and yet fit an essence that corresponds to the species. However, they also fit an ideal plan that sets the values for actual beings thus explaining how species can evolve according to the plan while also retaining the identity of the species according to the essence. Sauvagnargues argues that 'Ruyer's universe is unified universally through this formula: "there is always an [agent] working to realize an [ideal]". The agent is a primary consciousness passing through diverse types of complexity, realising either its type, its organic memory, or its spiritual value, by annexing functions and setting up organic or technical structures.'[28] Very similar to Uexküll's subjects, Ruyer's agents are therefore always between essence and ideal. They are fixed by both such that change is a shift from essence to essence according to an ideal realised by agents.

The concepts of pre-existence and eternity highlighted by Sauvagnargues are important because they show the Platonic aspects of Ruyer's philosophy. The ideal realm is not formed by the actualisation; it pre-exists it as eternal. In both Ruyer and Uexküll this does not mean that all eternal ideals are actualised at any given time. It is quite the contrary: actual forms realise some and discard other ideal forms. Ruyer and Uexküll can therefore hold to actual evolution while also speaking of transcendent ideals and plans, because evolution can be explained as change between actual things corresponding to different plans. That's why I will shortly be focusing on the problem of types of selection because it is how selection takes place in these explanations of change that makes the biggest difference to ideas of process.

Sauvagnargues draws our attention to the theological structure of Ruyer's model: 'Antecedent virtual and thematic actualization define a theology that retracts and petrifies itself in this static beat between actualizing forms and eternal essences.'[29] This is theological in the neo-Platonic sense of an eternal God and the worldly actualisation of his plan. The main concern, though, is not with any religious implication but rather with the concealment and withdrawal, the retraction, that leaves a petrified process. The beat is static rather than dynamic. The process has fixed points, relatively in the case of actualising forms and absolutely in the case of essences and ideals.

There are risks inherent to Uexküll's concept of the sign as fixed or petrified when it serves as a model for a process philosophy of signs. I will focus on two characteristics of the sign which follow from its definition and operation while also carrying far-reaching consequences for any realm or domain of signs as process. The characteristics are 'indifference' and 'neglect'. They will allow me to give a more precise definition of the individuation of the sign through abstraction which I attribute to Uexküll even where he speaks of a symphonic counterpoint of all environments and signs. It is this abstraction that leads to the petrification of process.

Uexküll draws attention to the characteristic of indifference when discussing the relation of tick to mammal. However, it applies to all sign processes and follows directly from the operation of signs and their limited number in cycles. Were there to be any doubt about its applicability once we move to the musical tropes from his philosophy, indifference is a consequence of the plan for the tick described as a formative melody: 'However great the meaning of mammals is in the tick's environment, the formative melody of mammals takes part to the same extent in the formation of the tick, to wit, as the odor of butyric acid, as the resistance of hair, as warmth, and as penetrability of the skin.'[30]

Four signs taken up in this melody are sufficient for a description of the tick cycle: 'It is completely indifferent to the tick that mammals possess thousands of other properties. Only those properties common to all mammals appear as motifs in the formation of the tick, where its perception organs as well as its effect organs are concerned.'[31] The motif is the rendering of the sign in the plan or melody. The key to understanding the sufficiency of a limited number of signs is in the affirmation that 'only' certain properties appear as motifs. Other properties simply do not register and hence it is correct to say that the tick is indifferent to them.

For Uexküll, the addition of other signs would be disastrous for the tick cycle. In turn, this commits him to a state-disaster-state model for evolution, where change occurs through the destruction of cycles and their replacement by others that use signs differently. Evolution by jumps between stable states is therefore a complement to the granular or bubble account of nature. Evolution cannot be smooth and continuous but must rather involve violent leaps because the things that evolve are closed in on themselves in fragile associations of sign cycles and environments. When change occurs these cycles and associations are broken in favour of others.

The idea of complete indifference is problematic, though, because the life of ticks as individuals or as a species is not completely indifferent to other signs in the mammal world. For instance, were the odour of butyric acid to be masked by a new sign then this would greatly affect the ticks. We attempt such masking against mosquitoes when we use citronella. It is not correct to say they are indifferent to the citronella, or to other more effective ways of stopping them. Those ways work through signs as defined by Uexküll since an effect such as masking is an operation on signs.

If by indifference we understand a lack of any effects, then it is not the case that sign cycles are highly limited because each sign works under negative and positive wider conditions through extended environments. There must be something in the tick, in any animal bubble and environment association, that allows for signs from beyond its closed cycle to intervene in it sometimes in a simple way, for instance in an effect of masking, sometimes in very complex ways, for instance when this leads to cross-species evolution. Uexküll has counterpoint as a resource for explaining such processes, but it cannot do this work if the processes are consistent and continuous rather than counter to one another. The concept of complete indifference requires counterpoint which allows for breaks and jumps between processes, but if processes coexist and connect more widely and seamlessly then Uexküll's conceptual frame is incorrect and counterproductive.

The deep problem with the characteristic of indifference lies with Uexküll's logical claim that there can be complete indifference to signs outside the cycle determining any given being. It is never complete, on the view I wish to defend, because there is always the potential for a minimally present sign from the environment to take on a greater role, for instance when there is an amplifying of a sign by another. However, I do not want to argue for ideas such as degrees of signs and the continuity of signs beyond assigned limits as biological facts. The point of the critique here is to draw attention to the lessons to be learned from Uexküll's definition of signs in biology for a parallel view of signs where natural things can be taken as signs without claiming they operate through them.

There is a similar difficulty to the claim about indifference in Uexküll's work on neglect, where there is again a claim to completeness. The discussion is important because it belongs to the explanation of the evolution of animals and change in environments. Instead of an account of degrees of influence of signs across cycles and environments Uexküll favours explanations of strict inclusion or exclusion. When there is a change between environments some signs are taken up and others fall into complete neglect: 'Anything and everything that comes under the spell of an environment is either redirected and re-formed until it becomes a useful carrier of meaning or it is completely neglected. Thereby, the original components are often crudely torn apart without the slightest consideration for the structural plan which controlled them to that point.'[32] So when an environment takes over another the selection of signs is strictly a matter of either in or out. The sign is adopted in a new cycle or it is fully discarded. Complete neglect is necessary in Uexküll's model because otherwise the account of closed cycles would collapse.

A state and break model follows logically from the commitments to completeness in closed environments, because were transitions smooth and connections extended, the range of signs for any given animal would extend much more widely than Uexküll can allow given his definition of animals and environment through a restricted number of characteristic signs and processes. Without a clear cut between them, a 'tearing apart', new environments and cycles extend into others and into the operation of their signs. My argument is that Uexküll's account of the sign is a detrimental model for the operation of signs as process because it misses a different potential for the idea of process and the idea of the sign as extended, continuous and differentiated according to variations in values.

To avoid the closed nature of circuits of signs in Uexküll's account, I have defined the sign as a selection against a limitless and continuous intensive substratum. This means that at least in its pure state, the environment for a sign is nothing like the plan, number and subject restricted environment in his biological definition. For the process sign to retain its reach and for it to remain as open as possible, there must be no transcendent elements to it or external restrictors. This also explains why stipulations over the sign are defined as general laws or codes imposed on the sign, rather than features of the sign proper. If they are included in the sign as legitimate elements of it, they become transcendent factors for the sign and serve to limit it.

Process Signs and the Process Philosophy of Biology

In their article 'Towards a Processual Microbial Ontology' Eric Bapteste and John Dupré argue for the importance of processes in biology.[1] Their demonstration has a critical element in seeking to offer a counter-model to an Aristotelian model of stable entities divided according to species.[2] Instead, stability is seen as relative, the result of a process of stabilisation. Process therefore becomes the primary ontological form. As such, they view it as leading to a pluralistic explanatory framework: 'a diverse set of processes including, for example, as well as phylogenetic relations, interactions that stabilise or destabilise the interacting entities, spatial relations, ecological connections, and genetic exchanges'.[3] Biological entities are relative to processes of stabilisation and destabilisation in this new process ontology.

There are strong lines of agreement between this modern process philosophy of biology and the process philosophy of signs. They share the priority given to process in ontology, the critique of Aristotelian models built on stable entities, the definition of process in terms of relative intensities (of stabilisation and destabilisation for Bapteste and Dupré, but of an unlimited series of changing intensities of relations for the process sign), and pluralism about explanation and commitment to multiplicity for biological processes and for signs. However, the first difference to draw attention to is methodological, in relation to the place of empirical research, metaphysical definition and philosophical speculation.

Bapteste and Dupré's work is for the main part empirical through close study of recent research on microbial systems and their evolution. Nonetheless, it also involves ontological definitions and hypotheses. I am interested in the latter because they illuminate how a process philosophy of signs might take inspiration from process philosophy of biology but also need to take some distance from it.

I want to consider how their research offers a different model to Uexküll's restriction of the sign and hence of process, but also how it has other methodological commitments which a process philosophy of signs will have to avoid. These commitments indicate some of the problems associated with scientific naturalism having too strong a hold on process philosophy.

The article begins with three far-reaching principles about the real, about living things and about the biological world. The principles are co-dependent since the second can be seen as following from the first, as the third follows from the second. When taken together they are the philosophical basis for the process ontology. The first principle advocates a distinction between a real entity and an 'artefact of our representation'.[4] This indicates a distinction between terms we invent in order to be able to describe and interact with the real and those that capture something that is necessary for real things.

For instance, we might need to distinguish between different directions on a territory in order to orient an investigation in it, though the directions need not play any essential role in determining what the territory really is. Thus, there are no real latitude lines on earth. They are artefacts of our representation. The directional aids are contingent and temporary with no necessary anchor in the real. For Bapteste and Dupré processes are real, whereas static entities are not. The concept of the artefact therefore allows for a distinction between the deeper reality of process and the illusory static representations we use to capture it.

The difference between artificial representations and real entities follows first from the idea of causal powers: 'We assume that real entities are those that have causal powers; complex entities are real if they have causal powers that are not merely aggregates of the causal powers of their parts.'[5] However, perhaps in recognition of the fierce controversies around the nature and reality of causality and hence the difficulty in taking it as a primary indicator of reality, Bapteste and Dupré settle on a minimal definition dispensing with the term: 'We don't want to commit to any particular account of causation; perhaps "having a causal power" means just "making a difference to something else". Making a difference to something is a minimal necessary condition for being the kind of entity we have any interest in recognising in formulating a biological ontology.'[6] The point is to defend the reality of entities such as processes because they make a difference to something else. Processes are not dependent on the components that come together in them and the components themselves do not make a difference.

To give a simplified example, the process of whistling produced by a steam whistle is the real entity, since the whistling makes the difference in noise leading to a warning to others; the whistling makes a difference to those at risk rather than the whistle. Taken as a set on the workshop bench or unused on the front of an engine, the components of metal whistle, steam from the boiler, lever, valve and bell neither whistle nor warn. It is only when the released steam courses through the valve actioned by the lever that the bell resonates: the process of whistling.

Note the counter-intuitive aspects of this move, since the whistling appears to be far less concrete than the components. It also depends on them. After each whistle, the sound fades away and the components remain to be set in action again. They have a concrete permanence the process lacks. Additionally, if any of the components fail, there will be no whistling, whereas the whistling does not instantiate the components. The process relies on the components and they persist even when there is no process.

Whitehead called this intuitive and philosophical objection the fallacy of misplaced concreteness. He traced it to seventeenth-century philosophy and science and their concerns for substances and qualities as related to the minds and bodies of human subjects: 'Thus I hold that substance and quality afford another instance of the fallacy of misplaced concreteness.'[7] The fallacy is to abstract from a process and to seek its 'simple location' in substances and their qualities as located in spaces we identify in relation to our minds and bodies. Bapteste and Dupré's artefacts of representation are cases of misplaced concreteness. Their argument demonstrates that for microbial biology process makes the difference rather than only apparently more concrete biological entities.

For scientific explanations the location in substances and qualities is a false illusion: 'There is no light or colour as a fact in external nature ... We ask in what sense are blueness and noisiness qualities of the body.'[8] Using Bapteste and Dupré's work rather than Whitehead's, we can see why there is a fallacy through their stipulation of 'making a difference'. Artefacts of representation such as species and organs taken independently of their process relations make no difference to other things. They have to connect and they connect through processes of stabilisation and destabilisation.

Varied and multiple processes make a difference in relation to microbial evolution rather than supposedly more concrete entities defined in relation to genetic lines, or the tree of life: 'The tree of life, we think, by insisting on the predominant importance of vertically transmitted origin as the defining feature of biological entities, has tended to promote just such an error [the distortion of basic ontology], marginalising evolutionarily significant entities that did not evolve along the single, privileged tree.'[9] In my simplified example, we respond to the whistling, rather than to the set of components, but we mistakenly attribute causal significance to the substantial components and to their qualities. We might say the bell made us jump, when in fact it was the ringing.

What of the reliance of the process on its components, though? Doesn't this reliance point to a greater reality for those entities even if we have to change them dependent on how scientific theories replace the fundamental entities we give precedence to? To answer these questions it is important to see the limitation of my example, since it relies on an opposition drawn between static entities and processes. Whitehead's work, like Bapteste and Dupré's, starts out from scientific theories where the existence of such static entities is called into question, for instance when we take note of all the ongoing physical subatomic processes underlying the apparent stability of a brass bell. The bell itself is only a multiplicity of ongoing processes such as deep corrosion, surface tarnishing and the effects of temperature stresses. A similar point could be made for something as simple as a bike chain. We might want to say that the chain failed because a particular link broke at a particular time, but it would be more accurate to say that processes of corrosion and wear, connected to wider processes linked to seasons and wider environmental road factors led to a process of snapping. The location of the problem is not the link as such, but the processes in and around it. The kinds of error associated with a non-process approach would then be to constantly replace failed links, the identified concrete thing, rather than analyse the processes at work across all of them and decide to replace the whole chain, or lubricate it differently, or avoid heavily salted winter roads.

The bike chain example and the concept of error based on misplaced concreteness point to the reforming nature of Bapteste and Dupré's argument. They are not making an abstract epistemological point but rather seeking to show how an ontological error can lead us to make mistakes in explaining evolution at a microbial level and hence also make mistakes in analysing problems of evolution, for instance in relation to the importance of microbial processes in the human gut for human life and illness. This shift from a simple process and static entity opposition to one of relative extended processes is made in Bapteste and Dupré's second definition and distinction about living things:

> A more abstract metaphysical distinction is also central to our thinking about biological ontology (and perhaps ontology generally). We understand living things to be most fundamentally the consequences of numerous interweaving (occasionally nested) processes. Although it is common to describe the domain of biology as consisting of things, for example organisms, cells, genes, and so on, we understand even these as ultimately processual.[10]

The metaphysical claim is carried by the qualifications 'most fundamentally' and 'ultimately' as applied to living things. Though living things might appear to be concrete stable entities amenable to distinctions according to classifications as static types of organisms, cells and genes, at a more fundamental level they depend on processes rather than the other way round.[11] I have used 'depend on' as a first step to explain the use of 'consequences of', but a more precise understanding comes from a return to the idea of making a difference to something. When living things evolve and relate to one another, processes make the differences in them.

In the main body of Bapteste and Dupré's paper the wide scope of these claims is underplayed because the argument goes from these opening abstract metaphysical distinctions to close work on some empirical cases and more tentative general suggestions. Nonetheless, these definitions and premises are the philosophical core for the new process ontology. It is then expanded through additional claims about the nature of process for living things. They are the consequences of 'interweaving and (occasionally) nested processes'.

The interweaving is very important, and the use of 'occasionally' is telling here because, without the interweaving, static entities and types can return as envelopes for processes. Though we assign a place for process in evolution, if we retain well-bounded lineages – as in the tree of life – process remains secondary to the things that evolve along well-defined lineages according to static genetic origins which provide a new basis for concreteness. The claims for the fundamental role of process, for the dependence of entities on process and for the artificiality of static entities as representations, then also fail, because processes are defined and explained according to the boundaries of entities redefined as envelopes and explanatory models for lineages. Things retain their ontological importance as ways of identifying and limiting the location of processes.

Bapteste and Dupré therefore develop their process philosophy in opposition to a standard model for evolution based on lineages. They seek to demonstrate the insufficiency of this model for explaining microbial evolution: 'In the microbial world, lineages of genes, or genomes, are not fully embedded in lineages of organisms, or even of species; lineages of genes can be independent from lineages of genomes.'[12] Interweaving of genes is therefore an essential part of their argument because it breaks down the boundaries of lineages and of genomes by drawing attention to the role of genetic processes that cross between them.

However, simply crossing between lines will not be enough to defend the process ontology since we might well situate the interweaving according to broader lines, classes and entities. A critical strategy would then be to try to define new lineages that take account of interweaving but situate it in static entities once it is complete. In which case, process will only have been a temporary state of uncertainty between a redundant set of lineages and entities and the new ones which come to replace them.

We must therefore distinguish between an argument that appeals to a new kind of entity – the limited weaving between entities X, Y and Z – and processes proper. Bapteste and Dupré do this by appealing to a core concept shared with the process philosophy of signs and recurring throughout recent process philosophy, notably in Deleuze and Guattari, namely multiplicity: 'This interacting multiplicity of kinds of lineage, with distinct stabilisation time scales and different degrees of obligate physical connection, introduces important limitations to the standard model that our alternative presentation of an extended evolutionary ontology aims to address.'[13] The multiplicity is not itself an entity regrouping a set of other entities. It is a multiplicity of processes that resists such identification or concreteness because it draws together different things in an ongoing transformation, as indicated by the core ideas of stabilisation and destabilisation over different times.

A multiplicity is many processes of stabilisation and destabilisation taken as continuous and resistant to a satisfactory explanation in terms of discrete entities or even stages.[14] Multiplicity precedes and exceeds entities which only appear as artefacts of representation when process is abstracted from. This is then the third premise of Bapteste and Dupré's argument, 'which leads directly from the preceding point': 'that the naturalness with which we see the biological world as composed of relatively stable things needs to be explained in terms of a variety of processes that stabilise these entities'.[15] Stable things are not fundamental explanatory units but rather call for further explanation through processes of stabilisation undermining any claim to explanatory priority for those entities.

Multiplicity plays a macro and a micro role in Dupré's philosophy. I have just outlined the micro role where multiplicity is recognised as an underlying plurality of processes of stabilisation and destabilisation at a microbial level. This is based on a scientific empiricism reflecting Dupré's naturalism where research in an individual science yields evidence for multiplicity and plurality as set out in the process philosophy. However, there is also a macro role for pluralism in Dupré's critique of philosophical monism and its dependence on supernaturalism.

As a claim about the unity of scientific explanation as physical explanation, monism depends on a myth about the unity of science:

> If this [commitment to the explanatory reach of science] is combined with the idea that science is a largely continuous and homogeneous activity, and even more specifically that its explanatory resources depend on its sole concern with the material structure of things, then we are well on the way to naturalistic monism. But monism, I claim, is a myth. And it is a myth that derives what credibility it has from its connection to another myth, the unity of science.[16]

The empirical demonstration of the myth depends on showing the diversity of scientific methods in relation to Popper's thesis about falsification. Through a brief study of well-known cases Dupré shows how sciences do not and cannot employ a unique method of falsification thereby justifying their methodological unity. Instead, we find a variety of methodologies: 'Methodologies have developed in wholly different ways in response to different kinds of problems, and the methodologies we have accumulated are as diverse as those questions.'[17]

There is therefore a multiplicity at a macro level for Dupré. It is the plurality of interconnected but irreducibly varied sciences and their methodologies. The two levels are allied in a vision of the natural world as a diverse field of enquiry for a diversity of sciences: 'More simply, our empirical experience of nature is, on its face, an experience of a huge diversity of kinds of things with an even huger diversity of properties and causal capacities.'[18] The commitment to the multiplicity of processes, methodological and biological, extends Dupré's commitment to process from an apparently restricted field in biology to a wider philosophical thesis: 'The way forward, I believe, is to recognise that an organism, human or otherwise, is not a thing or a substance at all, but a process.'[19]

The principle of the sufficiency of process explanation is very important in underpinning these ideas of methodological plural-ism and process multiplicity because it justifies the independence of process from static entities. It also discounts explanations situating process between stable moments, which then provide the ultimate explanatory frame and set of values. There are no finally stable enti-ties; they are always emerging out of processes and also disappear-ing with them. The gerund of the two verbs is important because it denies that the processes they describe should be understood as rela-tions between static terms.

It is not 'this' emerges from 'that', but rather 'these multiplici-ties are emerging'. It is not that entity X disappears to be replaced by entity Y, but rather 'there is a multiple disappearing and reap-pearing'. In response to the further objection that it makes no sense to speak of multiple processes if we do not know the compo-nents of the multiplicity, Bapteste and Dupré can answer that the multiplicity is constituted of many processes of stabilisation and destabilisation determined by speeds and directions rather than by settled entities.

This answer corresponds exactly to the process sign answer to the same question: it is always a matter of relative intensities of relations rather than transitions between fixed terms. Stabilisation and destabilisation are intensive terms; they are about increases and decreases in the intensities of relations, themselves understood as transformations in a multiplicity, such as emergence around a particular series of relations (particular microbial processes, for instance). Process is ontologically prior and continuous. Here, con-tinuous means that process is not a stage, between stable entities, but rather an underlying and irreducible reality, behind the artefacts of our representation.

I want to emphasise the contrast to Uexküll and Ruyer and thereby show the radical originality of Dupré's process philosophy. Multi-plicities of processes as explanatory for the emergence of relatively stable entities have no transcendent plan and no final stable represen-tation. Any plan would be a subsequent attempt at concreteness and a return to the stable entities Bapteste and Dupré have denied in each of their metaphysical principles.

Instead of individuals and species operating in environments through signs set by transcendent plans, Dupré privileges a multiplicity of intertwined processes:

> What we find in the living world are deeply interconnected and interdependent processes, and distinguishing individuals within these complex systems is difficult, can often be done in multiple ways and may be counterintuitive ... the best way of understanding these multiply intertwined cell lineages is in terms of hierarchies of *processes*.[20]

This problem of determination is an important one for process philosophies emphasising multiplicities, not only for the determination of individuals, but for any determination at all. Dupré therefore misses the fact that his identification of processes is already a cut into the multiplicity of processes thanks to priorities set by particular sciences at a particular time. Their scientific practice is already a way of determining what counts as a process and how it stands out from others.

However, his naturalism validates this kind of determination and the challenge is for other process philosophies to offer alternatives to it. It is in order to arrive at a different model for determination that the process philosophy of the sign works through the selection of a set that then determines a series of relations with its substratum. Diagrams for these signs also provide determination, but without the necessary dependence on the sciences following from Dupré's naturalism. It is for this reason that the diagrams are defined as always open to revaluations and situated in suites of diagrams which provide counter-cases and critical contrasts to one another.

For Dupré and Bapteste, and for the process philosophy of the sign, stable internal or external entities are not a necessary condition for process. It is the other way round: process is the necessary condition for the emergence of a strictly relative stability, a process of stabilisation. The difference between the two process philosophies lies in the answer to the question of why it should be the other way round, of why process is the prior condition. Is it for empirical reasons, or as part of a speculative account of the nature of the sign?

If a process philosophy of signs seeks to avoid the problems encountered in Uexküll and Ruyer, it should follow Bapteste and Dupré in making the sign a multiplicity of processes. That's why my process philosophy of the sign also focuses on multiplicities of intensive relations in the sign. As such the sign should be radically immanent to processes, that is, strictly dependent on processes unfolding with no external or transcendent presuppositions. However, this negative definition of immanence and process is still vague because process remains ill-defined in relation to immanence. How should any given process be free of transcendent or external determination? What are the reasons for the independence?

PROCESS PHILOSOPHY, NATURALISTIC PRINCIPLES OF DIFFERENCE AND EXPLANATION IN THE SCIENCES

The demand for freedom from transcendent determination raises a particularly difficult problem for process philosophy because opportunities for external determinations of processes return as soon as process is defined, or described, or given specific referents, or a specific role such as explanation. We have seen this in many forms in Uexküll and Ruyer: through the perceived need to ascribe limits to beings in order to define them (the animal's limited set of signs and proper bubble, for instance); through the role of transcendent plans as scores or maps for those definitions; through the role of those plans or of Platonic ideas in explaining the direction taken by evolution; and through the ethical role of transcendent plans and ideas in determining the proper identity or direction of evolution for living things.

It might appear that Bapteste and Dupré give us an example of a truly immanent account of process and hence a model for an immanent process philosophy of signs. Their definitions of multiplicity and of interweaving, along with the emergence of stability dependent strictly on process, seem to avoid any transcendent or external anchor points. They even hold off the possibility of such points by defining stability as always relative to stabilisation: 'Here we just reiterate that what we are inclined to think of as biological things are, on more careful inspection, specific temporal stages of stabilised biological processes.'[21] The key term here is 'careful inspection', meaning careful inspection of the evidence around microbial science, since it shows that the basis for the argument is the latest empirical research which gives support to the metaphysical definitions of process given at the beginning of their work.

A core facet of Bapteste and Dupré's approach shows that their work cannot satisfy all the demands for an immanent account of process. It comes back to the initial definition of 'making a difference to something' and to their approach to explanation, which in turn tie their approach to particular results of empirical research.

These define their philosophy as a naturalistic approach to process based on a version of supervenience. If we define explanatory super-venience as commitment to the explanation of observed differences of certain kinds through other more general underlying differences that explain them causally, then Bapteste and Dupré are committed to entity-process supervenience.

Differences in and between stable entities should be explained by more general processes of stabilisation and destabilisation across numerous and interweaved multiplicities. An observed empiri-cal difference, for instance between different types of stable living beings, supervenes on a difference between interweaved and trans-versal microbial processes – where transversal indicates differences beyond the boundaries and lineages of the entities observed at the first level. Dependence on this principle of difference, as based on empirical evidence, implies that process explanations should serve to explain observed differences through processes taken as the causes of the differences.

From the point of view of a speculative process philosophy of the sign, Bapteste and Dupré's methodological naturalism is to be avoided for a general reason with practical consequences for a specu-lative process philosophy. This methodological reason involves no critique of the process philosophy of biology as such. While natural-ism might well be the right methodological constraint for a process philosophy of biology, it is a bad model for a process philosophy of the sign because it overly restricts what we can take as process in the sign by limiting the explanatory target to empirical differences, limiting the explanatory theory to scientific accounts of process, and limiting the operation of process to a form of causality.

It is important for the intensive processes in the sign to be open to wide creativity in order to have as great a range of models as pos-sible for the representation of process. This range does not guarantee the truth of such models but it allows them a critical and analytical strength essential for the study of the power of signs and for the critical deployment of that power. Over the next three chapters I will demonstrate the type, value and function of these models through the concept of the diagram in the sign. The divergence from Bapteste and Dupré should be seen as pragmatic. Though they offer a strong model for process, it is not practical to take the details of that natu-ralistic model for a wider ranging speculative philosophy of the sign.

So my worry about the necessary role of natural difference in Bap-teste and Dupré's process ontology is about a limitation on the scope and form of process philosophy. This does not mean that I think the naturalistic principle of difference is mistaken or wrong for their project; that's not the purpose of this study which is instead to see what can be learned for the process philosophy of signs.

The work on signs makes no claim to direct critical input or philosophical framing for the sciences independent of the critical and creative opportunities provided by a given process sign. The flaws of any such moves in relation to the internal development of the sciences have already been highlighted for Uexküll's account of the operation of signs. Bapteste and Dupré's work on multiplicities of processes and on their interweaving provides a powerful rejoinder to his 'bubble and symphony' theory for the animal and environment relation.

In order to achieve this independence from the sciences, yet with a potential critical relation to them, the process philosophy of signs must allow for inclusion of terms from the sciences alongside other terms on an equivalent basis, even if this will change in subsequent debate around the sign. It must also be able to include elements not restricted to data taken from empirical research and avoid determination of the real by scientific enquiry and according to scientific norms. Yet it must also avoid commitments to transcendent criteria and allow for the possibility of what I have here called alarm. In the next chapter, the definition of the sign as multiplicity will respond to these challenges by allowing inclusion of any entity whatsoever in the multiplicity as a process of selection against a variation in intensities of values.

For Dupré and Bapteste, making a difference to something means to make a difference to evolution as stabilisation and destabilisation in and across lineages. More broadly, though, it means that process is designed to explain an external difference as registered by a science. There is therefore an essential role for empirical research which makes hypotheses about and then tests the wider processes involved. Process ontology of biology is therefore reactive, in the sense that there has to be a perceived change, where perceived is shorthand for change appearing as some form of datum or given, rather than appearing to the senses as such.

The philosophy is naturalistic because the data on which the deduction of process depends is taken from contemporary sciences, the theories to be approached critically are established scientific ones (for instance that lineages of genes are fully embedded in lineages of organisms), and the mode of deduction of the new process ontology is itself scientific (testing a new proposal as to whether it can provide new explanatory insights into the structure of the world as described by a science or set of sciences).

The problem is that this means that other processes that have no purchase in the data or in the theoretical unfolding and structure of debate of the sciences will gain no purchase and will be seen as illegitimate and extraneous to the debate. This is an undesirable outcome for the process philosophy of signs, if it is to allow for the possibility of critical alarm about the sciences, because the kinds of process it might want to appeal to will not be judged valid in relation to those drawing their legitimacy from the naturalistic model. It is also undesirable if the naturalistic model is taken as paradigmatic for all process philosophies, for instance in relation to art, politics and ethics. So the challenge becomes that of how to construct a process philosophy of signs that learns from the process philosophy of biology as outlined by Dupré, that can still relate to natural processes and to the sciences, but that is not restricted to scientific control over making a difference.

The Sign

WHAT IS A SIGN?

The process philosophy of signs offers a novel answer to the long-standing problem 'What is a sign?' Some of its motivation, and the underlying puzzle it seeks to address, concerns the historical resistance to the answer: the sign is process. In part, the neglect of this answer is due to its counter-intuitive nature and to the difficulties created by the combination of ideas of reliable signification and process. If the sign is to signify something dependably, how can it also be in process? What would we make of a red 'stop' sign suddenly changing its meaning to 'go' as we walk in front of impatient traffic, halfway across a busy junction? Signification – sense-based communication mediated by a sign – seems to require some sort of constancy between referent and meaning, if only to keep us safe on the roads.

The challenge set out in the first three chapters around the idea of a process philosophy of signs has therefore been how to design the sign as a workable process. The main features identified for the sign as process render it as multiple; as changing intensities of relations; as involving no fundamental distinction between sign and non-sign; and as allowing for critical and creative relations to the world. In addition, I have sought to avoid tying the sign to sciences or to a mode of identification of things in the world. I will now gradually introduce a more formal definition of the sign as a response to these different demands.

Formally, the sign involves two linked processes. First, a sign is a selected set, where selection is an ongoing process rather than the settled outcome of a choice. The process of selection emphasises a series of changing relations between all things brought about by a selection of some of them. It is therefore to pick out things by altering their relations, yet without detaching them from all others.

I used the concept of the substratum in Chapter 2 to explain this relation between a selected set and a wider background. A sign is a selected set and its substratum. For example, your name and two emoticons at the foot of a message are a selected set and therefore a sign {Renée, ☺, !}; its substratum extends widely through bodies, emotions, reactions and actions.

Second, the mode of relations in a sign is a transformation of intensities associated with the selected set and its background relations. Every selection is accompanied by a transformation of values which reflect back on the selection. Your name and two symbols are accompanied by changes in intensities such as your increasing joy at expressing happiness and the reader's growing delight at having caused it. The sign is thus always a selection accompanied by changes in intensive relations open to revaluations as those relations interact.

There is a process of intensive unfolding in the sign. In that sense, it is alive. Selection provides the initial material for revaluation. Revaluation plays out the selection and its intensive changes. Later, I will show how this playing out can be represented as a suite of diagrams around the elements of the set and its substratum. The exchange of messages after your confession of great happiness is a way of capturing and shaping this suite of diagrams of changes in intensity.

If you take a piece of paper and draw something on it, then stick the sheet facing out of your window, you are making a sign defined as a selection and transformation of intensities. We do this when we select a poster for our street-facing windows, such as a political statement ('Vote for independence', 'Save the common land', 'Violence is always the problem') or a piece of information ('The barbecue is around the back'). The marks on the paper are a selection against a background which then extends to a set of changes in intensities, such as the enthusiasm you might feel in drawing a red line across a hated figure, but also the shock a passer-by might experience at seeing a beloved symbol crossed out in red. Rising shock and hatred can be directions represented on a diagram that includes figures such as a passer-by.

The sign you have made is then not a fixed relation between something signified and a signifier, such as a loathed politician crossed out in red and the signified 'Do not vote for Professor Purple'. It is rather an ongoing and very wide process: a selecting and a changing of intensities of relations. There would be no point to writing and posting the sign if it wasn't accompanied by changes in intensity such as political doubt or relief at getting the right information. It is therefore inaccurate to think of signs as fixed connections between, for instance, a sense and a referent. This is because the sign is a process of selection before it appears to be a fixed relation. The sign is also a change in intensities before, during and after this merely illusory static connection between two terms.

I described the process philosophy of signs as counter-intuitive because we expect signs to be reliable connectors between things like meanings and referents. This is only partly true since I believe we have a deep sense of the sign as process, in the way we experience our lives in relation to the lives of others as the unstable and ongoing effects of significant choices concerning all of us. When we survive a selection and others do not, when we live on and others die, the lives lived in the shadow of the selection form a sign with it. Motionless images of death as terminal fail as signs of death because they depend on a false cut and abstraction from the other lives which make the sign significant.

A death spreads through the lives of those who live on. It is in this way that it is truly a sign. What is intensity here? It is shifting degrees of relief, gratitude and guilt as they haunt the survivors in the ongoing sign. These ongoing intensities in the signs of death explain why we have to work hard at getting memorials right. We want the memorial to be an appropriate response to ongoing intense feelings and desires, not merely the marker of the date of a death.

Or, to take a more everyday example, when we select something at a market, we change the intensities of relations between the chosen thing and all others; for instance, through growing scarcity or desirability. Market traders know this intensive aspect when they call out prices and descriptions of their wares. They are trying to alter the intensive relations of fear and greed, or need and avidity around prices and goods such that no price is fixed in the market. This static representation of the sign is an illusion hiding the ongoing and continuous flexibility of prices. This in turn explains how prices change. They do not alter in leaps between static price signs but rather change all the time, as intensities of relations shift continuously with the sign, for example when the intensity of fear increases rapidly with a new piece of information.

Thus when gold is taken for a universal currency the decision can be rendered through the following sign {gold, exchange rate, any commodity}. Any commodity will have an exchange rate with gold at a certain value. Irrespective of opinions about the true worth of gold as an ultimate monetary standard, as a process sign the decision involves a multiplicity of changing relations, for instance to the devaluation of silver. These changes can be rendered in a suite of diagrams, maybe with an axis showing acceleration from a silver direction to a gold one with respect to desirability.

WHAT HAPPENS IN A SIGN?

The relation between selected set, substratum and suite of intensive diagrams means that the sign can be thought of as a wide-ranging feedback loop from a selection and its changes in intensities to further intensive revaluations and back. However, this is an unsatisfactory model if it is presented as a linear feedback: selection – revaluation – selection. Instead, as we'll see from the formal model of the sign, it is concurrent and asymmetrical. So the sign will not be represented as S-V-S' but rather as S/V. The sign does not play out over time, but rather forward and back along a suite of intensive changes. A new intensive diagram changes the values of older ones, for instance in the way an intensive shift towards paper money alters the value of the confidence we once had in gold.

The revaluation runs alongside the selection and they alter one another as they unfold. They are concurrent. They cannot, though, be conflated with one another according to a set of laws or rules or functions. By definition such general laws are given as stipulations over the process sign. Selection and revaluation determine one another such that no overarching principle should be able predict or govern how they will unfold in relation to one another. They are asymmetrical in their concurrent operation.

The suite of diagrams should be seen as a concurrent determination and competition between diagrams. This cannot prove that stipulations over the sign are wrong. It situates them in a realm of critical debate over the sign. For example, a stipulation over the gold sign stating that gold gives the true value of everything because it is in limited supply when compared to paper money, is cause for debate around the gold sign and the sign provides the critical material for this debate.

Imagine a doctor asks you to pick out a picture among others laid out on her desk. You pick out a setting sun, and the doctor nods sagely, but also raises her eyebrows. The picking out is an element of the sign. The nodding is also an element. Something is selected against a background of relations, to other cards, to other gestures {setting sun, you, illness, doctor}. When this happens a series of values associated with different relations also begins to change; the selection intervenes in ongoing changes. The selection of the card strengthens its relation to your illness and to a possible cure. It also diminishes the hold of the other cards and of other things, such as ideas and objects. The selections set off value modifications in unpredictable and prospective ways, for instance in the burgeoning of hope and waning of despair, or in the excitement at the possibility of finding a remedy balanced by fear of failure, or in the beginning of shame at an unmasking and relief at exposure.

The selection of the card is a process, that is, for it to be significant it must not be simply thought of as 'this card here and now' but rather as 'this card against the background of all the others and as what it is doing to itself and to the others'. In this doing, the card is in feedback with the others. The feedback is mediated by revaluations independent of the selection, for instance the doctor's reaction, then your reaction to it. This process is not linear, though, and the selection as unfolding process runs alongside the shifting in values.

The difference is between representing the patient and doctor relation as P-D-P, as if a camera shifted from one face to the other and back, and P/D, as if two cameras allowed a filmmaker to produce a split-screen film where the faces run together for the audience. The split screen allows for two durations to unfold together as process rather than limiting each one to the start of the other. A sign is not a process of move-countermove-move which would commit the philosophy to a limited account of the sign according to a form of dialectics, since it would break and develop at each shift of perspective and topic.

The sign is a process of mutual, concurrent and, in principle, unlimited unfolding back and forth. 'In principle', given the practical requirements to treat signs within artificial boundaries, for explanatory purposes for instance. The selection decides on the ongoing perspective (P/D) rather than changes in perspective deciding on the limits of signs (P then D then P). This means that the sign as process is formally very different to the sign as a fixed relation between terms, where it is a 'sign of' or 'sign to' something. As process, the sign makes relations and values change, rather than indicating them as fixed in a particular space and time, or according to a wider frame such as a language game, a science of signs, or a series of conventions and agreements about meaning.

The process is a multiplicity of changing relations and values. It ranges over all things, not in the sense of everything being a sign, but in the sense of all things being open to be included in selections which make signs. So though we can speak of worlds and realms which are not those of the sign, where the processes are not those of selection and revaluation, nothing is outside the reach of a sign. Anything can be selected into a sign.

By definition, the selection of the set is unconditioned by the things and relations that are selected. The sign as process is not restricted by any rules, definitions, laws or qualities of the things it selects. So the sign as selection is not attached to a referent or to a meaning. It does not denote something reliably, but rather comes about as a connecting process, a change, that is not formally restricted by the fields the sign selects in. Instead of relating a limited number of things, the sign performs an ongoing operation on all of them by selecting some of them differently and with no necessary preconditions.

This lack of preconditions frees the sign from any essential, natural or logically necessary conditions. Anything can be included in the sign with any set of relations. No guarantees can be given about the mutual conditions of selection and revaluation on each other. Selection is unconditioned as to what it selects, how it unfolds and how value conditions that unfolding. So, for instance, among the pack of cards on the doctor's desk there are no images or associations which have a necessary hold on the selection.

If we followed the usual model for signs, we might think of an image with a picture of a dagger on it as signifying violence and referring to acts of violence we might be repressing, or of an image of a baby as signifying birth. We might think that picking one card with 'yes' on it and another with 'no' was a contradiction. But none of those conclusions would be necessary as properties of the selection; they would only be properties of wider descriptions of the sign according to diagrams of intensive directions and stipulations over signs.

As defined here the sign is partly unconditioned; its selections are free. Later, we shall see that when associations and negations are made in this process philosophy, they follow from intensive diagrams unfolding around the selection and from patterns imposed on signs, rather than from any features of the signs as unconditioned selection. The stipulated patterns define realms that are not those of the process sign proper, since they are determined by imposed codes and laws denying the free selection and the changing series of diagrams for the sign. The sign is therefore split between selected set, suite of intensive diagrams and codes and laws imposed on the sign, the stipulations over the sign.

The patterned realms and any of their components can always be included in a new sign, so the unconditioned selection in the sign maintains priority over conditioned patterns of signs. It is a limited kind of priority, because although each new sign can detach itself from a chain or pattern by selecting it, this secession does not disprove or break the pattern itself. The sign is prior because it can draw up different processes which provide the occasion for critical clashes of patterns but not their resolution. Any resolution is a matter for rules or patterns, but it remains subject to the differences, new potential and critical alarm carried by new signs.

When a patient's hand touches a card, on a given day and in a particular office, according to the definition of the process sign, this selection is always unconditioned. A conditioned arrangement of things in the world is made when we set laws or codes for how a sign ought or must relate, for instance when the doctor imposes a moral judgement on your selection or strictly follows a manual for the interpretation of signs. The patient might submit to a different pattern, perhaps an inner intuition about their illness or perhaps a delusion.

No sign can resolve the clash of rules, laws or interpretations, yet the clash itself is made possible by the unconditioned nature of the sign because it is what maintains a separation between the sign and the codes imposed upon it. The codes have to be imposed over the selection and its intensive diagrams because the speculative process defines them as unconditioned and resistant to transcendent laws or codes.

So it is not that reference and signification simply disappear from our ways of thinking about the world on this model of process. They are present in two ways: as things that can be selected into the sign and as ways of imposing patterns on signs. The sign can always include referents, meanings and other significations. They can count as things to be included in the sign as multiplicity, since anything can be selected and since the selection carries everything with it as background or substratum.

Referents and meanings are not simply discarded. They are articulated in new ways by any sign, sometimes to be given strong relations to other things, sometimes weak; there will be changing degrees of reference and signification, and the diagram of the sign will describe those degrees as intensive directions, as increases and decreases in speeds and connections. The process philosophy allows for the selection of a signifying sign such as 'dagger signifies violence' as a selected set {dagger symbol, violence}. However, the process version draws the signifier and signified into a much wider web of changing intensities of relations represented by a suite of diagrams without which the process sign will be incomplete.

Reference and signification are also rules or stipulations over the process sign. This is shown by propositions such as 'Every sign must indicate a referent' or 'There is no sign without meaning'. In the second chapter, I studied Wittgenstein's imposition of such rules in the distinction drawn between inert and living signs through use. In the third, I observed restrictions on the sign in biological cases where they were limited to specific circuits for Uexküll. In the fourth, I described how signs were given a limited empirical causal frame by Bapteste and Dupré.

According to the process definition of the sign, propositions and rules are false as adequate descriptions of the sign, even though they might be taken as important as rules or laws for imposing patterns on signs, for example in denying the usefulness of signs which have no referent (Oscar Wilde's second novel) or that can have no referent (Wilde's long and short novel) or that cannot be verified according to a form of life (Oscar Wilde's private language diary).

The definition of the sign as unconditioned is therefore not a commitment to chaos and lack of determination. First, the sign is the site of determined but changing relations. Though the selection is unconditioned, the relations in the sign are relative and there will be a qualified stability in the sign. When the doctor chooses to combine your picture and a common diagnosis, the selection is one of high relative stability among many terms in the selection and in its relation to a background. The diagram of the sign will indicate a strong pull between the direction of diagnosis and other relations. Second, though the sign itself is an unconditioned prior selection and process, series of signs can be given rules or laws which impose patterns on them and thereby define realms. Why then can't the relations in the sign be strengthened to the point where some take on a kind of necessity?

The sign remains an unconditioned selection despite prevalent patterns, trends and directions, because it is always in process. Changes in the unfolding of intensities recombine relations between things and disrupt supposedly stable patterns. For instance, though a medical practice can remain stable over very long periods, it is always possible for researchers to recombine symptoms and pathologies under the same name. It is because the sign is open to such novel groupings that we can refer to new entities while maintaining contact with many elements of the old. It is also for this reason that the sign has a critical and creative role, since its capacity to detach itself from prevalent states while including their elements allows for novel angles. A set of symptoms, the name of a disease, a pathology and proposed cures can be recombined in new ways offering critical and innovative angles in line with new discoveries or shifts in social practices and expectations.

It is essential, however, not to confuse the potential for the sign as invention and alarm with scientific demonstration. The fact that signs incorporate things in the world in no way justifies the validity of their relations as causal, probabilistic, or as reflective of forms of social consensus. The sign is accompanied by value shifts and these can take on weight as emotion or desire, but exactly because the sign is unconditioned these must be supported by other sources of validity before conclusions can be arrived at about states of the world that the elements of the sign are taken from. Since the sign is fundamentally unconditioned it is neutral with respect to validity. The fact that a sign has been proposed is no justification for the truth or importance of what is suggested. In Chapter 6 I discuss this important property of the process sign, as defined speculatively, in contrast to objective definitions for the sign in structuralism.

With the aim of providing an illustration contrasting with the sciences, it is helpful to turn to art to demonstrate the priority of selection over signification and reference. The arts can take familiar signs and recombine them in new and unexpected ways which point to novel relations and intensities of values for relations. This in part explains the ever-present critical potential of the arts and humanities as creators of new and disruptive signs when they are released from objective demands and from subservience to the sciences through forms of naturalism.

This iconoclastic power of the arts and humanities demonstrates the possibility of open selection in signs, for instance in the many ways artists have taken up national flags and symbols and transformed them to maximise an aesthetic and critical impact. Rules such as banning the burning of flags or associations of the flag with the nation as an homogeneous entity are brought into question by art and in novel concepts in the humanities because the relations in the sign can always be selected differently.

The process philosophy of signs claims that this openness depends on the unconditioned nature of the sign as selection and revaluation, but it remains opposed to ideas of essential truth for the arts or humanities in their selection of signs. Such arguments for the value of the arts are stipulations over signs rather than insights into the nature of signs as open process. The power of the arts and humanities is in creativity and critical alarm combined with debate with other claims to truth.

INTENSITY AND VALUE

The second reason for the intrinsic instability of the sign is more subtle than unconditioned selection and stems from the role of value as the second process in the sign. As selection, the sign is accompanied by an independent variation in the intensities of values of all relations. By value, I do not understand a given number or degree, but rather variation in the intensity of a relation. Whereas unconditioned indicates an absolute freedom in the sign, independence in the variation indicates a relative freedom. Revaluation varies independently over the selected relations of the sign and conditions their unfolding. To return to the example of survival, there are in principle no limits to how the selection of a sign might reassign relations between a survivor and an environment, from almost complete indifference to nearly total obsession with a death, for instance.

Nonetheless the sign is a selection of some things and their relations and revaluation is over the relations determined by the selection. Revaluation in the sign is therefore limited by given relations between the selected things. It is relative to them. Yet this provides it greater power over the sign, if by power we understand direct influence. Different signs can select different things and relations, such as survival around individuals or survival around blood lines. Variation in intensity then changes the emphasis within the different signs, for instance by emphasising particular types of individuals in one sign or particular aspects of blood lines in another.

A good way of understanding these points is through distinctions drawn between the freedom of an act of choice, the relative determination of any consequences of the choice, and the independence of those consequences in relation to what the choice might have hoped to achieve. Let's say you encounter someone who appears to be in need. You make the free choice to help them. The selection is defined as free, here, rather than deduced or observed as such; it is important to realise that stipulations over the sign can deny it, for instance by demonstrating unseen causes behind a decision. For the process sign the unconditioned state is given by definition, irrespective of whether there really is freedom of choice. The choice to help then determines a situation; for instance, the person is now helped, whether they like it or not. However, though the situation is determined by the choice, it is not determined in how it then plays out. Your intention might have been to help, but in fact you have insulted someone and they reject you. The sign is unconditioned selection, change in the intensities of relations determined by the selection, and revaluation of those intensities and of the selection.

Unconditioned selection works in part as a block or barrier to imposed order. Its power is to mark a point of unfeasibility, such as the impossibility for an imposed pattern of signs to lay claim to necessity when counter-signs can be selected against it. Conditional revaluation marks particular relations and its power is to pass into them. It only ever plays out independently, rather than marking a halt to a process or pattern. A revaluation such as an increase in the intensity of relations to guilt can destroy the claim to total indifference in a sign of survival. This is a greater and more precise power because it works on the potential of the sign, understood as an unfolding described by an intensive diagram.

Revaluation as change of intensities influences how a selection stretches out, how it acquires new potential and alters in current ones. If selection is defined as the process whereby relations extend between things, valuation is the process which disrupts selection as a smooth and determinate unfolding. It is why the sign cannot be taken as a causal process where an initial choice is followed by a set of inevitable consequences. It is also why a sign is not even a probabilistic process, since the revaluation reassigns intensities of relations and thereby reassigns distributions of probabilities. Yet it is also why the sign has some consistency since variation operates on the relations of a particular sign, on its unfolding diagram, rather than interrupting it and bringing about a new one.

When you select a card you make a new sign for the doctor and for yourself, but this sign always remains unstable. Something in it drives it outward unreliably. Its points of interest and importance shift. They are driven by changes in intensity independent of the relations of the selected sign. For instance, your selection might make her uneasy in her current diagnosis and generate a new line of thought. Perhaps she begins to suspect you are playing a game or harbouring some terrible secret. The sign as selection is completed and disrupted by this new potential, the change in values of the sign. Similarly, her reaction to your choice of card plays on your control over it. Her gestures show she knows you are faking, changing the many relations in the sign from your dissembling to her understanding.

Aren't these descriptions of patient and doctor objective claims, thereby contradicting the definition of the sign? When describing the sign and its intensive changes in relations, I am giving a description of a diagram for the sign rather than an objective description of a state of affairs. It is a suggestion for a picture of the changes brought about when selecting a sign and drawing up its intensive changes. The distinction is between speculative hypothesis, which can then enter into dialogue with matters of fact and other theories about them, and descriptions which lay claim to a different and non-speculative access to the matter.

In the sign, selection and valuation run in parallel, they are concurrent. They do not run on independent tracks, though, and instead determine one another differently. The selection provides the material for the valuation in setting up stronger or weaker relations between things. Valuation then works on these relations by varying their intensities. There is therefore an asymmetric relation in the sign as process, between the process as selection and an accompanying change in values. This asymmetry conditions both processes of the sign in so far as the ongoing selection is altered by a change in the intensity of its relations and the revaluation is constantly responding to the unfolding of the selection.

If we take the familiar image of a line-up of possible perpetrators of a crime in front of a victim, we might think of the sign as the fixed relation between the meaning 'That one did it' and the person identified in the line-up as articulated by a pointed finger. The sign is then a fixed meaning-pointing-thing relation. According to the process philosophy of the sign this is wrong because it misses how the selection unfolds and it abstracts from the changes accompanying this unfolding. The sign is a relative 'picking out' and hence also a 'leaving be' which reverberate through a world. It is also, though, a 'stirring of values', where stirring has its emotional sense of turmoil and mix of intense variations played out on relations.

When the finger points at the supposed perpetrator the others become blameless. That's not the only changing relation, though, since these know of no necessary limits. Some closer ones are easy to connect. Hypothetically, the crime becomes solved. The legal case begins. Those not picked out restart their lives. Their families become the families of unblemished citizens, just as the children of the perpetrator, in their homes and beds, become the offspring of a criminal, as a prison cell becomes a place for the guilty one, and lawyers, judges and jury members become those who will defend and judge, while an executioner is prepared and a new way of killing thought up and put into practice.

To take another example, from language this time, when a word is picked out as the right one to begin the next line of a poem, the word is selected against the background of all words and all texts and its relation to them is now changed because of its situation in the poem.

The word as sign is a new multiplicity of relations not only in the poem, but in principle in all things that can be selected. However, it is not only that the word has new neighbours and new associations. When it acquires these, it also changes values such that all things are not only related differently, but this new relation is the site of ongoing changing intensities, defined as the potential attractions and repulsions for the relations. So the positioning of a word in the poem is not only a process of selection, of a word against other words, it is also a process of valuation, of changing intensities of relations between words.

As sign, a selected word is therefore two mutually determining processes. On the one hand, once the word enters the poem or indeed any sentence, or crosses any lips, it sets off changing relations to all words and things according to the situation of its selection. The word is world. One way of feeling and understanding this is when our names crop up as names for others in unwanted or uncanny circumstances. The selection of 'James' for 'James the impaler' inflects my own name. We sense this burden and possibility when we choose names for our children or when we fight to renounce a patronym or gendered designator. On the other hand, once the word is selected as sign, it becomes open to variations in intensity beyond the directions of the selection and its situation; sometimes we become our name, sometimes we grow away from it. A name can fade on us to the point where we have to change it, or it can grow on us to the point of the folly of wanting it to live on unchanged forever.

We might think we select a word in an argument in an instant, as the right thing to say to indicate a meaning and bring out a referent at a crucial point. 'You fool' we say, assuming we have simply connected the meaning of 'fool' with our interlocutor in a particular moment and space. That's all wrong, though, because the selection of the word is a process sign. It spreads out beyond any instant and changes meaning and referent as it is uttered.

The word is accompanied by an intensive diagram of strengthening and weakening relations. We know this best when our aim is too good or too bad and the right word wounds or angers as it hits and for a long time afterwards. 'You fool' we say, and the face in front of us crumples or hardens. The face and its turmoil of emotions reflect back on the chosen word, shifting it from right to wrong as the sign unfolds. Words cannot be taken back, not because they pass away as past presents, but because as signs they continue to spread out in multiple relations as ongoing processes, always beyond our control.

Children and those new to a language are often closer to this effect of intensive revaluation in signs because they have a less well-grooved hold on the standard sense of words. They feel their strangeness and their power more deeply. It is easier to damage and delight newcomers to language because the effect of words running through relations and changing them is still raw. This does not demonstrate a lack of understanding and a need for better instruction in the proper sense of words. It reveals the way in which words are doubly unstable for all of us.

We might think instruction can rid us of this instability. We become grown-up language users, where language is a realm defined by the rules of language games. This is only an illusion, though, since the process work of signs is still there under the appearance of fixed meanings and referents, of grammatical rules and structural relations. Signs and their processes are the pressure point where novelty and critical divergence enter the game.

So maybe you think the pointed finger, the uttered 'he did it', and the indicated person in the line-up form a fixed relation, either something stable over an instant or a limited period of time, or something eternal or outside time. How then do you explain the fact that its relations move and spread out in waves of changes? Perhaps you think the children instantly become the offspring of a monster, and the executioner instantly the one who will rid us of an eternal evil? This is where variations in the intensity of values accompanying selection break with the idea of fixity in the relations of the sign.

Relations are not unchanging connections between terms but rather ongoing transformations as relations in a selection accompanied by revaluations. The sign as process is many lapping waves, a two-sided rippling of intensities, relations and things. The sadness of the child, regret of the perpetrator, guilt of the executioner and forgiveness of the victim grow and fade in the sign. Worlds do not change instantaneously at the whim of a sign. Signs change through worlds according to diagrams disturbed by variations in intensities.

Why aren't those variations in intensity open to some kind of linear treatment alongside the selection? Hasn't the line-up example given us two of them: one spatial and one timely. I said 'some are closer than others' and things 'grow and fade'. Doesn't this imply a spatial relation between elements in the sign? If it does, might there not be a causal account of the relations that can supplant the idea of the sign as process, for instance in tracing the causal chain from the identification of a parent as a criminal and the breakdown of a child? Do not growing and fading take place over time? If so, isn't there a single time or series of relative times allowing us to relate all the elements of the sign?

The definition of the sign given here makes no prior commitment to space or to time. The sign is outside space and outside time because the processes constitute the sign before it is situated at any particular spatiotemporal location. The sign is immanent to the processes rather than to a location somewhere and at some time. Immanent means there is nothing outside the unfolding and mutually determining processes as they make the sign become and as they are captured in successive and experimental diagrams.

The sign is therefore self-sufficient; it requires no prior space or time for its definition. This independence of the sign and strict immanence to its processes also applies to other determinations. There is no subject of the selection, or goal for the unfolding, or law governing it. The sign is defined as immanent process in an unstable double becoming determined by selection and revaluation. The relations in the selection are intensive in this definition, since they are a matter of greater or lesser emphasis and intensity, rather than a matter of extensive position in an external space. Closer and more distant are then metaphorical for the relations of the sign.

However, it is harder to dispel time than space, since when I use terms such as 'unfold' this appears to commit the sign to a kind of order which appears to be close to the linear kinds of time we tend to ascribe to human experience and historical events. They unfold as the present passes away and the future arrives. Yet there would have to be a different time for each sign because each one unfolds according to different intensive revaluations. They unfold according to different speeds and intensities. They also unfold in a dual and disrupted manner which takes the sign far from the idea of a homogeneous time in which all events occur. If the sign as process is to be taken as defining a form of time, it will be very different from any we are familiar with. Homogeneous time cannot be prior to the sign.

FORMAL DEFINITION OF THE SIGN

I have spoken about a formal definition of the sign but up to this point the definition has only been formal in the sense of giving a pared down description of the sign. The advantage of truly formal definitions of the sign is that they provide a model for wide applications and give a structure for understanding the implications of the sign. There is a downside though, from the point of view of process philosophy, since formal representations have a contingent yet strong tendency to reinforce ideas of fixity in the sign. This is because a formal representation appears to be motionless in its components and their relations. The lack of movement is purely dependent however, and hinges on shallow perceptions of movement in the image.

There is more movement in even a simple formal equation than in many dynamic images and we only miss this because we sometimes fail to sense and understand the implications of the equation; for an engineer, the equation of a wave is motion not rest. Process and stasis, movement and fixity, are not properties of forms such as representations. As images, it is down to the debate with stipulations around the lines, words and numbers as to whether formal models are fixed or in movement.

For instance, in the representation of the sign as relation between signifier and signified, as Sr/Sd, movement would depend on the meaning given to the bar '/'. It is usually given as Sr relates to Sd in a fixed manner under certain conditions at a certain time, for example 'Red' signifies 'anger' according to the following conditions. By definition, though, there is nothing to stop us defining the bar as a transformation 'By signifying "anger" with "red" the following transformation occurs'. I discuss the bar in relation to signification and structuralist theory in Chapter 6.

The process philosophy of signs is a limited speculative metaphysics which proposes a formal process model for signs in critical debate with other kinds of claims, defined as general stipulations over the sign. It works speculatively – creatively and critically – alongside the empirical sciences, common sense and intuitions, and against theological and philosophical claims to eternal certainties, whether formal or about specific content. The critical perspective and claim is two-way here, since other positions also challenge aspects of the sign: as material for selection in signs and as sources for possible rules and laws about necessary connections between them.

Here is the full formal definition of the process sign:

$$S\{a, b, c\}/Vs$$

Here are its sub-definitions:

{a, b, c, ...} is a set of elements selected against a substratum of all elements

S{a, b, c} is a multiplicity of changes of intensive relations around the elements associated with the selection. It can be represented by a diagram.

Vs is an open-ended suite of further diagrams for the selection
'/' is a two way determination between S {a, b, c} and Vs

If we want a simple name for a sign {a, b, c} will do; for example
{white dove, peace, love, now}. The sign is a set. But if we want to
draw attention to the intensive shifts in the sign and to call for its
diagram to be drawn up we should extend the notation to S{a, b, c,
d}; for example S{last dove, dead, climate, human-caused}. This combination of diagram and set is incomplete and potentially misleading,
because the intensive diagram is only ever a temporary proposal set
over an unfolding sign, a sign that is playing out (for instance, when
a more powerful symbol replaces the dove on a diagram). To indicate
the requirement for a suite of diagrams indicating the revaluations of
the sign we should adopt the full notation S{a, b, c, d}/Vs. The sign
is a set and a suite of competing diagrams for the unfolding of the
sign as process.

Here is a simple application:

Open your wardrobe and select one item of clothing, a turquoise shirt, say. This is {turquoise, shirt, today}. The set {tur-
quoise, shirt, today} is a selection of the shirt, obviously over
other items of clothing, but less obviously over all things (go
naked, or delay the selection, or go shopping, or select the shirt
with a tie, with that tie pin, while holding your lover's hand,
or cutting ribbons into the sleeves of the rest of his shirts). The
shirt colour sign is now named by a selected set rather than the
connection between two more different types of component,
such as signifier and signified, or expresser and expressed.

Intensively, the selection is a change in the relations around all things.
The selection changes intensities in other relations; for instance, in
your attachment to another colour as your favourite for Mondays.
Try selecting that cut off T-shirt for your interview, or that grey
woollen knit tie to get into the latest club and watch the intensive
repercussions of your choice spread out like the bow wave of all your
lousy sartorial choices. S{turquoise, shirt, today} is shorthand for a
diagram of all the changes in intensities of relation brought about by
the selection.

S{turquoise, shirt, today}/Vs indicates the way in which the selection unfolds subject to new assignments of intensities beyond the first
suggested one. As you select the tie, your interviewer selects the exact
same one, the bouncer of the club stubs her toe getting out of bed

and your lover reviews how they got caught with someone so drab he can only dress in shades of grey with ill-chosen punctuations of turquoise. In the formal definition of your selection, the sign is always accompanied by a revaluation that stirs up its unfolding diagrams.

As much as examples based on choices can capture the arbitrary and unstable nature of selection, they are also risky because they can reinforce a misunderstanding due to the leap we tend to make from choice to intention. By definition, there is no intentionality or subject in the sign. S{a, b, c}/Vs requires a differentiation of a, b and c from other things but does not indicate any requirement for a subject of an intending, in the intention to select or in the aim for the selection. To make out or deduce such a requirement is to fall back on a metaphysics of subjects, actions and intentions as an unnecessary presupposition for the process definition of the sign, for instance by stating that every selection depends on free human intervention and imagination.

Here is a non-intentional example. As you stare into your cupboard, a dark cloud passes by and changes the shades of the clothes. This is a new sign that includes the former one: Sdc{S{turquoise, shirt, today}/Vs, dc}/Vsdc, or in more simple notation {{turquoise, shirt, today}, dark cloud}. There is a new set which takes the shirt selection sign with a change in lighting 'dc' which was not intentional. The cloud selection does not require an intention of any sort and, again by definition, it can perfectly well include signs which appear intentional. Why only appear? Because the selection is defined as unconditioned even when it includes human subjects. This does not mean that such intentional acts are denied or impossible. They either belong to a different realm of stipulations over signs, in the same way that the science of cloud formations belongs to a different realm, or they belong in the sign such that choice becomes another element drawn out by the selection {choice by subject x, b, c}.

It could be objected that the problem is not whether signs can include intentional acts and non-intentional elements. By definition they can include such non-intentional things. The real problem is that any set has to be selected by a human subject, for instance in the way I choose a cloud element to go with the moment when a hand pulled out a turquoise shirt today. The answer is the same. There is no requirement for a subject in the definition of the selection of the set that determines a sign. We can discuss a given sign as intended or not and we can stipulate that all signs should be intentional or meaningful to humans, but there is no need for them in defining a sign as an undetermined set.

The non-intentional example raises new problems in the way it introduces the inclusion of signs in other signs, something always possible given the definition of signs as including any element and hence obviously other signs. This raises questions about the definition of the sign as selection of elements, and paradoxes such as Russell's paradox. It is also problematic in the way it makes the proliferation of signs more apparent. I will discuss the sign as involving paradoxes when I study paradox in Deleuze's philosophy of the sign in Chapter 7. Problems of proliferation will be discussed in the next section.

WHAT IS A SIGN? WORLDS AND REALMS

In setting out the process philosophy of the sign, I have used a language of selections and worlds, and a language of stipulated realms and patterns for signs. Each sign is a selection over all things. As such it is a perspective over a world: a selection within it. It is also, though, selected in other worlds: selected by other signs. These relations are therefore, first, those of the sign as a singular take on a world that is in principle limitless, $S\{a, b, c\}$ over all things. This sign is always in a process of change in relation to its own unfolding, $S\{a, b, c\}/Vs$. Second, there are stipulations over a sign which impose rules and laws for signs, which treat them as a coded or lawful realm. There is always a gap between the two manners of thinking about the sign, since realms necessarily contradict the unconditioned nature of the selection and the open, intensive, revaluations along suites of diagrams.

For instance, in discussing Uexküll, and Bapteste and Dupré, in Chapters 3 and 4, a distinction was drawn between Uexküll's limitation of the sign for different animals and the process definition. There was also a distinction between Bapteste and Dupré's inclusion of the sign under conceptions of empirical differences and the demands of naturalism, and the lack of such prior assumptions for the sign as process. The scientists and philosophers of biology define a realm for signs, with a dependence on limited plans in the case of Uexküll, or supervenience on empirical differences in the case of Dupré. There is nothing wrong with this dependence on its own terms. My concern is with the contrasts that can be drawn with a more open definition of the sign.

The limited number of signs for any animal and evolution in discrete leaps mediated through external ideal patterns in Uexküll and Ruyer could be an effective explanatory model. Difficulties arise when such models are taken as the basis for wider conclusions about the nature of signs because this eliminates their full critical and creative potential as process signs. The point of a realm is that even if it defines a sign as a perspective on the whole world, and thereby comes very close to the process definition, it also imposes a restriction on the sign as selection, containing its scope by stipulating which inclusions of signs by other signs are valid, empirically confirmed or possible.

The advantage of the process philosophy of signs over realms is that it allows for an approach where any sign can be entertained so long as it is not limited or given a fixed or stable set of relations for unfolding. The consequence of this is a definition of the world of the sign as a relational perspective on all things, solely determined by the singular aspect of the selection and by a suite of suggested intensive diagrams. This definition appears to come with a deep disadvantage, since signs are usually thought of as involved in discrete chains, such as linguistic combinations of signs that are in some way external to one another, for example, table + chair + room. Can the process philosophy of signs offer a viable alternative to accounts of systems of independent signs?

Rules, laws and realms are very good at handling combinations of independent signs because they give shape to them by stipulating which ones are allowed and which ones aren't, or which are empirically verified and which are not. I have taken advantage of this in order to draw a distinction between the sign as process and signs as used in science or logic. However, what if the stipulation for patterns is necessary for any sign? What if signs must be considered as external to one another and as dependent on chains for their existence? Might it be that the sign makes no sense when defined as a selection against a limitless substratum and as a perspective over a world?

The sign has an abstract role in philosophy, as a term for understanding kinds of reality and relation. It also has a practical role, as a way of understanding how communication works. In the first role, the problems of the sign are metaphysical; in the second they are semiological. The two connect since metaphysical claims can underpin theories in semiology. Equally, though, semiology can be presented as a theory about explanation, understanding and communication which does not require metaphysical underpinnings, either as an empirical approach to social and natural communication, or as theoretical and empirical theory construction about a special field: the field of signs. Given that the motivation behind this process philosophy is to give a metaphysical definition of the sign in order to allow for new ways of studying signs in practical circumstances, I am interested in both approaches.

In metaphysics, viewed as abstract speculation about the nature of reality, the main problems concern the plausibility of signs which encompass the whole of the world. If a sign is the whole of the world under the perspective of a selection and revaluation, how can it communicate with other signs which are the whole the world under a different perspective? If the sign is without limit, how can this continuity have an identity allowing us to make sense of it, since it seems that any grasp of the sign would have to cut into this continuity? If signs are selections on the whole of the world, and they are also selections of each other, won't this generate paradoxes where we either have an infinity of signs and perspectives, with no way of reducing it to some kind of order where we can speak of this world or one world, or we have rules for the inclusion of signs by each other which contradict the formal definition of the sign as unconditioned?

In semiology, viewed as a practical theory and handling of signs, the problem is that the process theory of the sign seems weak as an empirically determined and practical approach to signs. It also seems unpromising as a way to reduce and order the number and complexity of signs. If we define the sign as a limited and fixed relation we have a more straightforward methodology for the analysis of everything from words, to fashion, to advertising. All we need to do is look for the features identified in the relations and we have a repeatable structure for their study and critique. Thus traditional semiology and structuralism have offered many theories which allow statements such as 'Red signifies anger' or 'There is an analogy between colours and temperatures according to the following structure'. Structuralism and semiology have become common currency in cultural discourse and yet they have also fallen away as central approaches to social and cultural phenomena, perhaps due to the increasing influence of other natural and social sciences. One of the motivations for the process philosophy of the sign is to change the frame and justification for semiology in order to suggest a renewal of the subject as radical approach to signs.

I will leave the metaphysics of the sign to Chapter 7 where it will be discussed in relation to Deleuze and Guattari and Whitehead. Until then, provisional answers can be given to the questions raised about the plausibility of the sign based on its formal definition. Though the sign is without limits, it is not without determination because each sign is determined by its selecting set, and by its unfolding according to a diagram of intensive relations and its revaluations over this unfolding. It is also given a critical context by the realms seeking to control the sign.

The selection allows for a limited description of the selection S{a, b, c} with an ongoing and diagrammatic description of the unfolding and experimental hypotheses around further diagrams S{a, b, c}/Vs. Taken together, these are the basis for the description of a sign: selected set and suite of diagrams. These in turn must be completed by descriptions of the realms and rules or laws which stipulate limited relations within the sign, as well as limitations in its relation to other signs. Finally, these stipulations should be set alongside a critical and creative evaluation of the gaps opened up by the sign as selection. The sign is therefore an internal description and experimentation; an external description of claims on the sign; and a critical and creative response to those claims.

For example, a sign and world are selected in a generous welcome S{handshake, gift} which can be traced in a series of changing relations (increases in value for the gift, increases in mutual debt, increases in friendship, decreases in distrust, say). Equally, though we need to see how these strengthening relations are threatened by new valuations with experimental questions (How and why are these relations determined by the set breaking down?). Alongside these internal relations there will also be rules and laws stipulating how the sign might combine and unfold, for instance customs about gifts or social rules about corruption and graft. These can be in a critical and creative relation to a selected sign, for example in gifts attempting to reveal the role of corruption or bypass laws against it.

Or to give a non-human example, when a landslide blocks a stream thus giving rise to the sign S{landslide, blocked stream}, we can begin to trace changing relations in other things in their relation to the blockage – flooding, changes in plants, and so on – as well as trace hypothetical variations which break an emerging unfolding. Note how this is not limited by a scientific selection of salient facts, or a description of the unfolding from those facts according to causal or probabilistic models. Such a scientific model involves the stipulation of rules for a realm, rather than the description of a sign. The selection is unconditioned in the sign and its diagrams are drawn in an experimental and speculative way in terms of suggested variations in the intensities of relations.

The Process Sign, Structuralism and Semiology

ELEMENTS OF SEMIOLOGY I: LANGUAGE AND SPEECH

The sign as selected set and suite of diagrams is not only a definition of the sign as process. It is the basis for a method for describing and analysing signs: semiology. This method involves describing the selection, tracing its diagram or intensive unfolding, experimenting with revaluations operating on the diagram by suggesting further diagrams, and developing a critical study of the laws and rules that stipulate over the sign. How does this definition compare to definitions of the sign from the history of structuralism and semiology?

In his *Elements of Semiology*, Roland Barthes not only presents the main semiological positions, he also articulates them according to how their main features generate and respond to problems in the construction of a theory of signs, structures and language.[1] In addition, Barthes is interested in seeing how these theories can allow for a practical semiological approach. This aim comes through strongly in his examples and cases, not only of language use but also in the study of the common topics of food and fashion. So though the text can seem quite dense, it brings together a deep study of the philosophy of signs with a critical examination and practical applications as found in his other works on signs and myths.[2] The interaction of a range of theories, critique and simple practical examples can be seen as the frame supporting Barthes' very beautiful and subtle later readings of signs.[3]

Barthes' study begins with Saussure's distinction between language and speech. Language is a socially constituted system of codes and values that allows for communication, and speech is the individual use of language. As such, language is fixed through social conventions, whereas speech can vary individually. Speech has to use language and is therefore dependent on its codes and values, because elements of language are combined in speech and it is reliant on their repetition. The point of language is to allow for speech and speech contributes to the social construction of language. They are therefore dependent on one another.[4]

According to Barthes, Hjelmslev complicates Saussure's distinction but retains part of it by dividing language into pure form or pattern, norm as the social realisation of this form, and usage as the social habits of language use in a given society.[5] Within these distinctions, signs can be defined as operating in speech defined as the varied combination of recurrent signs. Signs are therefore in language as a relatively fixed structure of oppositions and in speech when it introduces the process of variation through combination.

This model is completely at odds with the process philosophy of the sign, since for Hjelmslev, as read by Barthes, signs are synchronically invariant when they are in language; their relations are structurally fixed at a given time. More precisely, in terms of Hjelmslev's method, variations in language can be drawn back to invariants through a method of reduction.[6] This means values and relations can be determined as fixed, even though they vary over time. This fixity is extended to the process of speech since it has to use repeated and repeatable signs taken from language.

Barthes attributes this basic structure to other structuralists, such as Jakobson, and to later philosophers such as Merleau-Ponty. According to Barthes, Merleau-Ponty sets out an opposition between structure and event as process; he also postulates that every process presupposes a system. Similarly, Lévi-Strauss uses the process and structure distinction to split sociological and ethnological investigation between the mechanical interpretation of language, where systems of oppositions are in play, and probabilistic calculus, which applies to speech. Where is the place for prior process in these oppositions, that is, process coming before structure and fixity rather than after them and dependent upon them?

It appears that there is no sense in defining the sign as process if we accept these definitions of language and speech since, even in speech signs defined as pure, process will neither be repeatable as the same sign, nor be able to be positioned within a structure of repeated signs. To be repeated they must take their place according to a system of oppositions taken from language. It does not make sense to posit speech without language. Nor does it make sense to speak of signs independent of a prior structure for signs and their values.

Barthes gives a semiological example showing the way in which signs taken as independent of language still depend on this kind of restriction. If we look at the signs of fashion, the way we dress is dependent on prior codes about dressing. We can make some choices, but the arrangements and types of dress are already set by social codes and by a restricted group of producers. The process of getting dressed presupposes prior structures of clothing and fashion. We cannot simply escape the language of fashion by dressing differently, since this difference is made in relation to the earlier established structures. In *Elements of Semiology* Barthes is particularly interested in how fashion journalism can inscribe new modes of dressing into a traditional structure of familiar codes.[7]

There are two steps to responding to this objection to the process philosophy of signs. The first is a critical point about the priority given to language over speech. The second shows how we can have a definition of the sign which is not independent of structure but that changes the way in which process and structure work together in the sign. The priority of language over speech is problematic with regard to this question 'Don't we require speech to bring about changes in the structure of language?'

Language changes as a socially determined structure. This change requires some kind of variation which does not come from within language itself as a settled structure. It comes from speech as a variation which introduces novelty into language. Therefore, speech events are the condition for changes in linguistic structure. The process philosophy of signs therefore needs to alter the place and function of signs in language and speech from fixed points in structure combined by speech to processes of change in speech introducing process into structure independent of prior and fixed structural relations.[8]

This does not establish the priority of process, however, since the relations between process and structure might well be dialectical in such a way that we pass from structure to structure through the input of process, so though the variation of signs might be necessary, so is the relative fixity of language. The sign then would not be process. It would be fixed in language. Process would still appear but only in a secondary manner, in the individual use of signs, or as events requiring a structure for their full operation. Process and speech would then be bridges between structures.[9] On this account, clothing would be given structure, such as meaning in a system of oppositions, but the meaning could change when individual users introduced variations acquiring structural relevance when they were adopted more commonly and entered into a social system.

For instance, in line with this dialectical model, the structure of clothing changed in the 1970s when punk appeared in individual and rare acts of rebellion (process and event), but this change required the earlier structure to work in and against. The novel process was then itself transformed into later structures as codified fashion, and even later into just one more set of codes within the larger structure of clothing. The same is true in the more commercially controlled shifts from new designers fresh from avant-garde schools who introduce novelty and process into the fashion world, such as the early Alexander McQueen, for example.[10]

These innovations introduce a disturbance into the system of fashion, but this then becomes a new code as each innovation becomes repeatable as a style within a wider structure. Capital has a central role to play in this dialectics because it requires novelty to release new desires and to bring distinctiveness into markets tending to uniformity and hence to decreased profitability. Markets need the difference and buzz of a new young designer to invigorate the marketplace with sharper differences in value and corresponding increases in desire.

However, to be fully exploited, a new style needs to be repeatable and positioned within a system of goods and value equivalences, not only for distribution but also for profitable sales and production. McQueen then becomes a name and a look, then a house style, and later an international brand of his own within a large fashion conglomerate.[11] This necessarily tends towards decreased interest and the market will begin to search for the next name and seek to sacrifice the current one. The turnover of ideas and names we associate with the pejorative sense of fashionable is a property of the dialectical relation between structures tending to stasis and forms of innovation associated with inventive designers, or the speech of fashion.

As described by Barthes, the dialectical interaction of structure and practice, or of language and speech, offers an alternative explanation for structural change and for the role of signs within that change. It is a challenge to the process model of the sign because the structural explanation relies on the identity of the structure which serves as a condition for the transformative role of aspects of speech, of the use of signs. Speech can negate some aspects of identity in the structure but not all of them, since it relies on their repetition.

ELEMENTS OF SEMIOLOGY II: DIALECTICS AND PROCESS

The process definition of the sign turns the dialectical account on its head by claiming process as ongoing and ubiquitous alongside secondary processes of relative stabilisation. There is an analogy here between John Dupré's defence of a prior process of stabilisation and the idea that process signs only allow for a relative stabilisation, rather than fixed structure.

Fixity is then only relative and it is false to claim that we ever have a stable structure prior to signs and as a necessary condition for signs. Determination in the sign does not depend on structure but rather on different intensities of relations which are not open to satisfactory analysis in terms of oppositions within and between structures. Instead, the sign is relative processes related to external reservoirs of things and stipulations. This means the sign is primarily process as varying intensities of relations, and structure enters the sign in three different but secondary ways.

First, structures taken as fixed entities can be selected to be included in the sign as process. This is important because it is one way of explaining how such structures are open to change in relation to the sign. Structures are set in motion by signs and this can reveal motion throughout the structure. It is not that signs require identical structures and elements to repeat, but rather that structures and elements are transformed when they are included in process signs. Repetition is not over most of the structure with a few novel changes. It is over all the structure as a variation carrying through all of its relations but at different degrees of intensity.

The difference can be understood in the contrast between two claims about speech. For a structural account, speech depends on repetition of identical elements and structures which then vary due to extrinsic properties and innovations in speech, such as intonation or the introduction of new words. For the process account, structures and elements are only apparently fixed and they are made to vary when they are included in spoken signs, so a spoken sign varies the whole structure and all its elements, even if for many of them this variation is hard to detect.

The recitation of a poem is a good practical way of understanding this. In the process account, when a child stammers or halts on a word this has intensive effects on relations through all aspects of the poem. The poem is itself an ongoing and continuous process, varied at each recitation. In the structural account, blocks of structure must remain the same for there to be any recitation at all. The stammering is located and its effect is restricted and explained on the basis of the structure.

A form of critique follows from this property of process signs as disruption through the whole structure. For instance, the process sign is always a potential revelation of the way structures teeter on the edge of change despite their claims to permanence, when an apparently fixed social structure is incorporated in a new sign which combines rigid distinctions with new intense relations revealing the motion present in the structure. *Are they allowed to kiss like that?* The appearance of fixity in the structure of the family has been subject to powerful critical challenge over the last half century from practices of the sign demonstrating how the familial structure can be combined with different entities and ways of life in a novel and transformative manner. As process sign the family was already in motion in multiple ways, rather than challenged as fixed structure and forced to change into another structure.

Second, this time itself defined as process, structure emerges as relative speeds and organisation within the sign. According to this view, structure becomes an emergent pattern in a diagram articulating different speeds, directions and singular points where intense relations are modified. These are special terms taken in part from Deleuze and Guattari; some of the debts and differences will be analysed in the next chapter.[12]

For my purposes it is sufficient to define the diagram as an articulation of changes in intensity taken as directions in the diagram. Singular points are then the neighbourhoods where these directions inflect one another, for instance, where an increase in one pulls others towards it, or scatters them. The child's singular stammer pulls and stretches rhythms and senses across the poem. The diagram is a map of these dynamic effects.

When structure is given as a system of oppositions it is static. As a diagram emerging with the sign, structure is dynamic and must be understood as multiple and continuous motion. The difference can be understood in the contrast between a grid map, which allows for positions to be determined and fixed, and a vector space (in Hilbert Space) which allows for directions and relative speeds to be determined. We have a strong intuitive understanding of this difference, for instance in our sense of the difference between being shown our position on a map and then being shown an approaching weather front or forest fire with our possible lines of flight. The first is a grid, the second a vector space. One is static, the other dynamic. One gives positions, the other gives directions and intensities.

Position is never enough where signs are concerned because our interest in them involves interaction with changing circumstances; hence the importance of knowing whether a weather front is a deepening low or whether an approaching fire is accelerating and increasing in ferocity in relation to our possible speed of flight or protection.

Diagrammatic structures emerging in signs are vector spaces where all the relations in the space are put in play. They communicate intensive changes rather than stable positions. They are therefore much more useful for understanding and reacting to changing circumstances, free of the illusion that some things remain permanent even when their borders and relations connect them to zones of intense disturbance.

Third, structures also make claims over the sign. This time the structure is not necessarily fixed but it is external to the sign. Stipulations over the sign are such structures. They come from outside the sign and seek to impose rules and codes on the sign as process. This imposition can be on a particular sign, for instance, when a sign of a changing sexual practice is set in an external order of normal and deviant which denies a continuity of changes and the multiplicity of practices. It can also be general when structures attempt to stipulate over the relations between signs in the way they can select one another and indeed any element; for instance, when contradictions are defined as nonsense.

External structure, such as in structuralist accounts of the priority of the structure of language over speech, seeks to control and dominate the vector space of any given sign or number of signs in order to render it as static and amenable to oppositions, fixed positions and absolute differences. As process signs, family or sexuality are dynamic vector spaces subject to intensive fluxes and continuous drift within the space. From these spaces, identity statements about families or sex are always a form of illegitimate imposition of limits and positions where only accelerations, decelerations, influences and directions exist.

Labels are frequently the site of such stipulations, for instance, when we are forced into a system of oppositions such as gay or straight by a questionnaire or by series of social norms and expectations. The deep problem is around the claims to absolute or relative legitimacy for any given stipulation. A norm, rule or code is always an imposition over process on this account of the sign. As dynamic, difference is always relative and in multiple motion. The power of the sign as selection is such that it can take external attempts to impose stasis on it and subject them to study as dynamic diagrams, thereby allowing for speculative critique of the effort to tame, control and exploit the sign.

I have used legal terminology around the stipulation of structures over signs. It is now possible to explain why I say structures that stipulate and impose fixity over the sign are doing so 'illegitimately' and that their claims are 'invalid'. The external structure defines itself with respect to the sign through the imposition of codes or laws. These are illegitimate, that is, go beyond the legitimate boundaries of those laws when they make claims to validly apply to signs as multiple processes.

It is not that the sign itself has a law or system of codes. It has a speculative definition at odds with any oppositional or codified legal framework which might lay claim over it. There is therefore an interesting question about whether a pragmatic and case-based legal basis might be consistent with the sign.[13] The definition as prior process means the sign is always a site of contestations in two directions: contestation over the sign when structures seek to impose themselves on it; and critical and creative alarm from the sign, when signs reveal process in structures when they include them in novel diagrams.

Before giving an example and then a more formal account of this reversal of the dialectical priority of structure as described by Barthes, it is worth pointing out how the process philosophy departs from scientific and objective claims for structuralism and semiology. Each sign is singular and is only open to a partial and speculative description. There is no valid generality of structure in this definition of the sign as process – even at a given time. I will give a more detailed definition and defence of this version of speculative philosophy in Chapter 7, in a study of the opening passages of Whitehead's *Process and Reality*.

This lack of fundamental validity also means that the sign is political rather than objective in four ways. First, it is originally political as unconditioned selection within the set of all things. Second, it is internally political as the site for disjunctions and differences as each sign unfolds. Third, it is externally political as a site of contestation over different ways of stipulating how the sign ought to be fixed. Fourth, it is internally and externally political in its ability to include stipulations critically and creatively within a new sign in order to reveal the dynamisms behind their claims to legitimate stasis. There will be a full discussion of all political aspects of the sign in Chapter 8.

As signs, clothing decisions such those made at the origin of punk right through to its inclusion in a long list of possible fashion styles are unconditioned selections. Each decision is the selection of a limited set of things among all things. In the sign, this selection sets off an unfolding of changing intensities of relations between all things: it defines a diagram. This diagram is also always accompanied by revaluations which alter unfolding patterns. The sign is, for example, S{k,l,u}/Vs where 'k' might be a series of slashes, 'l' a cloth texture and 'u' a type of fitting. This restricted set is never alone though. It is a way of identifying a wider change of intense variations across all things, for instance in colour, sharpness, care, feel, shock value, rebellion and reaction.

These changes unfold forward and back, sometimes according to very close relations, around music and social behaviour, for instance, and sometimes around very distant ones, perhaps around a street in London or the insubordinate curl of a lip. The use of 'around' is important because it underlines how intensive relations are not between identified terms but around singularities on a diagram. The picture is one of changing flows and movements around the singular points rather than connections between them.

External to this dynamism, rules and codes are proposals attempting to legislate over the sign in banning it, interpreting it, in ruling over it, denying it and passing judgement. However, any attempt to ban clothing or music can be taken up into a sign with the very thing it attempts to ban. This is often a good way of revealing and indeed triggering novel dynamic and continuous change, as those who attempt to ban frequently find out to their detriment when a novel sign mocks them.

Formally, change is internal to the sign as process. It is not in a dialectical to and fro between process and structure, or between what stands for language and what stands for speech in a sign. Structures of opposition and fixed relations now appear in the stipulations over the sign, for instance, in a rule about acceptable clothing styles or combinations, or more generally, in definitions of types of substitutions, contradictions or harmonies. Stipulations define structured worlds but these are not those of the sign as such. In descriptions of the sign they appear as claims over the sign and as alternative realms to the world of the sign.

The sign is in a critical relation of alarm with respect to these realms. It shows another potential world of a different kind to one where structure is a condition for process and hence one where structural stipulations are valid. This other world is one of process. It has only relative diagrammatic structures determined by selection and changing intensive relations determined by revaluations. As sign a novel mode of dress is disruptive and in perpetual motion. It will also therefore be the site of reactionary stipulations. The positive thing is that these stipulations are always open to be disrupted in new signs and taken critically by the signs they seek to control.

Barthes comes close to some facets of the process view when he considers how some signs retain independence from language. First, he notes the difference between language as structure, which should come about through a long interaction with usage and can therefore be called social and collective, and certain signs which appear to be given structure rapidly by a select group, for instance, a group of fashion designers or indeed a fashion police. This latter development of the sign is much closer to the idea of selection in the process sign, including its unconditioned or arbitrary nature: 'language is elaborated not by a "speaking mass" but rather by decision group; in that sense, we can say that in most semiological languages, the sign is truly arbitrary...'.[14]

Second, Barthes notes how some systems of signs are very different from language in the difference in scale holding between language and speech. Language has a restricted number of relations of oppositions and values yet gives rise to an infinite variety of types and instances of speech. In turn, this explains how a relatively fixed structure can change through the uses it gives rise to. The infinite variety of speech filters back into language and changes it. However, for a system of signs such as fashion, the language can be extremely limited and should in theory give rise to a limited number of uses within the scope of the original language. Yet fashion changes, why is this?

Barthes' answer is that limited structures such as fashion or food change due to a third term which we must add to language and speech. This term is matter, as in the material of cloth or foodstuffs. Matter explains why uses of fashion, or food in menus, can depart greatly from the original limited structure and hence allow it to change. In this case, Barthes' semi-materialist solution to the problem is some way from the process philosophy of the sign. This is because he situates material intensity outside the sign, in a form of matter, whereas the process philosophy situates it in changing intensities of relations internal to the sign.

Against Barthes, I would argue that intensity should be defined as an aspect of every relation in the sign because each sign is constituted by intensive changes across a set and its substratum. Intensive changes in the sign behave like Barthes' materials and cannot be seen as immaterial if that means lacking the richness he ascribes to materials. However, against the process sign, it could be argued that the sign should not be thought of as internal changes in relations but rather as determined by external relations to an empirically determined matter. Signs should be seen as signs of matter, not signs as matter.

For process philosophy, there is no such thing as the language of fashion or food in a chef's menu, as aspects of the sign to which we must add matter to explain change. Instead, any sign is always beyond the limits defined by a structured language. The mistake made by semiology and structuralism has been to limit signs to specific languages and forms of speech, to external matter and to social use. Every sign is a world of change and nothing is in principle excluded from it, though many things only appear at low intensity. This low intensity can always be contrasted with high intensity for the same relation according to a revaluation operating on the unfolding of the sign as process. The dialectical account of language and of the roles of signs is therefore a misrepresentation of process within the sign and of change across different diagrams of this process.

ELEMENTS OF SEMIOLOGY III: THE SIGN AS UNION OF SIGNIFIER AND SIGNIFIED

Having introduced and questioned the distinction between language and speech, Barthes turns to the sign proper in Saussure. The dominant feature of the sign is as union of signifier and signified. This definition of the sign as the bringing together of something that indicates and something indicated can seem obvious, but Barthes points out how Saussure was concerned to detach his definition from the great number of earlier uses of the term, for instance in religion or medicine, and from many near synonyms such as signal, index, icon, symbol and allegory. The main thing was to avoid the sign becoming identified as signifier alone, as the indicator rather than the union of signifier and signified. For instance, a sign such as a lightning strike or lethargy must not be a sign of something else, a god or illness, say. The sign is the lightning strike and the god, the lethargy and the illness.

Barthes adds that following Saussure the most important principle for theories of the sign is double articulation. The sign is always a two-sided union like the two sides of a piece of paper. Each side has its own structural complexity, such as the oppositions in a spoken sign of sounds on one side and of words on the other.[15] When we say 'chaffinch' there is not only the opposition of sounds, say to 'eagle', on one side, but also the opposition of types of bird, on the other.

The sign is an arbitrary double articulation because it brings together two different types of thing with no necessary relation to one another. Why should the sounds of the word chaffinch apply to this particular type of bird and not another? Barthes goes on to question this arbitrariness in many different ways and it is a persistent problem of structuralism that's easy to understand; for instance when we consider that it is possible to take a series of whistles as signifiers for birds. In the whistle case, the double articulation appears not to be arbitrary, though on closer inspection in can be made to be so. We could very well choose different sounds and have a perfectly workable structure. So long as we know that 'woof' corresponds to the chaffinch the double articulation will function just fine.

Saussure describes the arbitrary relation as holding between a signal and its signification, between the idea and the sound that signals it. This leads to an important remark for the idea of the undetermined selection of the process sign and for the arbitrary relation between signifier and signified in structuralist linguistics: 'Arbitrary must not be taken to imply that a signal depends on the free choice of the speaker ... The term implies simply that the signal is unmotivated: that is to say arbitrary in relation to its signification, with which it has no natural connection in reality.'[16] Lack of motivation is at the very heart of Saussure's work because it is 'the organising principle for the whole of linguistics, considered as a science of language structure' and 'the consequences which flow from this principle are innumerable'.[17]

Without the arbitrary relation, structuralist linguistics would always be caught in the trap of either constantly having to describe radically novel language use in speech and thereby change the structure of language, as a structure of significations, or having to limit the possibility of novelty in speech, as the production of signals, according to pre-existing structures in language. The arbitrary relation means that there can be a structural science of language and a descriptive science of speech where language has universal structure yet speech has untethered variability. This should allow language to change and retain its structural integrity.

Neither the process sign nor the sign in structuralism depends on free choice or free will. The relation between elements in the process sign as selected into a set and the relation between signifier and signified are undetermined or unmotivated because there is no natural connection for Saussure, and, by speculative definition, no legitimate law or code for the process sign. The difference in rationale is very important if we consider Jacques Derrida's criticism of the role of claims to naturalness and lack of motivation in Saussure.

According to Derrida, signals are motivated and have to be motivated for structure to apply to them in some way – for the two sides of the paper to be connected at all, if we follow the analogy. So the claim to arbitrariness conceals a deeper and contradictory claim to a motivation of signals and speech by language or writing.[18] The point of the speculative and definitional move is to avoid such problems by positing a single sphere from which signs are drawn by the selection of a set. There aren't two sides in the process definition of the sign. However, this comes at the price of weakening the objective and scientific claims allowed by the disassociation of the realms of signals and of significations, with 'no natural connection in reality' for Saussure.

Double articulation allows the sign to unite two different planes: the plane of expression of the signifier, and plane of contents of the signified. The signifier as expression relates to the signified as content. Hjelmslev then divides each plane into two strata: form and substance. Form is the system of oppositions which can be described by a formal science, whereas substance is the variable ways in which this form refers to something outside the structure.[19] So we can distinguish the sounds in 'chaffinch' in a formal manner as different from other associations, but in addition there are many different ways in which the word can be pronounced which do not change that underlying structure. Similarly, we can formally distinguish the different words for birds, and know that we have, for instance, twenty different words for them. In addition, though, there is the substance of all the differences between chaffinches and other types of birds which provide further material and distinctions outside the structure of those twenty.

The process philosophy of signs turns against all of these features of the structuralist definition of the sign. This should be a matter of concern, since as Barthes shows the definition is historically grounded in an effort to distinguish itself within historical usage and empirically grounded in an effort to represent how signs such as words work. Furthermore, this grounding is itself a step in defining a science of signs with objective and formally invariant aspects, as shown in Hjelmslev's additions.[20] The problem should not be thought as simply about the departure from traditional structuralism, but rather as a separation from its ability to give a convincing and effective realist account of the sign.

When defined as a selection, the process sign can always include and draw together signifier and signified or expression and content. It can also draw together form and substance. The difference is, first, that their association in the process sign must also include intensive relations to everything else, so the relation between a signifier and a signified is an emphasis on a relation in an intensive diagram or vector field. Second, the relation will be one of movement rather than stasis; signifier and signified will be united but with an attention to how they draw things together and apart through singular points and intensive increases and decreases. Third, this association in the sign will be open to a revaluation which can, if not break the association, at least subject it to lower intensification and changes in singular points and directions. The sign therefore becomes a selection which can be traced by an intensive diagram transformed by a revaluation and hence a suite of competing diagrams.

The difference can be seen in Barthes' claims about social signs which become fixed despite their supposed arbitrary union. He calls such signs function-signs and gives the example of a raincoat which immediately signifies a certain kind of weather:

Raincoat sign: Raincoat (signifier) – from the plane of expression/ Rainy weather (signified) – from the plane of content

In the process version this becomes:

S{raincoat, rainy weather}/Vs

The function-sign can seem fixed and immediate, at least for a given society. It is fixed at a given time and given place. However, as a process sign it is changing and we must draw the diagram of its intensive shifts around a particular selection, for instance around clothing and protection, how the selection changes social relations, how it relates to changes in wealth, sex, climate and locations. The objective aspect of the sign in the union and its validity shifts to a speculative aspect in the description of the intensive diagram with its singular points and intensive directions, as well as experimentation with revaluations through further diagrams.

Expression, content, form and substance are internal to the process sign as elements that can be included in a sign and as necessarily present but to different degrees on the intensive diagram for any sign. However, in Barthes' structuralist definition of the sign, as objective laws and codes for the functioning of any sign, they are externally imposed on the process sign; they become stipulations over the sign.

The sign for Barthes is a double articulation whereas for process philosophy it is a multiplicity of intensive variations subject to external stipulations. Though the process sign can include the terms from the structural sign, there is a great difference in how they can be applied to it. What does this imply for thinking about the process sign as signifier and signified, expression and content, form and substance, and double articulation? We can infer the following statements from the definitions:

1. The process sign cannot be a double articulation. It is always a multiplicity even when only two elements are selected for the set.
2. The process sign can select a signifier and signified and unite them, but only as multiple and extended process within the sign.
3. The selected set {a, b, c} can be defined as the expression and the process S{a, b, c}/Vs as the content for the process sign, but only if expression is defined as an incomplete representation of a content itself defined as ongoing process.
4. Selected set, singular points and diagram directions can be seen as the form of the sign and intensive differentiation can be seen as its substance, but any formal specification must be taken as speculative, temporary and incomplete in relation to its substance.

ELEMENTS OF SEMIOLOGY IV: SIGNIFICATION

I have used two concepts in and around the definition of signs which raise questions about their roles and necessity. First, in the sign, there is revaluation (Vs) which operates as a transformer across the suite of diagrams of the unfolding intensive relations for the sign and its world. Do we need this extra function if the diagram is itself a vector field which we only draw up by following intensive relations and their singular points? Second, around the sign, I have referred to a process of signification, defined as communication mediated by the sign. I showed how signification should not be thought of as outside the sign but rather, internally, as a process of relation in the sign and, externally, as a type of stipulation over the sign. Is this incorporation of signification plausible when compared to other ways of thinking about communication thanks to signs?

Barthes gives his own definition of signification and raises a number of difficulties for the sign around this definition. I will cite his definition at length, since it is complicated and rich:

Signification can be understood as a process; it is the act that unites signifier and signified, the product of which is the sign. Of course, this distinction has only a classificatory value (rather than a phenomenological one): firstly, because, as we shall see, the unification of signifier and signified does not exhaust the semantic act, since the sign gathers value from its surroundings; secondly, because the sign does not operate through conjunction in order to signify but by cutting out, as we'll go on to show: in truth, signification (semiosis) does not unite unilateral beings, it does not draw together two terms, for the good reason that signifier and signified are each time term and relation.[21]

The sign is made by signification; it is an act that brings both sides of the sign together. However, it is false to treat act and sign as separate, since the process of sign-making continues in the relation of the sign to its surroundings and since signifier and signified are relations to each other rather than independent terms. As phenomenon, we cannot distinguish the sign from the process of signification.

The sign is a signifying act and, since we cannot separate act and thing, the sign is process. Barthes therefore seems to come round to the process philosophy of the sign when he considers the process of signification as intrinsic to the sign. We can therefore draw a distinction between the sign as made by signification, the sign as a fixed double articulation, and the sign in its making, the sign as it emerges in acts of signification. For Barthes, signification as act is the genesis of the sign and the locus for understanding the sign as process.[22] What does this entail for structuralist accounts where they have to account for signification?

First of all, signification as process implies deep problems for the representation of the sign as a double relation because the relation must itself be seen as coming out of a prior act which does not depend on this duality. I have pointed this out earlier in my discussion of the 'bar' between signifier and signified, and in discussing the contradictions around arbitrariness and lack of motivation in Saussure's work. Their separation as independent yet fixed terms is an illusory, if perhaps necessary, means of capturing their process-like relation.

Barthes renders the problem as an ambiguity in the relation of signification and sign, at once different and the same, at once process and fixed relation between terms: 'This ambiguity is an embarrassment for the graphic representation of the sign that is nonetheless necessary for the representation of the sign.'[23] It is embarrassing because the graphic form strengthens the separation of static terms thanks to a dividing symbol: a bar or line. Arguably, Barthes' later semiology is distinctive because he is not embarrassed about the ambiguity. On the contrary, the ambiguity of signs is the gap in which he develops his sensitive and non-reductive reading of signs.

In *Elements of Semiology*, Barthes analyses ambiguity in graphic representations of the sign in Saussure, Hjelmslev and Lacan, and in non-isological systems, that is, systems where there is no direct and unique one-to-one relation between signifier and signified and hence where each relation is mediated through another system such as a linguistic explanation or analogy. Barthes is interested in the different ways each position extends the separation of signifier and signified by the graphic bar into a more process-like relation of signification. I am concerned about the ways in which this extension falls short of a full process account of the sign.

Following Saussure, process is introduced partly by spatial relation, where the sign and its bar indicate a kind of depth such that the signified can be described as behind the signifier, as a deeper meaning which we can access through the more overt signifier.[24] The deeper meaning of the dove is in the signified 'peace'. We can see how signification can become process-like through expressions such as 'the whiteness of the dove gets at the idea of peace'; there is a process of approach and a sense of deepening in the relation between signifier and signified as an act of signification, such as a poem on peace, draws the terms together as surface and depth.

However, according to Barthes, Saussure then renounces this spatial metaphor and its continuity and movement in favour of 'the dialectical nature of signification' where closure of the sign is only possible 'in discontinuous systems such as language'.[25] In dialectical signification, the sign is closed and fixed on its language side and set in motion between discontinuous language states by speech. This is the connection between system and speech which we analysed earlier but with the added description of their connection as dialectical and concerning the process of signification.

The key term here is 'closure' because it introduces a new condition on the sign and on signification which returns to the condition of repetition of the same. In order to function reliably language must tame the process of signification by fixing it. Signs become settled in a closed language which is only set in motion through the intervention of speech in a discontinuous movement between closed states of language and intervening stages of openness in speech. For example, when a poet introduces the idea of the red dove of war, the structure of language is made to change around ideas such as the idea of the war for peace, but only dialectically between states of language, pre- and-post the creation of the red dove of war.

There is a great contrast between this dialectical logic of discontinuity and the continuous and intensive definition of the process sign.

The difference is between a structure-process-structure presentation, synchronically static and diachronically dialectical, and a strictly process view where process includes all structures as mobile and multiple, and where synchronic states are illusory and temporary rather than the object of the dialectic. It is possible to focus on these states: either by abstraction when we represent the diagram as motionless and as a relation between fixed terms in the sign ('a signifies b'); or by stipulation when we take an imposed code as a legitimate part of the sign ('the signified and signifier are arbitrarily related positions from synchronically invariant structures').

As read by Barthes, Hjelmslev avoids the need for the bar indicating depth or for a commentary on the dialectical nature of the sign by opting for a 'purely graphical' representation where an expression (E) is related to a content (C) as ERC. This has the advantage of allowing for a metalanguage and the interconnection of separate systems through the nested notation ER(ERC). It is therefore not dependent on dialectics between language and speech or between structure and process because the relation R can itself be seen as process and that process is repeated in each nesting of a sign ER(ER(ERC)) and so on.[26] However, in seeking formal invariance in the persistence of expression and content as fundamental models for the sign, Hjelmslev still has an essential structural stasis within the system determined by the distinction between expression and content elements.[27]

Continuing with the theme of graphical separation, Barthes sees Lacan as retaining a form of spatiality with a dividing bar between S and s, rendered as S/s (or A/a), but this is different from Saussure on two key points. First, the signifier is global and allows for metaphorical connections between different levels, such that we have complex and layered signifiers. These are floating, in the sense that they are cut free from the signified and only connect at certain points. This version of the sign comes from psychoanalysis where the complex story (A) given to the analyst corresponds at significant points to a deeper repressed source (a).[28]

Another good way of thinking about the Lacanian version of signification is through fairy tales working as cautions. The tale can have many different storylines and themes. As global signifier it is therefore a complex series of layers, but as warning it only connects in a few points to the cautionary lesson, the signified. Second, the bar therefore has a meaning of its own since it signifies the process of repression of the signified, for instance when figures in a tale repress a threat or deep motivation which also becomes the point of the tale. It is important to note how Barthes reads Lacan in quite a reductive way in *Elements of Semiology*,[29] but also that this reading is plausible even when we consider the algorithmic nature of Lacanian formalism such as his 'matheme' for fantasy, $\$\lozenge a$, where the lozenge should be interpreted as an algorithm between the fantasy and object of desire 'a'.

Finally, in non-isological systems, process comes with the intro-duction of a mediating system between signifier and signified, where the non-isological nature is indicated by the mediating symbol $Sr \equiv Sd$ as opposed to an isological equivalence $Sr = Sd$. An example of a non-isological sign would be one where signifier and signified have to be connected by a translation or interpretation such as commen-tary labels in an art gallery. These mediate between the works (Sr) and the meaning they should have for the viewers (Sd). The works and their parts are not in a one-to-one relation to the set of ideas and sensations the viewer might have. Instead, the short commentaries describe and explain a restricted path from works to meanings, not one-to-one but many-to-one as mediated by the commentary. Non-equivalence can be demonstrated by the variance that occurs when different commentaries set out different paths, because each one is a restriction of signifiers to a more narrow number and structure at the level of the signified.

Process is doubly restricted in non-isological systems. It is rejected first through the operation of the mediating term, such as the labels in the art gallery, which sets up fixed patterns of relations for the art-work operating as sign. This is a formal restriction where a structure is imposed on signification as an open relation between signifier and signified. Second, there is a numerical restriction in non-isological systems because the operation of the mediating term depends on a necessary reduction of the number of related terms through the sieve effect of the mediation whereby only some features can pass.

This survey of the introduction of process into the sign shows how signification introduces process into the sign either as dialecti-cal (Saussure), relational (Hjelmslev), metaphorically and as repul-sion/desire (Lacan), and as analogical (for non-isological structures). Once the idea of signification is introduced, the process philosophy of signs does not seem quite so much at odds with other theories of the sign. It is even possible to discuss the process sign as defined here in connection with those attempts.

Nesting in the process sign S{S{a,b,c}, d, e} has the same advan-tages as Hjelmslev's nesting of relations of expression and content ER(ERC) in allowing for a metalanguage, or layers of signs which operate on and in one another. The full process sign S{a,b,c}/Vs shares

Lacan's floating away of one process from another, since S{a,b,c} as emergent diagram is always open to a revaluation Vs expressed in a suite of further diagrams at odds with the first one yet also transforming it. This means any diagram is provisional and floating away from itself due to the transformer Vs.

There are also significant differences. The process account has no need for the distinctions of signifier and signified, or expression and content, since these are replaced by a multiplicity of changing intensive relations between any selected things. These are not divided according to the plane of signifier and of signified, since all things are set in relation by the sign according to a selection and a revaluation.

This also means that there is no special character to the relations in the sign, either as depth or repulsion. The process philosophy does not depend on an explanation of the nature of the separation of signifier and signified. It is therefore far removed from the psychoanalytical roots of the Lacanian sign. Note also that there is no ladder of metalanguages set up as a hierarchy of greater inclusions, as in Hjelmslev's work, but rather the possibility of layers of language understood in a topological sense, that is, different paths of layers can be drawn up according to how signs include one another.

The process account also has no need for the mediating process in Sr≡Sd to avoid equivalence, since S{a,b,c,}/Vs is always an asymmetrical transformation. This is important because it brings asymmetry into all aspects of the sign. In the process sign as defined here, relations are multiple changes in intensity mapping out a diagram of directions according to vectors and singular points. The revaluation Vs is a transformer of emerging diagrams and hence relations, but it is neither one-to-one function nor analogical translation through another system. It is instead a constant potential for disruption of the diagram that can only be experimented with prior to its operation and mapped in a new state of the diagram afterwards. It could be called an uncertainty transformer, to capture its disruptive and yet uncharted role.

Take for example a wall topped with broken bottles, sunk into concrete to serve as warning: if we follow Saussure we can analyse it as signifier and signified in a simple way, yet also see it as part of a dialectics around visual signifiers and warnings. New acts such as indelible ink added to the top of walls change the structures of signifier and signifier; for instance the idea of warnings having to be sharp or cutting is extended through the idea of marking as deterrent. These are fixed synchronically, at any given time, but change diachronically, over time. Taken as a metaphorical system, a global account of defensive measures and threats can be seen as a form of repulsion of the threat of some unknowable and inadmissible otherness. Taken as an analogical relation, there can be a translation system between a few types of warnings and many different images according to a type of interpretation 'How to read the significant features of defensive measures'.

The process philosophy can take any one of these and include it in a new selection which allows a diagram of changing relations to be drawn in conjunction with the selection. For instance, S{glass, types of warning, repression of the Other}/Vs will be accompanied by a descriptive diagram of singular points, say relations around sharpness and injury, and directions (increasing and decreasing in this way and that), and experimental transformations (Where might it be going? How might it change? What if we do this?)

There are no classes of signifier or signified here, or content and expression, only an unconditioned selection and diagrams which then situate the selection – reintroducing relative conditions – and new transformers subverting those emerging conditions. The sign as multiplicity and process replaces all versions of the sign as duality. It also replaces the narrow concept of structural signification with ideas of selection, diagram and potential transformation which can include significations within the multiplicity of the sign. In addition, this process sign can also be the object of describable stipulations over the sign.

ELEMENTS OF SEMIOLOGY V: VALUE

Having defined signification as being about content, since it relates a given signifier or expression with a given signified or content, Barthes defines value as being about form. By this he means that value is about structures of oppositions or relations on a given plane. These are formal because it does not matter what a thing points to, in the sense of what it relates to on another plane, but only how it relates to similar things it can be distinguished from. Value is then about position in a system of relations or oppositions; for instance, before we think of what a glass-studded wall signifies we note that it is three times more prevalent than roll-topped walls and differs from spiked and barbed wire ones in how it is positioned in a certain number of ways and according to a certain frequency.

One of the enduring problems of structuralism is to defend the objectivity of this cutting out of value. When we look at the example of defensive measures on the top of walls we can see how the cutting out is in fact subjective, in the sense that the division depends on a choice of things to cut out and of which features to select among them. A truly formal cutting out should not be open to variation or debate. It should have a positivist character which would allow structuralist sciences such as linguistics to claim to be genuine, for instance in the claim that there can only be this basic structure of phonemes or these syntactic forms.

Even if it is possible to find formal units and a structure of oppositions or relations which are beyond arbitrary choice, there is a further problem when the formal structure is combined with others thanks to the process of signification, because it introduces variation into formally distinct structures. Note how the process definition of the sign as selection affirms this variation and abandons all hope for a true formal cutting out of structure, replacing it instead with the description of an intensive diagram of an unconditioned selection. The process sign allows for the generation of critical and creative signs, but it cannot be a positive science in its own right and it rejects the idea of a science of the process sign. Any such science will be a stipulation over process.

Given that signification is about the relation between two planes, value and signification must be connected aspects of the sign. Barthes renders this by describing a model offered by Saussure of two floating realms cut out simultaneously:

> In order to account for the double phenomenon of signification and value Saussure used the image of a sheet of paper: by cutting it up, on the one hand, we obtain different pieces (A, B, C) where each has a value in relation to its neighbours; on the other hand, each one has a recto and verso that were cut out at the same time (A-A', B-B', C-C') and this is signification. The image is precious because it allows us to conceive of the production of sense in an original manner, no longer as the simple correlation of signifier and signified, but rather more essentially as an act of simultaneous cutting out of two amorphous masses, of two floating realms...[30]

This is a preliminary simplification of the way structuralism must connect the scientific task of value, the charting of the formal differences, and signification, the relation of two realms in an act relating form to content. It does not resolve the basic ambiguity of signification, because the formal cutting out, the strongest version of which Barthes attributes to Hjelmslev, still depends on the simultaneity of two realms achieved through the cancelling of their floating relation through signification, or the process of associating the two. Even if we attribute simultaneous relation as holding between the formal aspects of both realms, the correspondence between them will also involve relations of changes in content dependent on signification.[31]

If, following Saussure, the cutting out of a two-sided piece of paper is the original model for structuralism, the right model for the process philosophy of signs will exploit the topological properties of a thin rubber sheet stretched out in the wind. The sheet is not to be cut out. Lines are drawn on it according to an initial selection. The process sign is lines on a mobile support. It is topological rather than structural. Directions and singular points shift and move according to the stretching of the sheet. This is the sign: not the stasis of a two-sided cut-out but rather the dynamism of lines in motion determined by an initial selection and a diagram of movements.

This model also shows the necessity for revaluation, since if the rubber sheet obeys laws about its stretching, even if these are probabilistic or emergent, the laws will become a way of determining the unfolding of the sign. This might well be legitimate as a process science of the sign, but it fails as a speculative philosophy of the sign unless the choice of the given science is itself presented as speculative. However, if that's the case, this choice ought to be open to a diagrammatic account in terms of signs, at least where the speculative selection is concerned. In which case, we still need the speculative process account of the sign, even if it is to present the sign as including the selection of a science: S{a,b,c, emergent science at epoch T}/Vs, or to present a science of the sign as a stipulation over the sign open to critical and creative counters.

For the process philosophy of the sign, the deep problem is not in the cancelling of form in signification, since signification as process brings the idea of the sign closer to a prior role for change over stasis. It is rather that the form to be cancelled might still be necessary for the process philosophy to get off the ground. This would follow from the claim that any semiology depends on the parcelling of a realm according to set relations prior to establishing process, even if the relations need not be taken to be oppositions. According to the terminology given here, it would seem to imply that a stipulation over the sign as process is in fact legitimate and necessary for there to be signs and signification. This problem can be stated in a pure manner as follows. Any definition of process in the sign must begin with a cutting out of the field or realm of signs as formal differences. Only afterwards can the sign be defined as process between the signs as variations which undo these initial forms.

My definition of the sign as S{a,b,c}/Vs seems to fall victim to this challenge in very basic ways. First, the selection {a,b,c} can be defined as an initial cutting out. Second, it is a selection over 'all things', where the expression all things also seems to presuppose a cut out ontology of things or objects we select among and then transform according to the selection S{a, b, c}. Third, formally, the process sign seems to be defined as a series of stages or moments: selection {a, b, c}; then diagrammatic transformation S{a, b, c}; then revaluation S{a, b, c}/Vs. These moments are therefore a fundamental ontological cutting out of different kinds of being. This might lead to an ontological order of being (cut), becoming (intensive diagram) and supra-becoming (suite of diagrams). The problem is severe because the radical claims for process fail in the definition of selected set, independent entities and ontological stages.

The third objection has already been answered earlier. There are no stages in the sign. The revaluation is concurrent with the diagram and any sign is both a description of the singular points and directions of the diagram and experimentation with the different ways it might be breaking down. The selection is itself concurrent with diagram and revaluation such that it is false to say the selection comes before the diagram, it is instead a way of giving emphasis to some relations on the diagram rather than others, of bringing some into the foreground and pushing others into the background or latent environment. Selection is a way of making some relations more distinct while others become more obscure. It is therefore not a selection of individual things, which is a feature of notation. S{a,b,c} is a rendering more distinct or an emphasising rather than a selecting of individuals. The naming of individuals is a preliminary step for revealing them in their real state, which is as directions and singular points on a diagram.

These preliminary answers lead into the next chapter. The language of distinct and obscure is taken from Gilles Deleuze's *Difference and Repetition*, and the concept of intensive diagram can be traced through many of his works. However, despite extensive work on structuralism, for instance in the essay 'How do we Recognise Structuralism?', Deleuze does not attempt a structural account.[32] On the contrary, it is arguable that Deleuze and Guattari develop a deeply critical reading of such attempts on political grounds.

From his work on Proust onwards, Deleuze often returns to the idea of the sign, but he never develops a full philosophy of the sign, let alone a process philosophy; in fact, it is hard to argue that the concept of sign is crucial to his metaphysics. There must be reasons for this, and Deleuze and Guattari might therefore give us the strongest critique of the process philosophy of signs, in the way one's friends can also be our most insightful and devastating advisers.

The Process Sign After Deleuze and Whitehead

TYPOLOGY OF SIGNS AND SPECULATIVE METAPHYSICS: DELEUZE'S *PROUST AND SIGNS*

One of the siren songs for the philosophy of signs is typology. There is always a temptation not only to divide signs into types, but to explain the importance and function of signs through the way they work as different kinds. In our sign-saturated world this is as close to a natural vice in relation to signs as we can get. A stroll down any street, but in particular one in an unfamiliar world, leads to troubling immersion in vast ranges of different signs: street signs, adverts, architectural features, natural topographies, human faces and bodies, signs from plants and animals, odours and sounds, visual textures, weather signals, ambient temperatures, barometric changes, machine racket, digital and analogue screens, familiar and strange languages both spoken and written, objectless messages from our senses, bodily joys and distress, the inner chatter of streams of consciousness and fluctuations of moods and drives.

It is natural to respond to this profusion and competition of signs with a desire to organise them. Which signs are important? How can we divide them into manageable categories? Which signs can be ignored? Which carry essential threats and risks? Which signs are under my control and how? What errors and faults are in these signs?

The arts are masters of this troubling wealth of signs because they themselves play on multiple layers of signs and find themselves at the centre of busy webs of interpretation. In coining new signs and inventing different modes of circulation for older ones, the arts help us live with them. Of the arts, literature and poetry are the pre-eminent teachers of the excess of signs. The conscious and unconscious flows of signs in literary arts keeps pace with the experience of the bombardment, distress and attraction of signs as met on a busy boulevard. This ability to match the rich order and disorder of signs explains why the novel or the sonnet has best captured and created some of the signs we search for most, like those of love and death.

This explains why Gilles Deleuze's initial work on signs studied one of the greatest works of literature of the sign: Proust's *In Search of Lost Time*. There, Deleuze develops ideas about learning as apprenticeship to signs which remain important for him through much of his later philosophy, though less so with the more group-oriented books written with Guattari. These drew Deleuze away from his taste for a kind of existential experience of signs and towards the more affirmatively political construction of radical movements.

Deleuze's *Proust and Signs* is the most obviously divided of his books, along with his work on Foucault, since it draws together two essays and a re-edition into a later publication.[1] The earlier part begins with the characteristically enticing and disconcerting claim that *In Search of Lost Time* is not about time and memory, or the famous ideas of remembrance or recollection, but about apprenticeship to signs: 'To learn is to be essentially concerned with signs. Signs are the object of temporal apprenticeship and not an abstract knowledge. To learn is first to consider a matter, an object, a being as if they emit signs to be deciphered, to be interpreted.'[2] Apprenticeship is a practice of the sign. Its constitutive problem is how to interpret them.[3]

For Deleuze, as reader of Proust, signs allow us to discover the truth of worlds, but since there are many different worlds there are also different systems and types of sign for each world: 'But the plurality of worlds is that these signs are not of the same type, do not have the same way of appearing, do not allow themselves to be deciphered in the same way, do not have the same relation to their sense.'[4] Each world calls for a different behaviour towards its signs. Worldly signs operate in a social milieu as proxies for actions or thoughts. These signs allow for access to the milieu – it is not how you act and think that is important for breaking into a social circle, but rather how you are seen to act and think in displaying and interpreting signs. The difference between old and new money is a good example of the operation of worldly signs. Wealth is not the key to entry into the old world. You have to know how to spend it in the right way and on the right signs.

Quite different from these worldly signs, love works by revealing a possible world to us through signs projected by the loved one. We can sense this revelation in the dreams we construct around the loved one's body. This idea of the expression of a possible world is also touched on in *Difference and Repetition*, in a more universal way, as the ethical relation to the other's terrified face and the manner in which it reveals a possible world we have no direct access to. The face unfolds into the world we cannot see; it is a terrified subject in the unseen world. In turn, the world folds into the face, when facial lines and contours are twisted by frights.

Signs from the loved one unfold a possible world; they express it. They are also folded into the world; it forms them. This determines a two-way – expressive and explanatory – relation where singular aspects of the loved one are explained by the world, or unfolded into it, and where the world is reconstructed from the features of the loved one, or expressed by a folding into them. The beach will meet the perfection of the curved back our fingers hope to track: it unfolds into the back. A curved torso has been made by the sun tanning it and the waves shaping it through hours of swimming and diving: it folds into the waves. The relations of expression and folding also explain the dependence of worlds on signs, since a world transforms when a sign flips. The beach suddenly becomes ugly and inhospitable without the right body to express it.

The lover's signs express a form of sensuality we have not yet tasted, or a way of living together we have not yet achieved. This allows for a deduction by Deleuze, following Proust, where the signs of love are said to invoke laws of jealousy and of lies. Jealousy rules over signs of love because the expressed world is always threatened by other lovers, by other suitors, since it is only a possible world we do not have direct access to, let alone possess. The possible world is always under assault from rivals, because it is only a projection from uncertain signs.

The theme of jealousy and suitors is picked up again in *Difference and Repetition* – in a different context, but also around signs – when Deleuze studies the role of pretenders in Plato. The parallel is a very strong one and connects to Deleuze's understanding of the importance of Plato and Platonism for the interpretation of Proust (and of Sacher-Masoch). The way to divide pretenders is according to which ones are true copies of an original and which ones tell a lie. Lies are also therefore a differentiating law for the signs of love. The unknown possible world is always open to the idea that the signs mislead us about it, as a world where our love is always thwarted and secondary to a better and purer love. So we jealously search for the true sign and for the lie in love.

The subtlety and insight of Proust's work on signs and Deleuze's interpretation are not in question here. It is rather that this powerful reading lures thought into a mistaken view of signs as many different kinds, with their own ways of functioning and their own laws. This pluralism leads to a philosophy of signs as a divided practice of signs. The practice is organised around two guiding threads: the encounter with the sign and the sign as a different form of truth. The problem is that the encounters divide into types and truth divides into modes of interpretation.

At least at this point in Deleuze's philosophy, apprenticeship to signs is partly defined as a response to a violent encounter with different types of sign. The idea of this forceful influence of signs is also present in *Difference and Repetition*, along with the apprenticeship to signs. In *Proust and Signs* violence is first situated in relation to love, but the lesson applies to all types of sign: 'There is always the violence of a sign forcing us to search, stopping us from being at peace.'[5] We begin to seek the truth after a sign makes us jealous and wonder about lies, or when a sign makes us feel excluded and wonder about the secrets of a world.

Deleuze draws two lessons from the violent encounter and the search for truth. First, the desire for truth is not pure and disinterested but rather driven by affects such as jealousy. There are no pure lovers of truth. Second, the search is not primarily conditioned by a method, but rather by the violence of the encounter. These points support the idea of the importance of kinds of signs. The search for truth depends on the way a sign drives us to interpret it. These ways vary and different kinds of sign draw us to them in diverse ways. Being driven to decipher the rules of a secret society is different from being driven to decipher the signals from a lover. The method for this search also depends on the type of sign because different signs call for different approaches. The interpretation of signs of love and lies calls for a different approach to that of the understanding of social games.[6]

Each learning practice therefore responds to signs demanding distinct approaches to its proper signs: the signs of the social world;

the signs of love; the signs of sensual matter; the signs of art; the signs in learning a technical skill or sport. There are convergences here, since the signs of art capture the essence of all signs as involving an ideal, and since all signs are about truth rather than pleasure, though truth is not about correspondence between an idea and the world, or about a valid inference. Truth for Deleuze is always about a chance disruption by a kind of sign, something that snaps us out of the received images governing our thoughts.

Despite truth and art indicating common aspects of different signs and worlds, Deleuze's work on Proust is split between introducing ideas that will become important components of his metaphysical systems, as developed in *Difference and Repetition* and *The Logic of Sense*, and his other talent for brilliant original classifications of philosophers, writers and artists (Proust, Masoch, Spinoza, Bacon, many filmmakers). He combines the genius of the engineer of metaphysical systems and the brio of the inventor of new types of vision, of ways of seeing differently ordered complexity in great works. These often complementary powers do not sit well together for the philosophy of signs, because the sign is at once a working component of philosophical systems and the tool according to which many classifications are made possible, as we have seen in the reading of *In Search of Lost Time*.[7]

The tension between descriptive classification and metaphysical speculation is even stronger for the process philosophy of signs, since if the sign as process is to be continuous and ubiquitous it should not allow for separate typologies of the sign. We should not have different worlds of signs, because every sign is a world connected to all others. The contrast is between a philosophy of signs which prioritises categories and one that prioritises individuals as perspectives on indivisible worlds. Categories should only emerge later, when placed over individual variations of intensities of relations.

The critical challenge is stronger than this though, for it translates into a critique of the very idea of the speculative process metaphysics of the sign set out here.[8] Shouldn't we aim to have many different pragmatic definitions of the sign adequate to different worlds, rather than a metaphysics defining the sign in the same way for all? The answer is that we can have many different pragmatic ways of thinking critically through signs, but these ways depend on a single common form for the sign. This formal definition combines absence of determination in the definition or naming of each sign with an incomplete and open determination in the description of its accompanying intensive diagram. This diagram is itself open to revaluations, since in terms of critical reflection it must be considered in relation to other potential diagrams. Finally, each sign takes its place in a wider network of claims or stipulations over the sign and its diagrams.

So we can be pragmatic in the selection of the sign. We can classify these selections as types of selected sign. We can also classify them in relation to their diagrams and the stipulations over them. However, we cannot see these classifications as fixed and restrictive of different ways of taking the sign. Any sign can be incorporated in new and different selections, but the selections themselves must not be divided into legitimate categories for signs. There are no essential or natural types of sign, because each sign crosses between types at different degrees of intensity.

We must therefore not use the classification of a sign as a way to determine borders for its diagrams. These are always without limit and borderless, only allowing for degrees of difference around intensities of relations, moving closer or further away, for instance. There are no final distinctions, such as 'this sign is never with this', or 'this sign is not that'. This means that signs come before and deny the logics of contradiction and opposition which allow for independent categories. It will never be satisfactory to say that such oppositions and contradictions can be subsumed in a later synthesis, because this still depends on the earlier logical distinction which inflicts mistaken boundaries on the sign. You do not make an unnecessary cut better by pretending to heal it.

The definition of the process sign denies foundational distinctions of the sign into, for instance, signs of love and worldly signs. Instead, we can pragmatically select a sign of love and draw up its diagram demonstrating that worldly signs are at a far remove from its most intense relations. This will always be open to challenge, either through a different naming and selection of the sign of love (for example, by including a worldly duty to family in the sign of love) or by showing how the diagram can be redrawn in ways that move its centres of gravity and distant points (for instance, by showing a strong and unexpected role for social conditioning around apparently pure and free love).

Finally, it is important to insist on the speculative, experimental and critical aspects of the process sign. It is always a suggestion rather than a claim to knowledge, a series of creative moves rather than positive objective description, and a critical position with respect to other stipulations over its components. This does not mean that the sign is not real. It means it is real as a speculative, experimental and critical intervention. We live among many such interventions around worldly signs and the signs of love, from great literary creations, through individual gestures and experiments, and on to novel or differently seen natural phenomena. Process signs are real and so is the changeability and impermanence of worlds.

STIPULATIONS OVER THE SIGN AND THE PROBLEM OF UNDETERMINED SELECTION

One advantage of classifications of signs into different categories is that they set the frame for critical debates. There is already some kind of shared basis for discussions about what a sign means and about how the sign relates to a wider world. By insisting on the individual sign as a selective naming and by claiming a universal transformation of background relations in each sign, the process philosophy of the sign seems to start all debates anew with each sign and thereby to cast the sign into an open-ended and chaotic series of claims over it. In the next two sections I want to show what this openness gains over more restrictive definitions and classifications of the sign.

This defence of openness in relation to various stipulations encounters a deep problem in relation to the claim for absence of determination in the sign. Is it really the case that a selection of a set of elements is undetermined? Can't we trace causes, influences, statistical trends or limits to this supposedly undetermined selection? The answer given in the previous chapter is that the selection is undetermined by definition, so the absence of determination is a premise for the process definition of the sign. Is that premise plausible?

In Chapters 3 and 4 I described the use of signs and process in biology. This study shaped the definition of the sign in two ways. First, the domain of the sign had to give a place to science and to other claims to determination over what can stand as a sign, reflecting their importance as critical opponents to the general definition of the sign. The sign must be set in critical relation to stipulations over it from science and other spheres. This means that the sign is only ever a prompt and critical move and not a well-founded claim to knowledge. It also means that the selection of a new sign is always possible in setting out a novel hypothesis in science and other stipulations about laws and codes.

The process philosophy of the sign leaves the nature of the critical debate around the sign and its external stipulations open. They could take the form of debates guided by different epistemologies and philosophies of science, or they could stretch wider to accounts of rational debate, or even wider to theories about the nature of truth. The point is that this speculation is made possible by the selection of new signs and experimentation around their diagrams which call for reflection on what will constitute a valid critical argument and criteria for rejecting or accepting suggestions for signs.

Take, for instance, the sense of a great wrong done to a group of citizens. Assuming the injustice cannot be recognised from within existing legal systems, then the task for an advocate for the group to will be to name the injustice, to select a new sign for it, and to describe the changes this naming will bring about, that is, to draw a diagram of intensive changes such as growing relief and reduction in harm. This naming of the sign will be strategic. The most effective selection needs to be made in accordance with an understanding of its accompanying diagram. Strategic considerations around naming and mapping are only part of the overall critical discussion. This is because they are moves in a wider dispute around, in this case, questions of justice. More generally, moves will be around debates between different claims as to what can be said at all and what can be said rightly about a collection of signs.

Even this might be to concede too much to the process definition of the sign. The problem can be seen through the example of chess. A chess move can be described as a selection; it is the selection of a piece and a place on the board. The move can also be described in intensive terms, for example in the way an attack puts stress on a particular defence and in the way a counter-move relieves the stress. However, this apparent confirmation fails on three counts. First, it is not the case that the chess move is unconditioned. On the contrary, it is constrained by the rules of chess about the movement of pieces. The appeal to some kind of absolute freedom in selection is therefore misleading.

Second, against the reference to intensity as describing different intensive pulls across a given situation, the use of intensity in relation to games can be seen as either metaphorical, since what is described as stress can be re-described in terms of the objective logical implications for any given move, or as external to the game proper, for instance, as a description of the emotional states of the players. If this is correct, then the appeal to intensive diagrams is unnecessary and they should be rejected on grounds of ontological parsimony. There is no need for any reference to intensities in diagrams.

It is worth giving advance notice of where some of these arguments lead, since the concept of intensity retains its importance in timed chess matches where time pressure can be thought of as increased intensity forcing players away from a purely logical analysis. Freedom from intensity might only be a reference to an ideal situation and to an abstraction: chess in some kind of unreal logical space. Though we can abstract from time and follow chess moves through to their completion logically, the concept of time advantage brings back an intensive aspect to the game. To say Karpov held the advantage in time is intensive rather than logical, since it bears no necessary relation to a given outcome and since it allows for dynamic and changing values, for instance of pressure, which can be mapped over the logical patterns of the game.

Third, it is not the case that the selected move opens up a debate between a suggested diagram and stipulations against the selection and diagram. There is no space for debate but only for moves to play out according to the rules of the game. The definition of the process sign independently of stipulations therefore seems the equivalent of a petulant child moaning about the rules of a game. You can moan all you like, but the rules aren't listening. In playing the game we agree to the rules and if we do not agree we should not play the game.[9]

There are two ready responses to these objections, but each one has to make broad concessions. We could respond that the process philosophy of signs addresses only certain kinds of problems and fields. It is possible to create new signs for questions of value, around the good, the just and the beautiful, for instance. But it is not possible to do so in fields where the implications are strictly logical or founded on a well-defined structure of rules. So we might be able to raise new possibilities through new signs in aesthetics, morality and justice, but certainly not in science, logic or fields with clear and limited agreed rules such as chess. We could also respond that it is only under certain conditions that new signs are valid moves, for example where there is a paradigm shift in the sciences, or where a rule change is suggested for a game that has become moribund or dangerous in some way. In the first case, we restrict the sign to a proper field. In the second, we limit it to a proper moment. The creation of a new sign then becomes something that occurs at transition points between paradigms, or when some kind of breakdown occurs in a structure of rules and laws.

I do not want to make either of these concessions, because they do not solve deeper problems about the definition of the process sign in relation to absence of determination and about the reality of changes in the intensities of relation around signs. In order to see why there might be another option, it is necessary to make the objection to the process sign even stronger. If we accept that the class of signs includes linguistic ones, can we still maintain that the selection of the elements of signs is undetermined and that signs are accompanied by intensive variations in relations?

Taken at a simple and immediate level, it seems that linguistic signs are determined and the relations they point to or imply are not intensive changes but rather structural relations of similarities and oppositions. Take the example of the selection of a name or set of words for a phenomenon. The name I can choose seems to be limited by the languages I possess, not only in their words, but also in their grammatical rules, their more loose idiomatic practices, their forms of inscription such as alphabets, and their forms of expression such as phonetics. I cannot select names from languages I do not know, or read symbols I am unfamiliar with. I cannot meaningfully push the rules of grammar too far or go beyond limits in my powers of pronunciation. What does it mean, then, to say that a selection of a sign is undetermined?

Furthermore, the signification or meaning of the sign I choose does not set off changes in the intensities of relations, 'more redness' for instance, but instead follows from relations to other significations, either in opposition, 'blue is not red', or in accordance with similar types, 'red is a colour close to maroon'. Even if we grant that such significations are changeable and relatively open, this mobility is determined by structural relations of some kind and not by an extra field of changes in intensity.

So even if we grant that there might be process signs, for instance in the way art practice can select very wide combinations of signs in order to trigger changes in the intensity of an emotion, it appears that when signs are linguistic, openness and intensities disappear in favour of structures. We might well argue about the source and nature of these structures – deep grammar or usage, say – but that does nothing to dispel their hold on the creation and reception of signs.

It is important to be precise about why these objections are troublesome for my definition of the sign as process. It is not because the definition might go against an established science of language or dominant philosophy of language. It is fine for theories of language to be stipulations over the sign, for their terms to be selected into a sign and for them to be placed on intensive diagrams. The process account is not a strict alternative to other theories of language. The problem is rather that theories of language make the formal definition of the sign as process highly implausible: there is no undetermined selection and there are no significant intensive variations.

To begin to understand how there might be an answer to these stronger objections it is helpful to restate the process definition precisely and with an emphasis on its completeness. The process sign is the undetermined selection of a set of elements against a substratum of all elements AND the drawing up of a diagram of changing intensities of relations around singular points and in different directions AND experimental revaluations of the diagram AND critical interaction with stipulations over the selected sign and its diagrams. I have capitalised 'and' here to indicate co-dependence. If we separate the terms we alter them when compared to their connected forms.

Selection in the sign is therefore not simply free extraction from a given background, in the sense of making the sign independent of the background or what I have called its substratum. It is exactly the opposite: the selection is only ever against the background. Indeterminacy is not about absolute independence, but rather about freedom to vary a relation between elements. Selection does not mean we can fully extract this sign from its background, or conjure up this new one out of nothing. The claim is quite different. It is that there can be a description of new relations within a set of elements thanks to a selection of some of them, independent of the relations said to hold between them prior to the selection.

For instance, novelty in naming does not mean coming up with a name that no one can pronounce, nor suggesting a name that no one has heard before. It is to connect the name to other elements in such a way that new relations appear across all elements in a manner that is not fully determined by earlier states. The name 'James-the-slippery-untrustworthy-sophist' is determined by the words I have learnt and their significations. I am suggesting it is undetermined in the new relations it sets in this book and beyond, because the selection highlights the elements in a different way against the background of all elements and their relations.

I am therefore interested in the idea that language has to have some kind of formal resource for expressing the new at the heart of each structure, taken synchronically, rather than between different structures, taken diachronically. The point is to situate this resource in the sign as process. How the process works as an undetermined entry point into novel signification is therefore of greater interest than the negative challenge to others around the moribund nature of language and communication if it cannot draw on novelty.

THE SIGN AS SELECTION AND INTENSITY: PARADOX AND SIGNIFICATION IN *THE LOGIC OF SENSE*

The nature of indeterminacy in the sign is tied to the relation between a selected set and its substratum. In turn, this is connected to the intensive diagram and its revaluations, since the selection determines the diagram and the diagram sets out the intensive changes for the selection. It is therefore in relation to the idea of selection, allied to intensive changes and their experimental revaluation, that the argument about absence of determination, structural predisposition and rules of signification must be made.

This is the point where it is useful to return to Deleuze's work and to his studies of signification and the sign in his 1969 book *The Logic of Sense*. In its twelfth series, 'On the Paradox', Deleuze sets up an opposition between paradox and common and good sense. This opposition sets the scene for arguments designed to unsettle a simple opposition between signification and paradoxical terms. There is paradox in signification and a place for novel paradoxical terms within any structure of signification. These statements are helpful for the claim that the process sign can be consistent with language, understood as a structure of signification, because, in Deleuze's definition of the term, structure emerges out of process rather than excluding it.

His argument begins by discounting a simple move. It is not possible to exclude paradoxes from logically consistent structures. This is because they continue to subsist within the structures they are supposed to be removed from. It is also because the structures can only function thanks to paradoxical terms. Finally, it is because paradoxes give a true and complex image of what thought is like, against the idea that thought can be shown to be logically consistent and simple in its structure of logical relations, such as the laws of non-contradiction and of identity.

To see how this connects to the debate about process and signification, it is important to note how the process sign is necessarily paradoxical in a number of different ways. First, given that the set selected in the naming of the sign can include any element, the sign can be paradoxical at that point, for instance in a sign including a contradiction {a & not-a} or in the generation of Russell's paradox when the set includes itself. Second, given that any selection is against a background of all other elements, there must be paradoxical relations operating in the process sign; for instance, any sign is in a positive relation to paradoxical terms such as contradictions, even if they are very distant and obscure background aspects for the selected set. The use of positive here indicates an effect of one upon the other, rather than a negative relation of opposition, contradiction or exclusion.

Third, given the claim that the diagram of a sign is a series of changing intensive relations across all elements, these changing intensive relations include paradoxical ones; for instance, the strong intensities around a given singularity on the diagram will have some relation to movements and other singularities that are paradoxical when taken in the close vicinity of that singularity. This is also trivially true of any revaluation of a diagram, but more importantly it follows from the relation between them, where the revaluation experiments not with an independent contradiction of a given diagram, but with another counterfactual state which connects to the earlier one.

Finally, the relations of the process sign as selection, background diagram and revaluation can be in paradoxical relation to stipulations over the sign, as for instance when a process sign contradicts a stipulation such as 'no sign should contain a contradiction', or 'no sign can make sense unless it is within current social language use'. It is here that we can return to Deleuze's argument, since his deeper point is that paradoxes are not contradictions to be excluded from valid forms of thought. Instead, paradoxes generate contradiction and hence play a part within it, even after they are repudiated by logical structures which seek to banish contradiction.

The role of intensity in Deleuze's arguments is underplayed in this series from *The Logic of Sense*, but there are two terms in which we can see its importance and necessity: 'The force of paradoxes is in this: it is not that they are contradictory, but rather that they allow us to assist at the genesis of contradiction.'[10] Force and genesis are intensive terms for Deleuze.[11] By appealing to force he is not making a metaphorical point, as if contradictions were forcefully meaningful because they are or are not contradictory. He is making a point about real power. Paradoxes bring about contradictions through intensive shifts, such as increasing doubt and decreasing confidence around something. They therefore work in the genesis of contradictions, as forms designed to fend off doubt and increase security within a structure.

Consider the role of copy editors on a busy news website. They have to rule over fast and varied flows of articles posted for inclusion on the site. They have a house style which allows them to correct entries efficiently. If you contradict the style you have to change your wording, or your contribution will be rejected. Deleuze's point is that uncritical acceptance of the style and its rule misses the genesis and forces around of the house style, or more generally around any logical and grammatical set of rules.

Rules emerge and grow over time as responses to problems and paradoxes, such as different uses for the same word. Problems and paradoxes therefore generate the rules and explain both the force in them, why we care about them, and the force outside them, why they are challenged.[12] The idea of unstable emergence is important because it captures the unstable and dynamic nature of these forces. They are in varying movements rather than static states; much as linguistic form is in a dynamic relation to idiomatic usage and biological processes are in process of stabilisation and destabilisation.

Deleuze's approach to good sense and common sense therefore involves a pincer movement. First, he seeks to show how there is a realm outside them that is not pure nonsense or something easily discarded. Second, he demonstrates that this supposedly barren and dispensable realm works inside the logical realms of common and good sense. Both sides of the movement can be seen in his critique of the law of non-contradiction: 'The principle of non-contradiction applies to the real and to the possible, but not to the impossible that it is derived from, that is, to paradoxes, or rather to what they represent.'[13] The 'derived from' is crucial here. It demonstrates the role and necessity of paradox.

Deleuze uses terms in different senses across his works and this is particularly true of 'real'. Here, he means real as actual. The actual and the possible are said to be governed by the law of non-contradiction. They should not entertain contradictions, whereas the impossible allows for them. However, this appears to confirm the opposite to what Deleuze is arguing, since we could conclude that the impossible should be disregarded because it allows for contradictions. His point runs counter to this on the grounds of function and form. The impossible is a full and important realm which we cannot simply disregard, because it has force by functioning in other realms and because as such the law of non-contradiction does not apply to it. The law does not legislate over the realm of the impossible, it can only claim to try – and fail – to banish it from realms where the law holds.

This force and failure can be demonstrated in the way the impossible generates the law of non-contradiction. It is because there are contradictions which have some kind of force, such as paradoxes, that the law of non-contradiction and other laws have evolved and have power. A good way to think about this is in terms of other, more familiar laws. It is because some people exploit the gullibility or lack of knowledge of others that we have laws about financial probity. The laws are generated and justified by the practices they outlaw and new laws emerge and are shaped by new versions of the practices, for instance, pyramid or Ponzi schemes.[14] With the same hubris of overconfident legislators declaring a certain kind of crime impossible, logical rules attempt to banish the very 'impossibility' that justifies their existence and explains their content.

A puzzle remains in Deleuze's proposition about non-contradiction. Why does he say paradoxes 'represent' the impossible rather than 'are' impossible? It is because paradoxes are a way of expressing rising and decreasing intensities in opposed, contradictory, yet connected directions. The impossible is not a simple contradiction but rather many different potential developments that cannot all be sustained in a possible world defined according to common and good sense. We are impelled in different ways. These ways are mutually exclusive and incommensurable when we try to impose a single order of measure over them. Nonetheless, at the point where we sense the force of the paradox the different ways are in play together. They are represented by the paradox.

The paradoxes express the ways and their genetic force, but they are not adequate equivalents for them, since the ways are more pliable and multiple than any given paradox can represent. The paradox is a bridgehead between the realm of the impossible and the realms of common and good sense. A paradox represents the impossible in a form that good sense and common sense can recognise as something to be excluded and yet also as something troublesome. Analogies for this model can be found in situations where an emotionally difficult choice is imposed over a number of mutually exclusive options. The impossible is the web of competing emotions across the different options. The paradox is the necessary yet nonsensical choice which draws out this competition. The realm of good sense and common sense is the representation of a world where the right choices can be made. *Choose one of these children...*

THE PROCESS SIGN, COMMON SENSE
AND METAPHYSICS

The deep interest in Deleuze's work on sense for the process philosophy of signs lies in his detailed description of the relation of the different parties to the emergence of language and thought through paradox. It allows us to understand why the sign cannot be reduced to the stipulations over it, but also why those stipulations are unavoidable and important. Here are features of good sense described in relation to paradox and to sense, understood as something impossible when viewed from good and common sense:

1. Good sense has a single direction. It goes from past to future through the present.
2. As direction, good sense goes from the more differentiated (the known past) to the less differentiated (the uncertain future).
3. Functioning in the present, the role of good sense is therefore to predict, to allow us to maximise certainty in the passage from the known past to the unknown future.
4. This prediction is done through a 'sedentary distribution', a cutting up of a present situation and its projection into the future through options that can be weighed.
5. So good sense ascribes a singularity to itself – the decision point in the present – but the singularity is then cancelled out by projecting it into the past and future as measurable distributions.

Decision points based around new problems are helpful examples of how good sense functions. Let's imagine you own a cycle workshop servicing a particularly sturdy type of bike. Your tools and manuals represent the past. They tell you exactly what to do when faced with misaligned gears and other faults. The instructions and implements are your reliable reserve of acquired knowledge based on past experience and practice. This reserve is put to the test when a rain-soaked cyclist comes into the shop with an esoteric hand-engineered bike. The bike's complicated gears are bent. Your present challenge is how to mend them even though they fall outside the range of your past knowledge.

The unique direction of good sense runs from the past (different types of bikes and tools for them), to the future (mended bikes), through the present (broken gears and the problem of the selection of the right tools and approach for a new kind of bike). The novel distribution is around the tools and techniques you think will adapt best to the strange machine. Prediction is in weighing up which course of action is the most likely to succeed. The singularity to be cancelled is the moment of uncertainty when you run through combinations of imperfect tools and techniques before you make the decision to use some of them in a new way.

The strength of Deleuze's analysis is in its closeness to our intuitions and experience about sensible courses of action, accompanied by great critical distance. He understands how good sense works, but he rejects it as an incomplete picture of action and thought. The argument is based on the idea that there is something prior to good sense and to objects of thought in good sense. He calls this event the donation of sense.[15] This donation should not be seen as something coming before other forms of sense and falling away once they hold sway; it is not like a question that calls for an answer but disappears once it is found. Instead, the donation of sense reverberates in other forms of sense with a transforming and generative force. So the argument is not about the presence of something else, something missed, by senses we have in common. It is that what we think we have securely in common in the form of our reflective actions is radically and inevitably transformed by another kind of sense working away within them.

The same argument holds for the process sign. It is not that there are some signs in process and others not. Every sign is in process and this is missed when we impose a stipulation about stasis or stable signification on the sign, when we apply the fallacy of misplaced concreteness, or when we confuse stabilisation with final stability. As defined by Deleuze, sense is given as movement and change within good sense and common sense and within signification and logical consistency. In opposition to the stipulations of good sense, the definition of the sign as process must therefore be equated to the donation of sense.

Metaphorically, we could think of donation as sensation prior to its ordering in terms of objects in a logically consistent field. It is like the experience of a dark vista requiring a slow adaptation to its initially imperceptible contents, or like an abstract painting or chaotic noise, prior to the recognition of figure, beat and melody. For sense as donation, these fluid and uncertain moments are never fully shaken off. They are at work within later order, denying it certainty and permanence.

The key points to retain here are, first, the claim about necessity. There has to be an initial chaotic perception for there to be the later well-ordered one. Donation is the necessary condition for later perception consistent with good sense. Second, there is a claim about inescapability. The donation of sense remains in later perception, in productive tension with it, like the abstract work we return to, in order to question the figures we have imposed upon it, or like a rich experimental field we go back to in order to check a new hypothesis. The process sign is a donation, because the sign is a condition for language and for understanding but also an unstable and mobile challenge within them.

The donation of sense is in paradoxical relation to good sense. A paradox expresses that there is a sense that tries to go both ways: towards order and towards disorder. However, neither way is a satisfactory resolution of the paradox and, instead, the paradox traps us in a multiplicity of directions, where we can neither go forward nor back once and for all. This means paradox works as a generator of insufficient yet necessary solutions. Directions are attempted, work for a while, but then fade as the paradox re-establishes its dominance. Paradoxes show there is a donation of paradoxical sense before good sense and in opposition to the direction of good sense towards a settled and consistent logical structure.

The passage from past to future is thought through thermodynamics, and Deleuze draws on the ideas of accelerating and decelerating viscosity and rising and falling temperature differences to explain different directions. His point is that good sense imposes a unique direction on two opposed ones. These are the direction we are familiar with (for instance, from more differentiated temperatures to less, when an ice block melts in a pool of water) and the opposite direction to good sense (for instance, from higher viscosity to lower viscosity as temperature decreases, such that cooking oil would become thinner as its temperature decreased). Good sense selects the direction which currently holds sway and the one that allows us to make correct predictions (from more to less differentiated, as temperature differences fall, from greater to lesser viscosity, as temperature rises).

It might seem that we should call the 'wrong' direction the paradoxical one, that is, the one going against good sense, order and shared belief. Deleuze explains paradoxes quite differently. Paradoxes make it impossible to distinguish the two directions so neither can be taken as the right one. There wouldn't be a paradox were this not the case, since we'd resolve each paradox by simply affirming the direction of good sense. Good sense and doxastic belief collapse when confronted by paradox: 'But paradox as passion reveals that we cannot separate the two directions. We cannot establish a unique direction, or a unique direction for serious thought...'[16]

The combination of passion and intensity in the paradox is what matters. We feel torn between directions by intense yet contradictory movements, such that neither direction is the right one and neither the wrong one. Instead, many directions take hold of us in a manner similar to a world where objects start to slip away of their own accord and at different speeds, driving us into a frenzied pursuit of the escaping objects. In order to be adequate to this combination of intensity and paradoxical pulls, the suite of diagrams of a process sign expresses motion in the sign as a multiplicity of directions around singularities and directions. The diagrams are representations of paradoxical and intense attractions. They express the difficult passion of signs.

This passion is portrayed as disarray by comic arts when they place a character in the midst of a world losing its logical order. This is why Deleuze puts greater emphasis on humour as opposed to irony and why he is interested in slapstick film and its portrayal of what he calls movement images.[17] Humour captures the motion and intensity effects of paradoxes, such as the instant flick from mirth to misery in slapstick, whereas irony pushes us towards a despairing intellectual consideration of detached puzzles. As gravity fails and familiar household objects fly to the ceiling, the first reaction is disarray and the second maddened activity in every direction: passion and intensity.

Paradox is therefore an intellectual problem and a sensual one. So when Deleuze uses the term sense as opposed to good sense and common sense he means sense as the sensation of increasing and decreasing intensities associated with an irreducible multiplicity of directions. Good sense emerges out of paradox as the suppression it, as an attempt to impose order, not on chaos but rather on intensive multiplicities. This is the parallel between the process sign as intensive diagram and Deleuze's concept of sense. It is also the connection between good sense and stipulations over process signs. There is an ongoing struggle between sense as given in paradox and the order of good sense. There is an ongoing debate between the unstable sign and stipulations over it.

However, there are two places where this parallel breaks down: the metaphysics of time and the boundaries of the sign. Deleuze's work on language and paradox is situated within a wider metaphysical account of time and a broader ontology of different realms related by an intensive surface. Both areas can be seen in the following passage which comes a few lines after the previous passage on paradox:

> Here we return to the opposition of Aiôn and Chronos. Chronos is the present existing alone. This makes the past and the future its oriented dimensions, such that we always go from past to future but only while presents succeed one another in worlds or partial systems. Aiôn is the past-future in an infinite subdivision of the abstract moment, which never ceases to decompose in both directions at the same time, forever slipping away from any present.[18]

Deleuze divides reality into two sorts of time. Aiôn is the time of sensual disorientation where we search back through the past and into the future among endlessly subdividing pressures and pulls. It is the time where our present location and action lose themselves under the weight of incalculable pressures from past and future influences. The present becomes a mobile point in Aiôn; it moves searchingly into the past and into the future. Imagine finding a new archive about your family, one in which a terrible crime is revealed. As you riffle through its documents and reassess all other documents as fast as you can, feeling your certainties and plans dissolve, you are in the grip of Aiôn.

In contrast to Aiôn, Chronos is the time of decision and action, where we take evidence from the past and predictions for the future and bring them to bear on an act in the present. Here, past and future are compressed into the present which, abstracted from the uncertainties of Aiôn, takes charge of the future and responsibility for the past. As you leave the distressing archive, you decide to burn it and free the future from its terrible secret. That decision and act are the mark of Chronos.[19]

Taken alone, the times necessarily involve different entities; they are ontologically separate. To be incalculable and multiple the pulls in Aiôn have to have an abstract and disembodied quality. In contrast, things in Chronos have to be discrete and concrete to be calculable and acted upon. Yet, Aiôn and Chronos touch and communicate through an intensive surface. What Deleuze means by this appeal to intensities and to a surface between the two times is that each one is subject to intensive changes. For Aiôn, they are in the speed and indistinctness of movement through all of the past and all of the future: the panicked flight through all our documents and memories as the police knock on the door. For Chronos, they are in the urgency of a single present pressure: the pain of unbearable heat, the search for the right escape, and the decision to take it.

Reality brings the two times together through the shared intensive surface, which explains why Deleuze is strongly opposed to simplistic accounts of the real as an actual identifiable world contrasting with identifiable but unrealised possibilities. In *The Logic of Sense*, the real is always intensive in its combination of infinite movement through the past and the future, and singular focus on the present. Acts and decisions in the present are undone by wounds from the past and from the future. Disembodied pulls in Aiôn are partially fixed when they are expressed in Chronos. It will always be wrong to dismiss Deleuze's philosophy as a dualist metaphysics, since everything significant happens at the intensive frontier between Aiôn and Chronos. There is a dialectics between the call of multiple abstractions and the need for secure actions.

The narrower claims of the process philosophy of signs need to be distinguished from Deleuze's work on time. This distinction is about the amount of metaphysical system-building required for an adequate definition of the sign in a process philosophy. My approach is minimalist and locally pragmatic. A speculative philosophy should involve no more metaphysical concepts than are needed to establish the sign as a process and to allow its application across a very wide range of cases of signs.

Deleuze's philosophy has much greater global systematic ambitions which mean that he constructs a system that maximises its conceptual reach across fields and across different kinds of cases. It is a philosophy of everything, including signs, as opposed to a philosophy of signs alone. If a philosophy concerned solely with signs can be accused of missing their connection to other phenomena, a philosophy concerned with everything can be accused of weighing down local phenomena with the conceptual framework required for all others.

My objection to Deleuze's appeal to a philosophy of time in relation to language and signification is that the sign is over-determined by a metaphysical structure. This occurs across all the main concepts in the definition of the sign. If we think of the process sign as a donation of sense in time, we theorise it in terms of his ontological distinction drawn between Chronos and Aiôn, whereas the naming of the sign as an undetermined set and the description of diagrams is metaphysically much more open because it avoids having to insert the sign in different processes mapped on relations of past, present and future.

In the process philosophy of the sign, the selection of the naming set is undetermined by definition. In Deleuze's philosophy, selection must accord with the different ways in which it takes place in time. Similarly, the diagrams of signs as process are not subject to restrictions according to time whereas, were we to follow Deleuze, all relations on the diagram would have to fit into relations across Aiôn and Chronos and their shared intensive surface. There are still restrictions through the concept of set and the idea of selection against a background for the process sign. This is also true for the specification of diagrams and of revaluations of diagrams. But each of these maintains much greater flexibility of content than a more strongly specified metaphysics.

The weakness of metaphysically heavy definitions of the sign is their lack of flexibility and accuracy in relation to the description of particular signs and in the structures they import into all signs. Flexibility is lacking because each sign must accord with the wider account of time and any narrow description of a sign will be inadequate if it does not extend to the full range of metaphysical concepts. The advantage of the process model is that it can extend and restrict the selecting set and accompanying diagrams to give wider or narrower descriptions of process and more accurate correspondence to specific features of a sign. Moreover, this does not discount the possibility of a metaphysics of time for a sign. It situates it at the level of a particular diagram. Deleuze's philosophy of time should be seen as a diagram, rather than the model for all diagrams.

There is a counter-argument to ontological and metaphysical parsimony in the sign, drawing on Deleuze's more comprehensive version. The fullness of his account provides an extensive explanatory frame. So when further questions are asked about features of particular signs or about decisions in describing them, they can be answered by referring to other aspects of the metaphysics. We saw this earlier in his concept of the folding and unfolding of signs according to explication and implication. It appears that the more narrow definition of the sign does not have such conceptual and explanatory resources to call on. This could be a serious flaw, as shown in following questions. How do we decide on the best diagram for a sign? What criteria are there for drawing the diagram? Where are we to set its provisional limits and what might constitute an error or infelicity in a proposed diagram?

The answer is that the process definition of the sign emphasises two aspects of speculative philosophy to allow for critical confrontation and discussion around the sign. First, each diagram is only ever a proposed model for the processes named by a given naming selection. It has to be open to counterfactual proposals. Second, each definition of a process sign is in critical relation to external stipulations and is open to a dialogue with them.

By definition, the process sign is internally speculative and externally dialogical, where neither of these limits is final, because external stipulations can be included in new signs and because any given internal description can also be taken as an external stipulation for all signs. For this process philosophy, the sign itself is always given provisionally, in a movable context and in critical debate with external suggestions for codes and laws about the sign.

The greatest contrast to the process definition as a way of following on from Deleuze's philosophy of the sign comes from Anne Sauvagnargues's work, with its debt to the French philosophers Gilbert Simondon and Raymond Ruyer and to their influence on Deleuze (despite her critique of Ruyer presented in Chapter 3). The best way of understanding the difference is to see Sauvagnargues's philosophy of the sign as realist, for instance in seeing the sign as constituted by real material forces and processes of individuation: 'It is then no longer a question of signifier or signified, nor of forms and matter, but of forces and materials, conforming to the Simondian principle of modulation.'[20]

From this point of view, my situation of intensity at the level of relations for the sign and my dependence on an open and speculative approach are anti-realist and mistaken about the material nature of forces and intensity. However, my concern is that Sauvagnargues's approach is either damagingly metaphysical in overloading the sign with limiting and unnecessary metaphysical concepts, or based on scientific approaches in ways that render the definition of the sign inflexible and in danger of rapid redundancy as sciences change. The deciding factors in moving away from a materialist account of the sign are to be found, first, in my critical reading of Uexküll and Ruyer with their loaded metaphysical imports into biology and their political and ethical consequences; second, in my encounter with Dupré's process biology which requires none of Deleuze and Simondon's metaphysical concepts; third, in my debt to Whitehead's speculative process philosophy.

WHITEHEAD AND A SPECULATIVE PHILOSOPHY OF THE SIGN

At the start of *Process and Reality*, Whitehead sets out his understanding of process philosophy as speculative philosophy. This is important because there is a link between the attempt to think existence as process and the aims of a speculative approach. We can begin to understand why this might be the case by starting from the definition of speculative given in the third sentence of Whitehead's book: 'Speculative Philosophy is the endeavour to frame a coherent, logical, necessary system of general ideas in terms of which every element of our experience can be interpreted.'[21]

This seems to be a definition suited to most kinds of philosophical metaphysics. The following could be a paraphrase of Whitehead's words: metaphysics should give a coherent, logical, necessary and all-encompassing world view. As such, his definition can easily be accused of the common dangers following from dogmatic images of the world. Experience shows that the facts of experience overshoot and belie the metaphysical images we try to impose upon them. When we insist on the correctness of the image against this evidence we commit a violent act of suppression.

Whitehead is aware of the dangers of dogmatic philosophy and of the need for philosophical modesty and caution. One of the aims of his process philosophy is to counter forms of dogmatism around, for instance, ideas of unchanging substance or ideas about disconnected ontological realms, such as the Cartesian mind and body. So we need to look at his definition a little more closely. The meaning of logical is the familiar one around logical consistency, but all the other concepts should be reviewed as new coinages of older terms.

Coherence is not another way of describing consistency for Whitehead. Instead, it implies an essential connectedness of the terms of the philosophy such that they complete one another and cannot be understood in abstraction from each other. As coherent, a speculative process philosophy suggests a multiple system without parts, if by part we understand a potentially independent entity in the system. It is therefore composed of necessarily interlinked processes where each sub-process must be referred to the wider system if its full role is to be given and if we are to avoid critical errors in understanding the immersion of smaller components in a wider system of processes.

This means that process philosophy is not satisfactorily summed up by metaphors of substitutable components or in a picture of the world where realms or atoms are independent. The interdependence of processes shows the connection between speculative philosophy and process, since movement within the system must be spread continuously throughout it; otherwise, there will be untouched zones able to exist independently and hence the possibility of divisions into discrete parts.

Continuity in process does not mean uniformity, in the sense of a continuity of pattern, scale, function, type or lawfulness. It would be wrong to say that process is continuous like the continuity of the frequency of a sine wave over different amplitudes, or the continuity of the scalar properties of a map, or continuity according to a form of logical reproduction such as a formula for syntheses of contradictions, or according to a general law or code. Continuity does not indicate a common mode of reproduction across the continuous processes.[22]

Instead, continuity as process has complimentary positive and negative features. Positively, process is continuous because a change in any one process implies a change in any other. Negatively, and as a corollary to the positive feature, process is continuous because it is not possible to detach, cut off or ring fence a process and leave it unchanged. Abstraction will always be a transformation rather than a simple subtraction or preservation. Continuity indicates a necessary common destiny of all processes, however strongly a subtracted zone or process lays claim to imperviousness or self-sufficiency.

This definition of continuity holds for the process sign, for the diagrams of signs and their necessary relation to naming sets. Stipulations over the sign make general claims such that process continuity is denied. So from the point of view of the stipulation, continuity does not hold because the stipulation claims an independence from process for itself and for its laws and codes. A stipulation transcends the continuity of the sign and makes a claim over it.

However, any stipulation can also be included in a sign, in a naming set and in a suite of diagrams. From that point of view, the stipulation is continuous and its claim over the sign as external general stipulation is denied: the stipulation shifts from transcendent to immanent to the sign. In addition, any stipulation over a sign can be included in a critical debate around the relative merits of process and of its denial. Depending on the terms of this debate, continuity can either be re-established or not, when the debate is itself focused on the relative pragmatic power or efficacy of different claims, or on absolute distinctions between them.

Whitehead's process philosophy provides a model for the process definition of the sign through the idea of a philosophy of organism:

> In the philosophy of organism it is held that the notion of 'organism' has two meanings, interconnected but intellectually separable, namely, the microscopic meaning and the macroscopic meaning. The microscopic meaning is concerned with

the formal constitution of the actual occasion, considered as a process of realizing an individual unity of experience. The macroscopic meaning is concerned with the givenness of the actual world, considered as a stubborn fact which at once limits and provides.[23]

Individual unity is always about process, rather than identity and stasis. The philosophy of organism is always about the combination of the processes of an extended individual unity of experience – with no intrinsic limits or valid divisions – with the given facts of an actual world which limits the experience, but only in the sense of determining it in different ways.

Think of all the processes taking place in and around you which come together to give an experience of change in your muscles, gut, lungs, cells and mind. The most varied and distant processes can be traced to it; like the poison from the bite of the spider, crawled from the bunch of fruit on the plate in front of you, the insect having been packed into the hold of a ship weeks ago and a thousand miles away. Yet all these distant and multiple processes are given determinacy by stubborn facts such as your here, now and this: a cramping stomach and rigid fingers, no longer able even to punch out an emergency code on speed dial.

I am concerned to retain the demand for coherence and the definition of organism from Whitehead. The sign must be an indivisible multiplicity of processes extending through the whole of the world, but it must also have its determining givenness, its close matters of fact. The first is expressed by the suite of diagrams of the sign; the second by the selecting set which determines the sign through changing intensities of relations around elements of the set of its substratum.

In defining actual things as a community, Whitehead makes this statement: 'The community of actual things is an organism; but it is not a static organism. It is an incompletion in process of production.'[24] The same should be said of signs. The sign is an organism, but not a static one. It is always in process of production and completion along further diagrams and in dialectical relation to recurrent stipulations. The stubborn fact is that the set has been selected. The processes of realisation are given in the suite of diagrams.

Whitehead insists on the possibility of intellectual separation of multiple microscopic processes from their macroscopic determination in order also to emphasise their real inseparability. Process is always multiple and infinitely extended but also limited and determined by feelings of givenness. Intensity of feeling plays a double role in this connection. On the one hand, feeling is intensity variation as a limit and determination; this is the intensive selection of a sign against a background. On the other hand, feeling spreads and varies through unbounded processes; these are the multiple intensive relations described by a suite or series of diagrams.[25]

Serving as a qualifier for the continuity of process, the second novel term in Whitehead's definition of the speculative is 'necessary'. This does not mean to respond to an external need, or to follow necessarily from something else, but rather to be applicable to every experience with no known exception. Speculative philosophy should put forward continuous processes proving to be applicable to every experienced case. There should be no exceptions, such as those afforded to a science when it has a defined field and makes no claim to wider ones, or to a theory about a portion of existence that discounts others. There is a contrast here between Dupré's pluralism, discussed in Chapter 4, and Whitehead's monism characterised by the demand for universal applicability.

The process philosophy of signs is ambivalent about universal applicability. It is common to limit signs to a particular field, to language or to forms of symbolic representation for instance. The aim of the speculative process philosophy is to define the sign as applicable to every sign when thought as process. To do this, the sign has been defined minimally as the selection of a set against a background accompanied by intensive changes in relations. However, the definition does not include stipulations over the sign or terms defined under them, that is, when the sign is defined against process.

Applicability is not universal, in the sense of unique, for the process philosophy of the sign. It is universally applicable as one way of defining the sign which must enter into critical debate with others. Every sign can be subject to external stipulations denying its internal processes through the imposition of codes and laws; these are meta-claims over the sign as a general field rather than forces among others on the diagram. Second, these external stipulations are a prompt for critical debate rather than elimination through inclusion in wider process philosophy: pluralism rather than monism.

If we take the concept of object, there are many philosophical definitions of the object which deny its description as process. Whitehead acknowledges this in Kant's philosophy and redefines the object and subject relation in two ways. First, he reverses Kant's direction of priority in the relation, from the subjective to the objective. Second, he defines the new relation around feeling, that is, around processes of subjective satisfaction whereby the subject undergoes an ongoing transformation with the object. The ground for experience is no longer subjective but objective, but the nature of the object also changes such that its relation to the subject is determined by the idea of feeling.

This reversal of Kant's model changes the role of emergence from a projection of subjective identity on to an objective world to a process of emergence which draws the subject into the world as process: 'For Kant, the world emerges from the subject; for the philosophy of organism, the subject emerges from the world – a "superject" rather than a "subject." The word "object" thus means an entity which is a potentiality for being a component in feeling; constituted by the process of feeling, and including this process.'[26] The subject is drawn into the world and changes with it; it is a superject in the sense of an emerging projection into the world.[27]

In the idea of the superject static aspects of subject-based philosophy around the continued identity of the subject are replaced by changing projections. This can be applied to the process definition of the sign in so far as fixed relations in the sign, for instance between a signifier and a signified, are projected and set in motion as variations in the intensities of multiple relations. Signifier and signified become elements among many others, immersed in a multiplicity of changing relations, stretched out and set in motion as something we might call a supersign.

For Whitehead, the object only becomes actual, as opposed to merely potential, when it jointly emerges with a superject, in a feeling which merges them in a world as process. For instance, a grape should not be thought as a separate object available to a subject for consumption or inspection. Instead, in eating the grape or crushing it in our fingers the superject emerges with the changes brought about by feeling with the fruit and the many microscopic processes working with it. The subject and object opposition is exchanged for a merger as process where the superject is drawn out by the feeling.

The diagram of the sign is a description of a world as emergence where intensive relations do not hold between entities, but rather describe the emergence of joint and relative transformations. Everything is intensive emergence on the diagram; for instance a sign that includes water has an intensive direction around quenching on its diagram. My objection to Whitehead's approach is rather about what happens to Kant's account, or any other non-process claim, in the process philosophy. The Kantian concepts of subject and object are explained away by Whitehead. By this I mean they are subsumed into process rather than set alongside it as a form of evidence to be considered on its own terms.

This explaining away and inclusion into process could be justi- fied on the grounds that Kant is wrong. If we are presented with a mistaken theory, is it not right to set it aside and give the correct alternative position? I think this approach is mistaken on three counts where the process sign is concerned. First, alternative claims which deny aspects of the sign should be taken to be real counter-positions, a form of givenness, but where givenness can take two forms. A coun- ter-position can be a direction or 'player' in the intensive diagram itself, but the counter-position can also be a denial of the selection and diagram of a sign.

This second role cannot be reduced to the first, because to include a code or law directly in the diagram is already to prejudge the scope of its claim and to situate it as a direction and emerging series of intensities among many, rather than as a generally applicable rule over the sign. The nature of the general claim is that it is not con- sistent with process, multiplicity and intensity as indicated on the diagram. This leaves us with a decision to make which is not simply resolved by arguing that all is process, since this would be to pre- judge the validity of general claims running counter to the suggestion of process in a given sign. As speculative, the process philosophy must leave a place outside process for debates about the validity and worth of ideas suggested by process signs.

For example, we could have a sign around an ethical act such as a lie. On the one hand, rules against lying can be presented as one direction and intensity on the diagram, like the pull of conscience as we reach out to steal an apple. On the other hand, the rule asks us to resist our hunger and to put a maxim or law about theft above all desires. From this second point of view, the diagrammatic repre- sentation of a pull of conscience is a misrepresentation and it should be possible to indicate this in our understanding of the sign. It is therefore wrong simply to set general anti-process positions aside by offering an intensive and process-based explanation that makes them redundant.

The counter-positions or counterfactuals represented by laws and codes denying the sign as process can be included in new signs that offer alternatives to them, but they should also be presented as part of the oppositional context in which process signs operate. This is to recognise the speculative aspect of the philosophy of process in a different way to Whitehead, by acknowledging the experimental, hypothetical and provisional aspects of a speculative claim within the model of process itself. Whitehead's idea of the speculative involves global oppositions, for instance between process philosophy and Kant's critical philosophy. The right philosophy is designed to subsume the wrong one. On my definition of the sign, opposition should be presented locally within process itself and globally in a debate around denials of process.

This local and global operation for counter-positions leads to my second objection to Whitehead's account of process as ubiquitous and as explaining away other positions. It is not only that the effective role of these positions is denied. It is that this role is not given a specific function in relation to process itself. This is why the definition of the process sign gives space to stipulations over the sign as laws and codes running counter to process in given signs by giving general and contrary analyses of the sign as static. These need not be seen strictly as philosophical opposition; the main sources of opposition to process could be scientific, as shown in my study of Uexküll in Chapter 3, but they could also be moral, logical or philosophical.

My third objection concerns the mode of encounter between this non-process context and set of positions and the sign itself. It is not enough to offer a process explanation that supposedly avoids any non-process accounts or ideas. There has to be an argument between positions setting out the stakes and implications for a particular sign and the stipulations made over it. As such, speculative philosophy must have a place for varied and open debate across many different modes of argumentation allowing for challenges to any given claim to process and scrutiny of its claims in relation to opposing positions. The Whitehead approach is too metaphysical and not pragmatic enough, not internally open enough to challenge and experimentation, because it imposes a blanket image of the world over a multiplicity of changing signs and stipulations over them.

We can see how the difference between options for a speculative philosophy plays out when we turn to Whitehead's idea of applicability to all experiences. This idea leads to the final and most important claim in Whitehead's definition of speculative process philosophy around interpretation and general schema: 'By this notion of "interpretation" I mean everything of which we are conscious, as enjoyed, perceived, willed, or thought, shall have the character of a particular instance of the general scheme. Thus the philosophical scheme should be coherent, logical, and, in respect to its interpretation, applicable and adequate.'[28] The aim of a speculative philosophy should be to propose a general scheme applicable to everything in the form of an interpretation.

Whitehead makes this assertion more precise and more onerous in stating that 'everything' does not mean all things we happen to have included in the interpretation, but all things in the sense of 'all experience'.[29] Adequacy is therefore universal. It means adequate to all 'enjoyed, perceived, willed, or thought' things with no exclusions. Moreover, this adequacy is itself accompanied by a stringent condition around the form of interpretation and hence the nature of the schema: '[Adequacy] means that the texture of observed experience, as illustrating the philosophic scheme, is such that all related experience must exhibit the same texture.'[30] This is a complex claim because it combines three different conditions for experience: it appears with a texture; illustrates a scheme; and all 'related' experience exhibits the same texture.

I am going to assume that related refers to any experience rather than particular experience here, since otherwise there would be a contradiction with statements about 'all' experience in Whitehead's definition of speculative philosophy. This means that the ideas of texture, illustrated scheme and sameness strongly condition the speculative model. The philosophy gives a structure for experience, even if this structure is one of process. The structure is replicated between philosophical scheme and experience and the texture is the same for all experiences. This is an exclusive definition of speculative thinking in two fundamental ways. It leaves nothing out and everything that it includes must accord with the same basic pattern.

The process definition of the sign seeks to avoid this exclusivity by replacing it with a minimal and more modest model where a frame is offered for the sign: selected set, suite of diagrams, stipulations over the sign, and debate over their different merits. This frame is much more flexible than Whitehead's demand for adequacy because the process sign incorporates challenges to it whereas adequacy aims to exclude them.[31] Signs should not be forced into an all-encompassing metaphysical scheme and, even when defined minimally, they should be open about the hypothetical and temporary nature of their representations. The process philosophy of the sign offers an architecture for a maximally pragmatic approach to the sign as process and to the denial of that process.

The Process Sign is Political

THE SIGN AS POLITICAL

I define the political as an event bringing diverse positions into conflict with one another. In the political, something happens that draws out different standpoints and throws them into conflict. The uses of 'political' rendered secondary by this definition are therefore those concerning types of government or political ideals, the politics of parties and factions, and questions about social consensus.

The political is not primarily about how best to rule or the nature of political society. It is not about the conflict of left- or right-wing parties. The political is not defined first by the problems of the distribution of finite resources or of the representation of majority and minority voices. In the process sign understood as political event, difference or conflict is prior to these traditional approaches; it is a condition for them.

The political sign gives rise to more stable and familiar ideas of the political. It stands in excess of them and thereby determines them as insufficient and forgetful of a deeper truth, if by truth we understand prior conditions and more complete explanations. For instance, the event of a new form of exploitation or exclusion can cause disagreement between a pragmatic politics of acceptance and one of unconditional resistance. The event gives rise to and shapes the divergence. The exposure of a crumbling sweatshop, in which fleeing workers are confronted by locked fire doors, is political in my sense; it triggers and shapes ensuing debates and actions. The event of a new government questionnaire with a box to tick for 'born in the Union', and the event of destitute migrants living in vast camps on the borders of our nations, alongside debates about true and false belonging, are similarly political. They are events which force political disagreement.

What of the objection that for an event to appear as condition for political disagreement it must presuppose prior political awareness and theoretical positions? For instance, awareness of the concept of exploitation matters for an understanding of the nature of work in a sweatshop. The point of my definition of the political is that the event diverts and repositions the world it arrives in. When it does so, current debates and positions are disturbed and rearranged. So any political world can be seen as a history of events and positions conditioning one another. The events are primary because they are the source of divergence and novel significance.

A political event is like an imprudent stamp on an icy pond, drawing new fault lines, potential paths to safety, and arguments about which dangerously unstable track to attempt. There would be no urgent debate without the intensities of fear and hope accompanying new fissures on the ice sheet. It is a mistake to limit the political to settled paths and abstract questions, and to the arguments about which is best, which is right, which questions are most serious and which most pressing. The sign as political event initiates a new challenge and calls for different modes of response. These enter into conflict with one another around the event and the difficulties it has raised.

This definition of the political redirects its urgency away from political ideas, bodies and structures towards political occurrences and effects. Once this happens, the sign becomes political, in the sense of generating the political, rather than standing as an object for pre-established political consideration. The distinction is important for this work on process signs because it moves the political from ideal structures, normative claims and social factions to significant happenings accompanied by scissions and the struggles following from them.

The political is then no longer a problem of the reproduction of theoretical frames, where events are placed according to prior political theory. Irrespective of whether the frames have an empirical or rational basis, they prejudge the nature of the political. A process sign determines the political as a problem of description and succession after a novel event which occurs within established frames, where signs shape and give rise to the political as conflict calling for new hypotheses and models.

SIGN, SETTLEMENT AND DIAGRAM

According to the definition of the political outlined above, a new datum or given, such as a new discovery, is always political since as an event it challenges current patterns of thought and action. For example, the advent of novel and expensive medical treatments raises questions about costs, benefits, access and bearable effects. Patients are pitted against doctors, doctors against other specialists and managers, economists and politicians. The important thing is that this given difference is political in advance of and as a condition for later settled factions and positions.

The dynamic concept of settlement is important because it draws a line between recognised positions and nascent ones. The sign as event is accompanied by a diversity of ways of capturing the event and by a diversity of callings, in the sense of demands coming from the sign. It is fluid, not as a transition between decidable camps and ways of seeing, but rather as a visceral wrench within a situation.[1] The sign is therefore an unsettling occurrence emerging in established positions. These positions are not static. They have emerged according to processes of settlement where the diversity of processes acquires relative stability.

To return to the discussion in the previous chapter, the event is a donation of sense, following Deleuze's usage in *The Logic of Sense*. It is something that happens prior to good sense and common sense, disturbing them through intensive changes in relations which appear paradoxical to established political distributions and values. This gives rise to different attempts to resolve the paradoxes. These attempts constitute the different conflicting positions of the definition of the political as event.

Does this mean the event and the new problem always come from the outside to challenge an established order? It is rather that the event reveals internal flaws and renews an existing and perhaps hidden problem. An event cannot be completely external. How could we even recognise it as such, if it wasn't already adapted to our powers of recognition? Instead, the event works through pre-existing flaws and insufficiencies.

So the discovery of a drug or the naming of a syndrome is not a completely new factor. It responds to demands from ongoing illnesses, to the need for health and treatment; it occurs within them, against a background. To set necessary limits for this background is always wrong given the definition of process defended here. For instance, the context of health events cannot be restricted to a medical field. A medical discovery has continuing economic, technical, social, environmental, ethical and existential environments. Their inner disjunctions, clashes, changes and resistances provide the pliable matter for the impact of the novel event.

The process sign is therefore political across each of the stages of the definition of the political, against politics understood through established orders and questions. The naming of a sign – the selection of its set – is a facet of the political event. So are the suggestion of a diagram and the experimental speculation on further and different diagrams. These are the location for conflicts and stresses between different directions around singular points and across fields within each diagram. Finally, the debate around stipulations over the sign is political through the conflict between the sign as process and externally imposed codes and laws.

Here is the formal definition of the sign S{a, b, c}/Vs rendered as political:

- the event of the selection of the set {a, b, c} and of its accompanying intensive diagram S{a, b, c}
- conflicts between different directions on the diagram
- the speculative experimentation with different diagrams S{a, b, c}/Vs
- internal conflicts within these further diagrams
- conflicts between different diagrams for a given selection
- and, from outside the formula, clashes and dialectics between these connected events and stipulations or settlements over them

Imagine a village with a strict rule for the colour of house paint – the same shade of ochre catching the greens of the surrounding hills in pleasing contrasts. An incomer arrives (city folk and foreign) and paints their house a fluorescent orange. The painted walls are an event. The selection of the sign {house, 'fluorange'™, village} against a background of all wider elements (hills, sun, visitors' gaze, weathered patina of other dwellings and so on) is a political event. It is accompanied by a diagram with singular points around places, people and acts: increasing and decreasing outrage, loathing, defensiveness, incomprehension, resistance, banning, sympathy, clans, betrayals, optimism, inspiration, greed and anxiety.

This is the most obvious diagram, but there are other more speculative counterfactual ones to set alongside it, perhaps a diagram where the fashion for colour catches on smoothly, or one where an older way of life and set of people are pushed out by wealth and its individualistic bourgeois foibles. There are laws and codes in the diagrams; for instance around a parish bylaw. But there are also stipulations over the sign, such as general claims about the nature of light and colour, or claims about natural aesthetics, or theories about the proper mode of resolution for local conflicts. The difference between external and internal codes is whether they work within the diagram as a force among many, or whether they claim to be an overall law for selection and for diagrams. Stipulations are generally applicable and to be obeyed across the entire process.

The village example shows the flexibility of the idea of an intensive diagram. The pure form of the diagram would be a vector space in n-dimensions in Hilbert space indicating intensive accelerations and decelerations around singular points and neighbourhoods. In the case of the painted house, the diagram might radiate from the orange house, not to other houses but around groups of villagers, actions, places and objects: anger around the mayor, hatred around incomers, petitions on the village square, petty acts of violence and retribution. The diagram will have a whirl at its centre and vectors from this to further pools and eddies, forming attractions and repulsions in the more sparse spaces between them. The diagram is intensive and in movement. It runs parallel to the dynamic conflicts it comes to map.

This pure form should not be seen as exclusive. In Chapter 2, I gave a literary version of the diagram and I have just given a descriptive rather than graphic one. For the village scandal, a film, accompanied by a translation into the components of a sign, could express the features of the event and the pulls and drives it sets off among the villagers. It is possible to think about diagrams through painting. My description of vortices with pulls between each other might be captured by swirls across a starry sky or a field of flowers. A diagram for a particularly focused and violent sign might be captured by the gulfs, abysses and ridges of a thickly painted abstract expressionist canvas.

Some works are explicitly diagrammatic in their combination of figures, names, colour and intensive directions. This does not mean they are always the best for a given sign. Highly figural works by Bruegel might be strong diagrams of village sensuality and intrigue. The symbolic shock of Picasso's Guernica, or the dream-reality of Chagall's wanderers and lovers, could be better suggestions for eruptions of violence, affect and displacement around new signs. The artwork plunges a named event into a web of forces, with the advantage over a mathematical representation of a more direct and sensual communication of intensities.

The contrast between mathematical and painterly expressions of the diagram, and the mention of works and artists attached to historical massacres and persecutions, raises the question of its objectivity. Is a diagram an objective, positivist representation or a subjective and contingent translation of an unreachable phenomenon? The answer is neither and both. By this I mean that a diagram is a map that can make use of positivist and creative resources, but as a speculative proposal its status is dependent on later and uncertain juxtapositions. The diagram is a projection and the sign as intensive multiplicity comes prior to its real effects.

I use phrases such as 'might be' and 'could be' out of concern for the speculative nature of any diagram. The diagram is a prompt and a suggestion; it is dependent on later arguments and responses. Within the definition of the process sign, these take the form of new named signs, further experimental diagrams, and the dialectical context of arguments with external stipulations. Strict objectivity and subjectivity are two extreme versions of such stipulations, opposed to the idea that the diagram of a sign is essentially speculative.

No matter whether the diagram is given in its pure form or through a different aesthetic medium, the sign is political across seven different processes: the selection of the sign; the initial diagram as speculative suggestion and as internal differences; counterfactual diagrams as speculative and as differential; the conflict between diagrams and with stipulations. These must be taken together when the sign is described and taken up as political, because each one can only give a partial view of the sign as political event.

UNDETERMINED SELECTION AS POLITICAL EVENT

The first point to make when considering the selection in the sign as political is that the concept of selection is independent from a selecting subject. Whether or not a subject can be taken as the instigator of the selection has no bearing on its status as event or on its lack of determination. The best way of putting this is to say that there is a set which defines a selection that is not determined by anything other than the selection. A set appears against the background of all other things as an event with no predetermination. This set names a sign.

It could be objected that the set {a, b, c} is nothing like an event or a process as we commonly understand them, because the set is neither something that happens, nor something that becomes. It is merely a static collection. This would be a mistake because it would be to abstract the detachment of the set from the background of all things. A more cumbersome way of describing the set would be EVERYTHING ⇨ {a, b, c}. This notation would still be misleading, since each selection is a two-way process. The selected set changes the relation of its elements to each other and to all other things. It also changes all other things, for instance, by pulling its elements away from them.

A better notation would be EVERYTHING ⇔ {a, b, c} indicating a reciprocal determination between the two sides. Each set determines the other with no linear order such that we could say one comes before the other and with no reversibility such that we could describe the conditions as reversible. So an even better notation is EVERYTHING ⇨⇦ {a, b, c} to indicate irreversibility and disorder.

For example, we could introduce a gender neutral third-person personal pronoun into English named by the set {she, he, sih}. *The pilot landed the plane. Sih then headed to taxiway 32B.* The new sign would change language and linguistic practice, for instance, around our attachment to or dislike of other pronoun options such as 'they' used in the singular or 's/he', but it will also have much wider repercussions, around gender expectations and associations, and poetic possibilities. The new sign will also encounter resistance and be shaped by that too. So the fuller notation for the political event of the sign would be EVERYTHING ⇨⇦ {she, he, sih}.

As defined, signs are the whole of the world under a certain perspective which itself changes because the sign is process. How then can we refer to signs reliably? The relevant version of this problem here is around my use of the concept of a name. In common usage, a name is a reliable identifier, allowing us to refer to something across different situations, across time and space. *Hey, isn't that James?*

The version of a name I have given appears to fail in two fundamental ways: for the diagram, as a name for the process; and for any discussion of the sign, as a name for the sign. If the selected set is a name for an intensive process that includes the set, then the changing processes the name refers to also engulf the sign as referent. So the set {a, b, c} is changing when we use it to refer to the diagram and therefore it refers to a different diagram in different instances. This problem could be called the inexistence of the sign as named or its fleeting quality as duration. The sign the set selects is always receding. The solution to this problem is to insist on the incomplete nature of the naming set without accompanying diagrams.

The next problem is that as a name for the sign the set fails as an indicator connecting the discussion to a stable and reliable referent. This is a deeper problem than a contingent difficulty around naming, that is, a challenge to find agreement about names. It is not that the discussants have difficulty agreeing about what their names refer to. It is rather that the names cannot refer to the same thing by definition. The name fails as a connection between sentences and a referent, because the name is never the name for the selfsame thing. If the name stays the same, it fails to correspond to the changing process; if the name keeps changing, it fails as a stable referent. The deepest and most commonplace problem of a radical process philosophy reappears. If all is process, do we not also lose the capacity to identify these processes?

We can draw a distinction between a traditional use of names and a naming set. The naming set picks out an undetermined selection against a background which is then described by a suite of diagrams. The traditional name is supposed to pick out a stable object in the world. So when we meet a friend at the airport after a year away and phone home saying 'James is back' it is understood that in some sense it is the same James as a year ago.

For the naming set this supposition is by definition mistaken if we assume that the set reliably refers to things across different situations, because the naming set is in a different process across the situations. We'd need two different diagrams to name someone a year onwards, but then the set plus diagram solution to the earlier problem causes even bigger difficulties because we have two names rather than the same one across different periods.

The solution to the problem is to separate ordinary naming and the naming of process signs. In the process sign, the naming set is a way of entering into a series of connected processes extending to a perspective on the whole of the world. The ordinary name is a way of identifying components of these series, across times and places, as if they are not in motion. The naming set is a simple and direct way of describing an unfolding process. The ordinary name is an abstraction from these processes requiring an additional marker to indicate process, for example by adding a time to draw attention to a change: James in 2000 and James in 2010.

So why not call the naming set an ordinary name? What advantage is there in adding to the number of name types? An ordinary name would miss the process described by the undetermined selection of a sign and it would miss the relation between elements of the naming set and its diagrams. It's the difference between saying 'James is out of prison' and adding 'He's even more cantankerous than before but with less humour.' The second statement connects to the intensive changes on the diagram ('even more' and 'with less').

Why not dispense with ordinary names and just have naming sets? Setting aside aesthetic motives, the main reason is indexation; that is, a fixed name allows for the recording of place within an unfolding multiplicity of processes when a 'go to' or 'go back' function is required. It is these jumps that I am referring to when I use the expression across diagrams and across situations or time. Were we to use the naming set across something, we would make a falsifying assimilation because the set names different processes when it is reused.

What reasons are there to call either of these uses of the name political as defined earlier as event, difference and conflict? The selection of the naming set is always an event because it is the arrival of a new process between the set and all other things; first of all, as this simple selection. In despair or fear someone else takes your hand and presses firmly. Why is this political? It is because it redirects the element of your life, independent of whether it works or not, in the sense of helping or curing; something new has occurred at the crux of different pulls and thrusts.

We can see this political effect in emblematic gestures such as kissing an outcast. The kiss is political and intervenes in ongoing political debates. The process philosophy of the sign picks up on this political aspect and makes it a general feature of all signs, thereby calling into question any hard and fast distinction between emblematic and ordinary signs. The touch of two 'ordinary' bodies is political in the same way as the hands of a pope on dirty feet: they are event, difference and conflict.

LANGUAGE AND THE POLITICAL

In the early 1980s, Jean-François Lyotard made problems of political discord around events the centrepiece of his work on language and the concept of the differend. A differend is a difference between two or more positions that cannot be resolved by appeal to a common understanding, for instance shared knowledge about a referent. There are lessons here for the process philosophy of signs as a claim about the political nature of the sign as prior political difference.

Lyotard's 1983 book *The Differend* is more representative of his philosophy than the better known *The Postmodern Condition* from 1979. The postmodernism book can be seen as a tentative forerunner of ideas that are properly developed and grounded in the later work. For instance, the concept of a grand narrative from the earlier book is translated into the idea of a genre in *The Differend* as part of an extensive philosophy of language that no longer speaks of the end of grand narratives but rather of the conflict between linguistic genres and of differends arising from the need to follow sentences with others but with no final rule as to how. We encounter sentences that challenge us to do justice to them, but they also present us with many different and irreconcilable ways of doing so. The concatenation of sentences becomes the locus for political conflict and the end of grand narratives.

The conflict and its demands are summed up in two principles from *The Differend*: we have to follow on from sentences, but there are no rules for their concatenation, for the way sentences form chains; we must testify to the differends that occur with sentences. For example, according to Lyotard, a sentence such as the order to hand over someone to the police is necessarily a cause for uncertainty but also a call to act, with no dominant way of solving the ambiguity between different ways of acting. The first political duty is therefore to testify to this impossibility and hence to the illegitimacy of claims to a final just act or resolution.

These statements are significant for work on language as political because of the political context of the end of grand narratives and the illegitimacy of overarching genres in relation to the concatenation of sentences. The end is a collapse of dominant forms of rationalisation across many different modes of justification and explanation, for instance in the unity of a communist state or of modern nations constructed around Enlightenment ideals allied to state-based versions of capitalism. It is political because it marks a shift from a centralised and unique combination of power and justification to many different and incommensurable social, ethical and political claims. The state is shattered with the end of grand narratives.

The common measure of a single narrative shifts into a postmodern fragmentation of communication and explanation, into many ways of understanding and explaining existence, all out of sync with one another. However, where *The Postmodern Condition* based its argument on broad observation of the failure of unifying narratives and growth in disparate modes of understanding, *The Differend* takes a close study of linguistic forms as the ground for its main political conclusions and for its statements on concatenation and testimony.

The main shift is around history and philosophical arguments. The postmodern work can be misunderstood as making the claim that grand narratives failed at a particular time thereby dividing the modern and postmodern into two epochs. In fact, Lyotard's argument was that they coexist but sometimes with grand narratives dominating and sometimes postmodern fragmentation. The end of grand narratives was a local and relative statement rather than a final historical statement, which could not be justified on the basis of particular observations in any case.

Why does any of this matter for the process philosophy of signs? It is because the turn to the philosophy of language as a basis for political divergence is common to Lyotard's concepts of the sentence and genre and to my definition of the process sign and stipulations over it. It is also because the detail of Lyotard's philosophy of language provides a strong critical test for the claims made for the sign as political. I defined the process sign as political because it is event, difference and conflict. This echoes the statements about the concatenation of sentences and differends made in *The Differend*.

A sentence is an event leading to unsolvable differences between the ways we can follow it. Here, 'to solve' means to give a legitimate way of following on from a sentence that does justice to all other ways, not in the sense of conceding to them, but in the sense of recognising their claims and either accepting or dismissing them on shared grounds. So the imposition of a particular way is not a legitimate solution, nor is any way which depends on enforcing its account of justice on others without recognising their alternative claims. These differences are the basis for the political as primary conflict covered up by stipulations. The different directions on the diagram of a process sign and the suite of conflicting diagrams represent such differences. They come up against stipulations designed to impose an order on the sign.

An objection to these definitions is helpful for understanding them. It could be claimed against the idea of the process sign as political conflict that the just solution is simply the best one, rather than one that can claim some kind of ultimate and generally applicable justice. We have to do something, since not acting is still to follow a sentence. The best thing to do could be to seek the least harm, or maximise happiness, or achieve peaceful coexistence.

Lyotard grants the first part of this objection. It is indeed the case that a sentence of a sign has to be followed; even inaction is to do so. He also grants the second part but with an important proviso. There are better and worse ways of following on from a sign and from a sentence; some forms of maximisation or paths to more fair and rational solutions might indeed be the best way to proceed. However, these ways must record the fact that they cover up an original difference, rather than legitimately do away with it. They must also take account of those continuing differences and of new ones in the form and specific content of any now relative solution.

This allows for further clarification of the way in which the process sign is political. It is not that the general form of the sign suggests a particular politics. Nor is it the case that a particular process sign calls for a particular political movement or act. Instead, the sign is political in making any sign the site of differences that cannot be eliminated but must instead be incorporated in any political reaction to the sign as degrees of directions which can be increased or decreased but never fully discounted.

Connecting back to my earlier definition of the role of the sign as alarm and critical movement, the sign is the site where general and universal claims must enter into a debate with a multiplicity of directions which resist external rules and codes. We can therefore think of the process sign as a kind of political fact: there will always be multiple and recurring differences; and as a kind of political conscience: any political act should do justice to the multiplicity and recurrence of differences in the sign.

LANGUAGE AS POLITICAL

Lyotard is helpful in understanding the process sign as political because he combines political motivation with linguistic study. This invites a criticism that could apply equally well to my work on the process philosophy of signs. Cannot language be a-political, in the sense of a politically neutral structure and vehicle for communication that only becomes political after the fact, as a field for later and distorting political intervention?

Language can show us the wrong turns of political discourse, for instance, where rhetoric is used to advance a false idea. It is not made by political discourse. It is not a matter of what we might want language to be like according to our political inclinations. It is a matter of how a correct science identifies linguistic structures and thereby allows for a critique of false political claims. So it is only the misuse of language that makes it political.

This critique does not depend on denying that language and signs can be political. Instead, the first point is to distinguish political and a-political language. The second point is to show how the latter can act as a critical tool against political misappropriation of language. It is a familiar argument which turns on the idea that a correct use of language, dependent on its deepest structures of grammatical precision and logical rigour, allows for an escape from politically motivated confusion and deception. On this view, the statement about political necessity in language and signs becomes doubly blameworthy. It is wrong about language and therefore politically negative too.

In reply, Lyotard takes the concepts of name, reference, presentation and situation to demonstrate a necessary political dimension to language. He seeks to show how any reference is unavoidably dependent on a conflict between regimens of phrases, that is, different grammatical categories of sentences such as descriptive sentences (It is so), sentences of prescription (You must), and sentences of obligation (You ought). Regimens are incommensurable because their validity depends on incommensurables rules, for instance correctness in terms of descriptions, obedience in terms of prescription, and moral validity in terms of obligation.

So when an officer tells you to hand over your driving licence, it matters whether the order is taken as a prescription or an obligation. Lyotard's point is that there is no overarching rule for deciding which regimen is the right one. The licence can be taken as the object of a prescription or of an obligation and there is a conflict between the two. We are familiar with these kinds of conflict where outlying yet strong moral or religious beliefs enter into social and legal realms. For instance, in the case of conscientious objectors to military action, the prescription to serve the nation at war clashes with the obligation to take no lives.

A name ('Citizen Smith', 'driving licence') can be included in different regimens of sentence and this leads to conflicts between diverse claims about the name which cannot be resolved by referring to the regimens themselves, since they are incommensurable. For Lyotard, these first-order conflicts are partially resolved through genres of discourse. A genre is a set of rules for the articulation of phrase regimens that allows them to fit together in well-ordered chains of sentences aiming towards a common goal. For example, the economic genre submits different phrase regimens to the aim of gaining time.

The roles of alarm and critique in the process sign stem from a similar property of the name and its inclusion in different regimens of sentences. When included in a process sign, the name does not have a straightforward relation to a sense and to a referent. Instead, the inclusion is through a set and a transformation against a background represented by a series of diagrams. The name is part of the process which is open to different representations and resistant to any final or legitimate representation.

A sign such as {Jacques Delors, smiling, means well, European flag} is determined by a multiplicity of pulls around ideas of European unity, good and bad intentions, and an individual bureaucrat.

A certain politics might want to make the sign simple and unique. Many in the British press did this to Delors; for instance with *The Sun*'s headline 'Up yours Delors!' designed to make Delors, the President of the European Commission, a demonic and anti-British figure akin to early nineteenth-century cartoons of Napoleon. However, as ways of rendering the multiplicity in the process sign they will always be falsifications if they deny its multiplicity and seek to impose a single pattern on it.

This appeal to political cartoons raises another objection to the definition of the process sign and by extension to its understanding as a primary political fact and conscience. The cartoon has a simple message to append to a number of simplified referents and ideas. If it can do so, then the sign is not multiple and open-ended but simple and closed. For instance, in a cartoon of Napoleon on his way to Elba, with a broken sword and facing the wrong way on a donkey, the message is straightforwardly the reference to a defeated and disarmed tyrant. Furthermore, if some signs can have this simple form, is it not better for all of them to? If we can find a way of eliminating ambiguity from language and multiplicity from the sign, will that not lead to more effective and rational communication?

Lyotard owes much to Marx. The aim or law of gaining time can be seen as an extension of the general formula for Capital where surplus-value appears as the positive difference between M and M' in the formula M-C-M' (money-commodity-money + Δ money). If we submit all linguistic activities to this meta-law then a description, prescription or an obligation can be combined according to the rule that different chains of phrases can be judged in terms of their contribution to the positive difference in capital coming from the exchange into a commodity and back again.

In the economic genre, an obligation and a prescription can be weighed up and combined according to their overall profitability. The conflict between the description 'You need to rest ten hours per day', the prescription 'You must work as hard as possible', and the obligation 'You ought to care for your employees' is resolved by ignoring the description and the obligation, given the better contribution of the prescription to profitable activity. The moral obligation to allow for rest and the medical description of a healthy life become negotiable and are replaced by the notion of 'possible' from the prescription to work as hard as possible. This notion of possible is itself negotiated in relation to the ultimate law of increasing surplus-value, as Marx described well in his accounts of the nineteenth-century struggle to achieve even the most basic living conditions for workers in a legal vacuum. When the economic genre is unbridled, the limit of 'to work as hard as possible' can be extended even to the idea of the possible replacement of exhausted workers by new flesh.

For Lyotard, we can replace the role of money in the formula from the first volume of *Capital* by a difference in time. The law of the economic genre is to gain time, where any sentence is judged according to how it contributes to a gain in time between an input and an output. The decisive question becomes 'Does this obligation or this prescription, or any other sentence type, contribute most to gaining time across this work activity?'

In the following remark from *The Differend*, Lyotard's critique of a politics based around genres such as the economic aim of gaining time is connected to the most basic claims of his philosophy of language: 'Politics is the threat of the differend. It is not a genre, but rather the multiplicity of genres, the diversity of ends and, above all [*par excellence*] the question of concatenation.'[2]

Lyotard's argument is that the political as deliberative discussion around differing claims cannot claim to be the supreme or commanding genre. He calls such a claim vain, in allusion to the vanity of political and parliamentarian assertions about control over society. That's not where power lies and, if there is a genre with a plausible hold on supreme power, it is the economic genre rather than the political one. 'Follow the money' or 'follow the logic of gaining time' are the ubiquitous contemporary ways to an understanding of other regimes and genres; they work behind and through the political.

So where are truly political resources to come from? Lyotard's answer is that the political comes about with the threat of the differend. It is important to distinguish this from the threat of a disagreement. He does not mean that the political emerges when there is a difference of opinion. Such a difference is easily handled by an overarching genre with, for example, a judgement over which saves the most time. Instead, the threat is not from a recognised difference, but rather from an event initiating multiple differences within genres and in a way they cannot handle. Something occurs that shows there are many genres and many different aims we could ascribe to them.

The reason this is above all a question of concatenation is that the thing that occurs has to be set into a chain of things in order to impose an end to it. For instance, the demand of an obligation to sustain a certain standard of living as a moral obligation is bent to the rule of gaining time by following it with a series of economic sentences imposing their rule and asserting their legitimacy to do so. The petition for moral standards is followed by the request to

'Show us how this obligation allows us to gain time and therefore raise living standards as a general measure of increased productivity over time.'

However, the thing that occurs does so with a gap or vacuum around it. It is defined as a sentence by Lyotard and as a sign in this process philosophy. The threat of the differend is really the threat of an occurrence which calls for further sentences and shows their necessity but does so in such a way as to demonstrate that no way of following is legitimate. Lyotard's formula for this is that to link on from a sentence is necessary but how to link on is not. The threat of the differend is therefore not about different regimes and genres but rather about an event making the occurrence of differends inevitable and striking. It is the sense of threat we get from a psychological blow or an unwelcome form of evidence running counter to any possible action. This is the demand of the process sign as political: it is an event calling for a just way to follow on from it, but with no law or code for that justice.

Conclusion

I have given formal and philosophical reasons for turning to a process philosophy of signs. Sometimes it is helpful to have an insight into some of the wider motivations for a new take on a well-established field. Over recent years in my academic work, university life and wider social engagement, I have observed new waves of signs slowly taking over and transforming practices, institutions and values. I was struck by the way words such as 'excellence' or 'performance' exercised a kind of gravitational pull across many different ways of doing things, changing them at different speeds but leaving them profoundly altered. The problem was that these signs did not stand up to scrutiny as simple meanings and referents. They were nebulous and quite random in their limits and associations. As a sign, 'in the top ten' seemed both very important and yet also quite empty to those who swore by it, since the judgement behind the ranking was often crude and unreliable when compared to the thing to be ranked. It would be absurd for me to rank the top ten human beings of the hundreds of students I have taught over the last twenty years. Yet some of the richest and most complex areas of human endeavour such as philosophy and education were not only subjected to crude signs, they were organised around them, and allowed to thrive or wither under their control.

There were real forces behind this organisation. Financial pressures, changes in technology, and the demands of capitalism above all. My concern, though, was with the sign. How should we define the sign to make sense of its power as a forerunner, as the avant-garde, of political and monetary forces? It could not be as a sign with a straightforward meaning or indicated thing, since these were extraordinarily varied. 'Excellence' seemed to apply to everything from the mending of a leaking tap to the counselling of a student in deep distress. 'Performance' applied to poems, professors and silicon chips. How should we define the sign to take account of its speeds, from the insidious poisoning of a cultural bastion, to the calcification of the minds of colleagues?

The sign had to be defined to reflect two features. First, each sign was plural. It did not have one meaning and a limited number of similar referents but rather many connections across disparate things. The sign extended widely and in an undiscriminating manner. A phrase like 'we have to rationalise' touched everything from paperclips to research time and the strength of coffee. Second, the reason the sign mattered and how it operated were not instantaneous, like a statement of fact or a pledge, but rather about increases and decreases of intensity. You felt the grip of 'excellence' tighten like a chokehold. Signs seeped and crept, preparing the ground for acts and decisions.

Though my examples might seem gloomy, there were other positive signs waxing and waning in multiple directions: 'equality', 'tolerance' and 'change' for instance. Nor were signs strictly verbal. Images and sounds were signs too. Perhaps they had greater powers of influence and transformation, from the awakening brought about by images of torture, to the shared joys of new voices and beats, and the double-edged influence of new digital platforms.

I required a model for signs capable of capturing their variety, movement and plurality. Process philosophy was the most promising approach available, because it combined a plural view with an insistence on process over stasis. In very different ways but with intriguing connections, Whitehead and Deleuze offered philosophical explanations that could underpin a new philosophy of signs. There is a chapter here explaining my closeness to and distance from their ideas. I wanted to borrow the idea of process from one and the idea of a diagram from the other. The sign is a process of selection and a diagram of the intensive variations of relations unfolding around the selected sign.

For example, institutions had begun to insist that every presentation by an employee should have a template and the institution's crest on every slide. This new sign could be given as the selection {slide, template, crest, every talk}. It was a process drawing out these elements against a background of all others, such as more personal styles, senses of independence, colour and format choices and so on. How could this formal model represent the changes in intensity in the relations between elements in the set and all others? How could process be shown?

The answer was to accompany every selected set, every sign, with a diagram showing directions as changes of intensity of relations around elements. So when I wrote earlier of the gravitational pull around a sign, the idea was that this kind of attraction and repulsion, acceleration and deceleration, should be shown on diagrams. For example, when an institution deploys a sign such as 'total staff performance management' there is acceleration, an increase of the intensity of vectors, away from individual freedom and towards institutional control around a large number of individual elements or neighbourhoods. The diagram would be a picture of the changes in intensity of relations around elements.

A very deep problem arose at the point of defining the sign as the selection of a set and as a diagram of the processes of intensification of relations between many elements. What was the status of the representation given by the diagram? Was it an objective description, or a more subjective impression? What was the relation between the model for the process sign and the sciences?

The answer was quite simple and familiar within process philosophy, but its repercussions were broad. The process philosophy of the sign was to be speculative rather than objective. It proposed a model for the sign. Within this model, the representations of individual signs as processes were themselves only suggestions. This meant that the sign as selected set would be accompanied by an open number of diagrams. There is a suite of diagrams which not only compete with one another as representations of the sign, but also interact with one another in changing the intensive pulls around the elements they represent. Each sign is a selection and a suite of diagrams. They are competing ways of mapping the effects of the selection of a sign: how do you see this sign changing our world?

This answer raised new problems, because it meant that the process model clashed with theories and descriptions coming from the empirical sciences. As hypotheses, diagrams could vary widely and therefore clash with scientific accounts not only of signs but also of the fields they referred to. This explains why the core of this book involves chapters on biology and signs, through the historical work of Uexküll, and on process biology, through contemporary work by Dupré. It also explains why other chapters engage with the claims to scientific status and objectivity of traditional structuralism after Saussure. The process definition of the sign learns from but stands apart from these positions. It is in a critical relation to them.

This critical role is also creative. Signs introduce alternative positions and potential into debates and activities. The process sign is a critical and creative tool working alongside others ways of studying our world. Unlike the fully scientific and objective aims of some versions of structuralism and of the sign and process in the sciences, the process sign is defined in counter-position to different kinds of claims coming from the sciences and other sources of universal laws and rules. This means the sign as selection and diagrams must be taken in critical debate with propositions that deny the picture given in the sign. I have called these counters 'stipulations over the sign' and the full description of any sign should include external stipulations alongside its selection and diagrams.

As critical and creative, signs take on a function of alarm and innovation in conjunction with other claims to knowledge and to truth. The process philosophy is not a universal model. It argues for a limited place for signs within wider debates, rather than for a central function within an all-encompassing system or metaphysics. This is a break with the philosophies of Whitehead and Deleuze. I felt this was necessary because the extension of the sign into all fields seemed hubristic, foolish even, when so many sciences relied on different accounts of the sign, or on no signs at all.

This does not mean that the process philosophy is devoid of all bold claims, despite its relative methodological modesty. In chapters on Wittgenstein and Barthes, I have argued for the life of signs independent from human forms of life and meaning, against Wittgenstein's dictum that the sign is dead until it is in human use. Against Saussure, Jakobson and Hjelmslev, I have also argued for the independence of the sign as process from prior structures. The plural process sign is a condition for the emergence of relative structures, rather than the opposite.

Finally, I have argued that the sign is essentially political. Every sign is a political event, whether it is the appearance of a new code word in the workplace ('a *learning* organisation'), the disappearance of another species ('the golden frog on the way to extinction'), or crosses at our borders or on our doors. We have many intellectual resources for understanding the events associated with these signs; some will deny they are events by defining them as facts, others will claim to have the last word on them. The point of the process philosophy of signs is to define the sign as process in order to make space for critical resistance, constructive debate and creative innovation – thanks to signs.

Notes

CHAPTER 2

1. Ludwig Wittgenstein, *Philosophical Investigations*, trans. G. E. M. Anscombe, Oxford: Basil Blackwell, 1953, p. 128.

2. The process philosophy set out here does not draw a distinction between linguistic signs and other signs such as pictures. Sabine Plaud argues that, even if we accept the distinction between linguistic signs and pictures, there is a parallel between them where life and death in relation to natural use is concerned: 'We may thus briefly summarize the parallelism Wittgenstein suggests between words and pictures. In both cases, pictures and words cannot live in isolation, but need to be integrated in a natural environment.' Sabine Plaud, 'Life and Death of Signs and Pictures: Wittgenstein on Living Pictures and Forms of Life', in From the ALWS archives: A selection of papers from the International Wittgenstein Symposia in Kirchberg am Wechsel, available at <http://wab.uib.no/agora-alws/> (accessed 6 August 2015).

3. Note that my discussion of signs in Wittgenstein is concerned with his later work. For a discussion of the earlier work on signs and work on the distinction between signs and symbols in the *Tractatus* see Eli Friedlander, *Signs of Sense: Reading Wittgenstein's Tractatus*, Cambridge, MA: Harvard University Press, 2001, pp. 71–6.

4. To read Wittgenstein against the grain: 'The book is full of life – not like a man, but like an ant-heap.' Ludwig Wittgenstein, *Culture and Value*, trans. Peter Winch, Oxford: Blackwell, 1984, p. 62e.

5. I am concerned with the life and death of signs in relation to use, rather than the different claim, criticised by Cora Diamond as a mistaken interpretation of Wittgenstein by Dummett, that 'meaning is nothing but "use"'. Cora Diamond, 'The Face of Necessity', in *The Realistic Spirit: Wittgenstein, Philosophy and the Mind*, Cambridge, MA: MIT, 1991, pp. 243–66, esp. 243.

6. Ludwig Wittgenstein, *The Blue and Brown Books: Preliminary Studies for the Philosophical Investigations*, Oxford: Basil Blackwell, 1993, p. 4.

7. For a discussion of signs and use in response to the idea that signs are dependent on individual thoughts and minds, see David Stern, *Wittgenstein on Mind and Language*, Oxford: Oxford University Press, 1995, p. 109: '[Wittgenstein] argues that the meaning of two sentences differs because we give different explanations of their meanings, and that fact has to be understood in the context of the overall system of signs, not the speaker's or hearer's thoughts.' My argument is that this point can be conceded without having to concede that signs are only meaningful through use and its context.

8. For a very helpful presentation of some of the differences between Deleuze and the early and later Wittgenstein in the context of a study of intensive differences, see A. W. Moore, *The Evolution of Modern Metaphysics: Making Sense of Things*, Cambridge: Cambridge University Press, 2015. Moore develops a sympathetic interpretation of intensity in Deleuze and then shows how this leads into an understanding of sense very different from Wittgenstein's in the *Tractatus* (pp. 557–67). He also argues that the problem of anthropomorphism is the key to the difference between Deleuze and the later Wittgenstein. While I agree with both these remarks, the process philosophy of signs attempts to take inspiration from Deleuze in order to avoid the restricted meaning of sense from Wittgenstein and the appeal to some kind of fundamental role for humans in setting value around sense and signs.

9. Though Wittgenstein was critical of religion he was also interested in religion and religiosity. Given this and Wittgenstein's Jewish background in Vienna and family ties to Prague, the references to Genesis and the Kabbalah make sense. There are also interesting notes on the Word and God where Wittgenstein discusses Kierkegaard in the remarks collected in *Culture and Value*: 'The Spirit puts what is essential, essential for your life, into these words' (p. 32e).

10. For a helpful discussion of Wittgenstein and Hebraic thought, including Wittgenstein's Jewish background, see Tim Labron, *Wittgenstein's Religious Point of View*, London: Continuum, 2006, pp. 99ff.

11. Genesis 2:7 (KJV).

12. Elberfelder Bibel rev 26, Genesis 2:7.

13. There is an interesting reading of the remarks on the life of signs and Aquinas by John Haldane that points to the possibility of a wider interpretation connecting to religious sources and ideas: 'What of the claim implicit in Wittgenstein's questions about the life of signs. For one thing, I think we need to be more cautious in glossing Wittgenstein's text ... That leaves space, however, for acceptance of a subtler interpretation of Aristotle's dictum that spoken words are signs of passions

in the soul. I have suggested that such an interpretation is to be found in Aquinas's reflection on the *verbum* in the *Summa* and elsewhere.' John Haldane, 'The Life of Signs', *Review of Metaphysics*, 47:3, 1994, pp. 456–70, p. 470.

14. 'You cannot draw the seed up out of the earth. All you can do is give it warmth and moisture and light; then it must grow. (You must not even *touch* it unless you use care.)' Wittgenstein, *Culture and Value*, p. 42e.

15. See Paul Patton, 'Sovereignty, Law and Difference in Australia: After the Mabo Case', *Alternatives: Global, Local, Political*, 21:2, April-June 1996, pp. 149–70.

16. Bruce Chatwin, *Utz*, London: Jonathan Cape, 1988, p. 42.

17. This passage and Wittgenstein's debt to Frege around language and numbers is discussed by Erich Reck in 'Wittgenstein's Great Debt to Frege', in Erich Reck (ed.), *From Frege to Wittgenstein: Perspectives on Early Analytic Philosophy*, Oxford: Oxford University Press, 2002, pp. 23–5.

18. Wittgenstein, *The Blue and Brown Books*, p. 6.

19. Jim Hopkins discusses the question of code, signs and content independent of use in his helpful and comprehensive discussion of Wittgenstein and the life of signs. See Jim Hopkins, 'Wittgenstein and the Life of Signs', in Max Kölbel and Bernhard Weiss (eds), *Wittgenstein's Lasting Significance*, London: Routledge, 2004, pp. 110–47, esp. 143.

20. Wittgenstein, *The Blue and Brown Books*, pp. 16–17.

21. To set my objection to the cut between sign and use in a different context, it is possible to understand it as an objection to this remark on meaning and use by Marie McGinn: 'For now we see that the same picture might come before our minds and the application still be different: the picture doesn't, after all, *force* a particular use on us.' I agree with McGinn that a variety of uses can follow a sign. I also agree that no 'particular' use is forced upon us. However, this does not entail that no range of uses is forced upon us or that the sign does not have a meaningful force prior to use. The sign is a multiplicity of forces which bridge between a living state, prior to use, and any subsequent use. See Marie McGinn, *Wittgenstein and the Philosophical Investigations*, London: Routledge, 1997, p. 85.

22. Wittgenstein, *Philosophical Investigations*, 208e. ' "Substratum" here does not refer to something corresponding to the experience, or to a causal dependency, but to a conceptual one. This mastery of a technique (or of a practice) is what knowing the meaning of words consists in.' Gilead Bar-Elli, 'Wittgenstein on the Experience of Meaning and

the Meaning of Music', *Philosophical Investigations*, 29:3, July 2006, pp. 217–49, esp. 237. Bar-Elli's rich and insightful article also insists on the process of meaning in Wittgenstein, as a process opposed to any idea of psychological process: 'However, Wittgenstein was also interested in what he called "the process of meaning," which should be distinguished from the (psychological) process accompanying an act of meaning' (226). This process is an expressive side to words and sentences which cannot be separated from them but adds 'the "soul" of a word and the way it "feels" to us' (227). Again, this is not process in the sense that I am using it, since for Bar-Elli process is an inseparable part of the word, whereas my claim is that process is the sign. This refusal to situate process in one expressive aspect of language connects the difference with Wittgenstein with the contrast I wish to draw between a thoroughgoing philosophy of process and the more limited role of expression in structuralism and the use of speech in Saussure and Hjelmslev.

23. With a more positive slant on the possibility of reconciling Deleuze and Wittgenstein thanks to a development through Stanley Cavell, D. N. Rodowick offers a counter to the more critical approach to Wittgenstein given here. Significantly, Rodowick ascribes a positive creative and critical role to signs and in particular to the signs of art as interpreted alongside an ethical enquiry. He uses the following expression, inspired by Cavell, to capture the power of signs: 'Sign of possibility and a world to think are apt characterizations, as good as any, for whatever happiness philosophy can bring to human existence.' D. N. Rodowick, *Philosophy's Artful Conversation*, Cambridge, MA: Harvard University Press, 2015, p. 294.

24. In continuation of the preceding note on Rodowick, to defend this sceptical role of philosophy with respect to its own metaphysical overreach and attraction to unanswerable questions, Cavell describes Wittgenstein's later philosophy as an attempt to avoid philosophy's attraction to domains beyond human forms of life: 'For Wittgenstein, philosophy comes to grief not in denying what we all know to be true, but in its effort to escape those human forms of life which alone provide the coherence of our expression.' Stanley Cavell, *Must We Mean What We Say*, Cambridge: Cambridge University Press, 1976, p. 61. My worry is that the definition of these forms of life and their relation to signs is a mistaken imposition of a model of what a form of life and a sign can be. This imposition, then leads to a limited conception of coherence that becomes a bane when we come to depend on signs as critical tools.

CHAPTER 3

1. Jakob von Uexküll, *A Foray into the Worlds of Animals and Humans*. With *A Theory of Meaning*, Minneapolis: University of Minnesota Press, 2010, Kindle edition. References are to the Kindle location numbers, here 1283–4.
2. Ibid., 492/2765.
3. Ibid., 556/2765
4. Ibid., 486–90.
5. 'The synthetic unity of consciousness is therefore an objective condition of all knowledge', Immanuel Kant, *Critique of Pure Reason*, trans. Norman Kemp Smith, Basingstoke: Macmillan, 1985, p. 156.
6. Uexküll, *A Foray into the Worlds of Animals and Humans*, 1379.
7. Ibid., 1379.
8. Ibid., 1344–8.
9. Ibid., 1262–4.
10. Ibid., 1445.
11. Ibid., 699.
12. Ibid., 938–9.
13. Ibid., 1313–14.
14. Ibid., 1533–9.
15. Ibid., 1533–9.
16. Elizabeth Grosz, *Chaos, Territory, Art: Deleuze and the Framing of the Earth*, New York: Columbia University Press, 2008, p. 42.
17. See Gilles Deleuze and Félix Guattari, *A Thousand Plateaus*, trans. Brian Massumi, Minneapolis: University of Minnesota Press, 1987, p. 51.
18. Heidegger's most extensive engagement with Uexküll is in *The Fundamental Concept of Metaphysics*, where Heidegger is concerned to defend his statement that the animal is poor in world against the objection based on Uexküll's work that animals have a world as shown by the concept of the animal's environment: 'Indeed, at first sight, our thesis seems to run directly counter to the most penetrating fundamental reflections in biology and zoology, when we consider that ever since J. von Uexküll we have all become accustomed to talking about the *environmental world of the animal*.' Martin Heidegger, *The Fundamental Concepts of Metaphysics: World, Finitude, Solitude*, trans. William McNeill and Nicholas Walker, Bloomington: Indiana University Press, 1995, p. 192.

19. Jeff Malpas, 'Heidegger, Space and World', in Julian Kiverstein and Michael Wheeler (eds), *Heidegger and Cognitive Science*, Basingstoke: Palgrave Macmillan, 2012, pp. 309–42, esp. 325. See also Jeff Malpas, *Heidegger and the Thinking of Space: Explorations in the Topology of Being*, Cambridge, MA: MIT, 2012, pp. 126–8.

20. Malpas, 'Heidegger, Space and World', p. 326.

21. Heidegger develops this point over a full section of *The Fundamental Concepts of Metaphysics* around Uexküll and Hans Driech. Heidegger's main point is that the difference between human and animal is not qualitative or quantitative, in the sense that we could say that the human relation to environment is deeper or richer, for instance. It is rather a matter of being. Animals are tied to their environments in ways that humans are not, so for humans there is a world that they form, whereas for animals there is an environment they are essentially adapted to, rather than adapt to: 'The organism is not something independent in its own right which then adapts itself.' *The Fundamental Concepts of Metaphysics*, p. 264.

22. *A Foray into the Worlds of Animals and Humans*, 1999. Elizabeth Grosz has drawn the connection between Uexküll, Ruyer, Simondon, Deleuze and Guattari and music in 'Deleuze, Ruyer and Becoming Brain: The Music of Life's Temporality, *Parrhesia*, 15, 2012, pp. 1–13.

23. Uexküll, *A Foray into the Worlds of Animals and Humans*, 1995.

24. For a detailed and insightful discussion of the ethical and political positions directly drawn from biology by Uexküll, including his religious views, anti-Semitism and relations to the National Socialist Party in Germany in the 1930s, see Anne Harrington, *Reenchanted Science: Holism in German Culture From Wilhelm II to Hitler*, Princeton: Princeton University Press, 1996, pp. 34–71.

25. Anne Sauvagnargues, 'L'averse de sable, l'atome et l'embryon', *Critique*, 804, 2014, p. 413.

26. Ibid., p. 413.

27. Ronald Bogue, 'Raymond Ruyer', in Graham Jones and Jon Roffe (eds), *Deleuze's Philosophical Lineage*, Edinburgh: Edinburgh University Press, 2009, pp. 300–20, esp. 308.

28. Sauvagnargues, 'L'averse de sable, l'atome et l'embryon', p. 413.

29. Ibid., p. 413.

30. Uexküll, *A Foray into the Worlds of Animals and Humans*, 1898.

31. Ibid., 1898–9.

32. Ibid., 1269–71.

CHAPTER 4

1. I will be reading this article by Bapteste and Dupré closely because of its careful definition of the idea of process in biology. This work is part of a much larger and ongoing project around John Dupré's Centre for Genomics in Society at the University of Exeter. Other arguments for the importance of process in biology can be found in his recent article on animalism, the persistence of identity and process, 'Animalism and the Persistence of Human Organism', *The Southern Journal of Philosophy*, 52, Spindel Supplement 2014, pp. 6–23, and the earlier collection *Processes of Life*, for instance in his work with Maureen A. O'Malley criticising the role of hierarchies of entities in contemporary biology: 'Our view is that these problems reflect a more fundamental difficulty, that life is in fact a hierarchy of processes (e.g. metabolic, developmental, ecological, evolutionary) and that any abstraction of fixed entities must do some violence to this dynamic reality.' John Dupré and Maureen A. O'Malley, 'Metagenomics and Biological Ontology', in *Processes of Life: Essays in the Philosophy of Biology*, Oxford: Oxford University Press, 2012, pp. 188–205, pp. 188–9. The process definition of the sign shares the concern with dynamism and the critical stance with respect to the abstraction of entities from process. However, it does not seek to ground this idea of process on the sciences or an ontology drawn from them.

2. This critique of substance ontology and of Aristotelianism is where Dupré's work joins classical process philosophy, and the following statement from Whitehead could be endorsed equally well by Dupré: 'Aristotle introduced the static fallacy by another concept which has infected all subsequent philosophy. He conceived of primary substances as the static foundation which received the impress of qualification.' A. N. Whitehead, *Adventures of Ideas*, Harmondsworth: Penguin, 1948.

3. Eric Bapteste and John Dupré, 'Towards a Processual Microbial Ontology', *Biology and Philosophy*, 28, 2013, pp. 379–404, esp. 379.

4. Ibid., p. 380.

5. Ibid., p. 380.

6. Ibid., p. 380.

7. A. N. Whitehead, *Science and the Modern World*, Harmondsworth: Penguin, 1938, p. 68.

8. Ibid., p. 69.

9. Bapteste and Dupré, 'Towards a Processual Microbial Ontology', p. 385.

10. Ibid., p. 380.
11. Dupré's definition of life as process has become more radical over time as a shift away from organisms. In *Processes of Life*, he sometimes defines process around the idea of a life cycle: 'This organism is a process – a life cycle – rather than a thing; it may be a community of distinct kinds of organisms rather than a monogenomic individual; and it must be understood as conceptually and of course causally linked to its particular environment, or niche, which both contributes to the construction of the organism in development, and is constructed by the organism through its behaviour' (p. 99). This is a greater restriction on the extent and multiple nature of processes than in the work with Bapteste because in their definitions the organism disappears as the principle of unity of processes, as seen in the earlier use of the idea of a 'community of organisms'. Those organisms are themselves communities of processes.
12. Bapteste and Dupré, 'Towards a Processual Microbial Ontology', p. 383.
13. Ibid., p. 384.
14. The concept of stabilisation is not only important at the microbial level for Dupré. He sees it as essential for understanding process for all organisms. See his 'Animalism and the Persistence of Human Organism', p. 16.
15. Bapteste and Dupré, 'Towards a Processual Microbial Ontology', p. 381.
16. Dupré, *Processes of Life*, p. 23.
17. Ibid., p. 29.
18. Ibid., p. 37.
19. Dupré, 'Animalism and the Persistence of Human Organism', p. 8.
20. Ibid., p. 12.
21. Bapteste and Dupré, 'Towards a Processual Microbial Ontology', p. 381.

CHAPTER 6

1. Roland Barthes, *Elements of Semiology*, trans. Annette Lavers and Colin Smith, New York: Hill and Wang, 1986. Roland Barthes, 'Éléments de sémiologie', *Communications*, 4:4, 1964, pp. 91–135 (all translations are mine).
2. I have chosen *Elements of Semiology* as a short-cut and guide through the different positions in the structuralist accounts of the sign. My view of Barthes is in fact that he is much closer to an intensive definition of

the sign than a purely structuralist one. His work combined a surface of structures with its disintegration in the intensive matter of individual signs. Here is his diversion of the structuralist slash between signifier and signified into a complex multiplicity of interactions between S and Z in his reading of Balzac's *Sarrasine*: 'Hence the slash (/) confronting the S of SarraSine and the Z of Zambinella has a panic function: it is the slash of censure, the surface of the mirror, the wall of hallucination, the verge of antithesis, the abstraction of limit, the obliquity of the signifier, the index of the paradigm, hence of meaning.' Roland Barthes, *S/Z*, trans. Richard Miller, Oxford: Blackwell, 1990, pp. 106–7. The intensive panic function sets each of the relations between S and Z into dynamic movement: slashing, hallucinating, rendering oblique, shimmering on the surface, anything but a direct relation of signifier to signified.

3. See for instance Barthes' melancholy yet also gorgeous meditation on the uncertainty of signs in *A Lover's Discourse: Fragments*, trans. Richard, Howard, London: Vintage, 2002, pp. 214–15.

4. This co-dependency of language and speech is not symmetrical, however, and Saussure defines speech as the lesser term as individual (as opposed to social), ancillary and accidental: 'By distinguishing between the language itself and speech, we distinguish at the same time: (1) what is social from what is individual and (2) what is essential from what is ancillary and more or less accidental.' Ferdinand de Saussure, *Course in General Linguistics*, trans. Roy Harris, London: Bloomsbury, 2013, p. 16. This privileging of language over speech by Saussure was one of the topics of Jacques Derrida's early deconstructions where Derrida shows the contradiction in Saussure's use of the idea of the 'natural' in relation to speech as audible and to language as visible: 'It imprudently makes of visibility the tangible, simple and essential element of writing. Above all, in considering the audible as the *natural* milieu within which language must *naturally* fragment and articulate its instituted signs, thus exercising its arbitrariness, this explanation excludes all possibility of some natural relationship between speech and writing at the very moment that it affirms it.' Jacques Derrida, *Of Grammatology*, trans. Gayatri Chakravorty Spivak, Baltimore: Johns Hopkins University Press, 1976, p. 43. The precise connections and differences between deconstruction and the process philosophy of signs will have to wait until a later work. The seeds of this current research were no doubt sewn some time ago when I was writing an earlier book on post-structuralism with a chapter on *Of Grammatology*. See James Williams, *Understanding Poststructuralism*, Chesham: Acumen, 2005.

5. This is a simplification of Hjelmslev's account of the structure of language with an added complication around the translation of technical terms like form, substance and purport, and their relation to expression and content on the one hand, and rules such as commutation and substitution on the other: 'A similar universal applicability to sign systems ... as a whole is found in the study of functions and their analysis, of signs, of expression and content, form, substance and purport, of commutation and substitution, variants and invariants and the classification of variants.' Louis Hjelmslev, *Prolegomena to a Theory of Language*, trans. Francis J. Whitefield, Madison: University of Wisconsin Press, 1961, pp. 102–3.

6. 'At each stage of the analysis we must be able to infer from variants to invariants with the help of a specially prepared method that establishes the necessary criteria for such a reduction.' Ibid., p. 62.

7. Barthes had a longstanding interest in semiological and structuralist studies of fashion; see Roland Barthes, *The Language of Fashion*, ed. Andy Stafford and Michael Carter, London: Bloomsbury, 2013, and Roland Barthes, *The Fashion System*, trans. Matthew Ward and Richard Howard, London: Jonathan Cape, 1985.

8. The priority to be given to process and variation over structure runs counter to the opposite structuralist method of reducing variety in speech, for example where Hjelmslev seeks to 'exhaust' variation through analysis: 'The peculiar fact is that the division into varieties and the division into variations are exhausted by turns.' Louis Hjelmslev, *Language: An Introduction*, trans. Francis J. Whitfield, Madison: University of Wisconsin Press, 1970, p. 113. The point of the idea of a multiplicity of intensive relations as described by a diagram for a process sign is partly to define variation in the sign as resistant to such methods of reduction and exhaustion. Roman Jakobson lauds a similar linguistic invariance in his work on universals in language: 'Our century has witnessed the gradual stages of a spectacular rapprochement between linguistic and mathematical thought. The gratifying concept of invariance, which in synchronic linguistics had first been applied to intralingual comparison of variable contexts, was finally expanded to interlingual comparison.' Roman Jakobson, 'Implications of Language Universals for Linguistics', in *On Language*, ed. Linda R. Waugh and Monique Monville-Burston, Cambridge, MA: Harvard University Press, 1990, pp. 152–63, esp. 153.

9. The subservience of change to structure is summed up in the following statement by Jakobson which could stand as a credo for the structuralist reduction of difference to structural difference: 'Changes must be

examined from the standpoint of the linguistic system which undergoes these changes: this means, in short, that they are subject to structural analysis.' Jakobson, 'Current Issues of General Linguistics', in
On Language, pp. 49–55, esp. 54.

10. 'The fashion press was looking for the "new punk" in October 1993,
    wrote Marion Hume in her review of his second show, the hottest in
    London Fashion Week. But they didn't find it in the clubs of Soho
    or Kings Cross, but on McQueen's runway.' Judith Watt, *Alexander
    McQueen: Fashion Visionary*, London: Goodman, 2012, p. 61.

11. 'With the pressure for expansion on, for the next two seasons McQueen
    produced collections by the Gucci Group that were commercially
    driven to the detriment of his scene setting and the feats of craftsman-
    ship now expected of him.' Ibid., p. 223.

12. I haven't drawn a connection between structuralist and formalist lin-
    guistics and Deleuze's work here because of my close focus on signs.
    It is however a very fruitful area of study as shown by Helen Palmer's
    recent work on Deleuze and Jakobson, among others, see her *Deleuze
    and Futurism*, London: Bloomsbury, 2014.

13. Readers will note that I have not discussed Charles Sanders Peirce in
    this book. This omission might be seen as a glaring one where I raise
    the question of pragmatism and the sign. The absence of Peirce is in
    part due to my related work on Barthes, Deleuze and Peirce on the
    sign which I do not want to repeat here; see my 'Barthes, Deleuze,
    and Peirce: Pragmatism in Pursuit of the Sign', in Sean Bowden,
    Simone Bignall and Paul Patton (eds), *Deleuze and Pragmatism*,
    London: Routledge, 2015, pp. 38–54. In order to further mitigate
    this lack, I will restate my critical approach to Peirce here. My
    objection to Peirce's definition of the sign, as given in 'What is a
    Sign?' and many other texts, is that signs are divided according to
    triads, not only with reason and truth at the top but with all other
    aspects of the sign directed towards the aims of reason and truth.
    This means that there is a categorical structure and value system for
    the sign rising from likenesses, to indications and then to symbols.
    In that sense, signs are tethered to particular sensations, functions
    and modes of thought. So Peirce's pragmatism (or pragmaticism) is
    restricted where signs are concerned; for example, by the function
    of indication or by their roles in particular kinds of sensation. So,
    though Peirce has a sense of process in his account of the sign, this
    process is secondary to other considerations: the demands of reason,
    the types of sensation and the kinds of indication. His great merit
    is to see these as changing, which therefore introduces process into

the sign, but the process comes from a relation to things outside the sign: it is generated by the use of reason, as shown for instance in this passage from his 'What is a Sign?': 'It [the modified symbol] is not a dead thing, but carries the mind from one point to another. The art of reasoning is the art of marshalling such signs, and of finding out the truth' ('What is a Sign?', in *The Essential Peirce: Selected Philosophical Writings, Volume 2*, Bloomington: Indiana University Press, pp. 4–10, p. 10). A lot turns on the meaning of 'carry' in this passage. If the sign carries the mind in the sense of drawing it in a multiplicity of directions that reasoning must then impose order upon, according to my use of stipulation over the sign, then Peirce's definition of the sign comes closer to the pure process definition I have given. However, I think another sense is more plausible and this is that signs change in use by reason, as shown in another passage from 'What is a Sign?': 'In use and in experience its meaning grows' (ibid.). This skews process in the sign towards human use, meaning and experience, whereas my speculative claim – where the meaning of speculative takes the approach away from Peirce's pragmatism – is that it is the other way round: process in the sign draws meaning away from restricted human uses and towards a multiplicity of becoming. Despite his attentiveness to sensation in the sign, Peirce's pragmatism maintains an intellectual frame and human function for the sign. It serves more than calls.

14. Barthes, 'Éléments de sémiologie', p. 101.

15. Barthes is giving a formal account of Saussure's analogy on articulation, developing it, while moving from Saussure's ideas of thought and sound to later structuralist developments on language and speech, in order to produce a unified structuralist theory across a number of its main thinkers and concepts: 'A language might also be compared to a sheet of paper. Thought is one side of the paper and sound the reverse side. Just as it is impossible to take a pair of scissors and cut one side of the paper without at the same time cutting the other, so it is impossible in a language to isolate sound from thought, or thought from sound.' Saussure, *Course in General Linguistics*, p. 132.

16. Ibid., p. 78.

17. Ibid., p. 78.

18. Derrida makes this argument by introducing the idea of a trace which crosses between signal and thought, or signifier and signified, as a necessary condition for their practical connection that is hidden in their abstract arbitrary relation. The other must appear as other in what it is not, or the arbitrary relation must nonetheless allow for

a connection between the two sides of the arbitrary relation: 'These oppositions [between nature and convention, symbol and sign] have meaning only after the possibility of the trace. The "unmotivatedness" of the sign requires a synthesis in which the completely other is announced as such – without any simplicity, any identity, any resemblance or continuity – within what is not it.' Derrida, *Of Grammatology*, p. 47.

19. 'That the sign is a sign for something means that the content-form of the sign can subsume that something as concept-substance.' Hjelmslev, *Prolegomena to a Theory of Language*, p. 57.

20. The search for objectivity and status as science is all important for structuralist philosophies of language and the sign, see, for example, Hjelmslev's claim for objectivity at the start of *Language: An Introduction*: 'Our presentation is *not subjective*' (p. 6). Or see Jakobson's praise for linguistics as a paradigm of scientific precision in the social sciences: 'linguistics is recognized both by anthropologists and psychologists as the most progressive and precise among the sciences of man and, hence, as the methodological model for the remainder of those disciplines.' Jakobson, 'Linguistics in Relation to Other Sciences', in *On Language*, pp. 451–88, esp. 453. First presented in 1967, the dated quality of the claims for the dominance of linguistics in psychology made in the essay show one of the problems of the structuralist approach to the sign in its desire for a place among the sciences. The rapid changes in the status and theoretical frames of those sciences introduce ageing and redundancy into linguistic sciences belying their objective and universal claims. The more modest speculative approach seeks to avoid that kind of redundancy by scaling back the weight of those claims to alarm and potential critique rather than objective certainty. The sign becomes an opportunity for a critical and creative pause rather than a fundamental element in a universal science.

21. Barthes, 'Éléments de sémiologie', p. 110.

22. Barthes' emphasis on signification as individual process is noted positively by Derrida for its reversal of the Saussurian order from language to sign: 'The Barthesian reversal is fecund and indispensable for the description of *the fact and vocation of signification* within the closure of this epoch and this civilization [of phonetic writing] that is in process of disappearance in its very globalisation.' Derrida, *Of Grammatology*, p. 52. This process philosophy of signs seeks to replicate the reversal by defining the sign independently of any linguistic structures and by focusing on signs as individual selections and diagrams rather

than as belonging to classes of signs. The genesis of the individual sign comes first.

23. Barthes, 'Éléments de sémiologie', p. 110.

24. There is conceptual depth in the signified below the mere sound of the signifier in an act of signification. See Saussure, *Course in General Linguistics*, pp. 76–7.

25. Barthes, 'Éléments de sémiologie', p. 110.

26. 'Thus we see that there can be languages of different degrees: first-degree languages, and second-degree languages, or metalanguages. Theoretically, of course, we can continue the progression: a language that describes a metalanguage will be a third-degree language, or a second-degree metalanguage (also called a meta-metalanguage).' Hjelmslev, *Language: An Introduction*, p. 132.

27. 'We may take it as given that every language has two, and only two, planes: the content plane and the expression plane.' Ibid., p. 106.

28. Though from a paper that was published later than Barthes' work in *Elements of Semiology*, one of the clearest statements by Lacan on the signifier, signified and bar of signification can be found in the 'Agency of the Letter in the Unconscious'. Lacan's presentation of a series of algorithms for signification is considerably more complex than the version given by Barthes: 'Secondly, $f(S'/S)S \cong S(+)s$ the metaphoric structure indicating that it is in the substitution of signifier for signifier that an effect of signification is produced that is creative or poetic, in other words, which is the advent of the signification in question.' Jacques Lacan, 'Agency of the Letter in the Unconscious', in *Écrits: A Selection*, trans. Alan Sheridan, London: Routledge, 1989, pp. 161–97, p. 181. The important thing to retain from this is the poetic production of signification in a metaphoric structure such that signification is both process and creative production rather than simply an arbitrary connection of signifier and signified.

29. Given the extent and complexity of Lacan's work, this very brief discussion can only be a preliminary step in the study of process signs and his work on language. Furthermore, it relies on work by Barthes which passes through the intermediary of Jean Laplanche and Serge Leclaire's quite brief references to Lacan's work in *La psychoanalyse*, IV and V, 1958 and 1959. Laplanche and Leclaire confirm the essentials of Barthes' short interpretation, in particular around the metaphorical nature of signification and its passage through a restricted number of signifiers: 'But we also see, and this is what interests us, that something has fallen below, has been "simplified out" in the algebraic sense

of that term – the original signifier. It is to the extent that the fate of this signifier "S" is distinct from a pure and simple suppression that metaphors offer poetical resources creative of meaning as opposed to mere "nominal definitions".' Jean Laplanche and Serge Leclaire, 'The Unconscious: a Psychoanalytic Study', trans. Patrick Coleman, *Yale French Studies*, 48, 1972, pp. 118–75, esp. 156.

30. Barthes, 'Éléments de sémiologie', p. 114.

31. Roy Harris takes the arbitrariness of the relation between signifier and signified, as given through the sense of floating, as the condition for linguistic change in Saussure. To connect back to the discussion of signs and use from Chapter 2, Harris argues that Wittgenstein's philosophy lacks this connection: 'All that need be pointed out for the moment is the connection between arbitrariness and linguistic change, which Saussure sees but Wittgenstein ignores.' Roy Harris, *Language, Saussure and Wittgenstein: How to Play Games with Words*, London: Routledge, 1998, p. 52.

32. Gilles Deleuze, 'How do we Recognise Structuralism?', in *Desert Islands and Other Texts, 1953–1974*, ed. David Lapoujade, trans. Michael Taormina, Cambridge, MA: MIT, 2004, pp. 170–92.

CHAPTER 7

1. For an outstanding reading of Deleuze's *Proust and Signs*, see Jean-Jacques Lecercle, *Badiou and Deleuze Read Literature*, Edinburgh: Edinburgh University Press, 2010. I was strongly influenced by Lecercle's situation of Deleuze's account of the sign against Saussure's structuralist definition at the outset of this project: 'But the concept of sign escapes this general demotion [of the centrality of language]: the Saussurian sign, that is the linguistic sign, is dissolved but other signs increase and multiply' (p. 75).

2. Gilles Deleuze, *Proust et les signes*, Paris: PUF, 1993, p. 11 (all translations mine). Gilles Deleuze, *Proust and Signs*, trans. Richard Howard, London: Athlone, 2000.

3. Following Deleuze, Miguel de Beistegui argues that this commitment to learning makes *In Search of Lost Time* a Bildungsroman, rather than a work of recognition. See Miguel de Beistegui, *Proust as Philosopher*, trans. Dorothée Bonigal Katz, London: Routledge, 2013, p. 94.

4. Deleuze, *Proust et les signes*, p. 11

5. Ibid., p. 24.

6. For a succinct and very clear account of the connections and differences between signs for difference encounters, see Ronald Bogue, 'Deleuze and Literature', in *The Cambridge Companion to Deleuze*, ed. Daniel W. Smith and Henry Somers-Hall, Cambridge: Cambridge University Press, 2012, pp. 286–306, pp. 290–1.

7. I agree with Eleanor Kaufman when she notes the importance of an abstraction and structural repetition which allow Deleuze to extend and complete Lévi-Strauss's structuralism: 'Deleuze's study of Proust therefore stages in more than one fashion the triumph of form and abstraction, presented in what follows as the perception of the law of the series above and beyond the amorous self.' Eleanor Kaufman, *Deleuze, The Dark Precursor: Dialectic, Structure, Being*, Baltimore: The Johns Hopkins University Press, 2012, p. 107. However, despite the recognition of a two-way exchange from concrete signs to abstract series, I am critical of the way in which this leads to the dominance of typology through abstraction in Deleuze's philosophy of the sign.

8. My argument has been based on the early edition of Deleuze's *Proust and Signs*. Though written later, the other editions confirm his focus on the classification and division of signs into types according to apprenticeship. See Patrick M. Bray's detailed and very helpful reading of the book and its different parts: 'Six years after the first edition of *Proust and Signs*, Deleuze added a new section entitled The Literary Machine. This new section clarifies the arguments of the first edition, such as distinguishing Proust from Plato, and explores in depth the production of signs in the novel. While the first edition catalogued the types of signs and their relationship to essences and time, Deleuze's addition argues for the diversity of signs themselves, their proliferation, and disruptive function.' Patrick M. Bray, 'Deleuze's Proust and Signs: The Literary Partial Object', in *Understanding Deleuze, Understanding Modernism*, ed. Paul Ardoin, S. E. Gontarski, and Laci Mattison, New York: Bloomsbury, 2014, pp. 11–20, esp. 15.

9. This discussion of chess connects to Saussure's analysis in *Course in General Linguistics*. Saussure's analogy is supposed to demonstrate the priority of synchronic structure (language) over players' past moves (changes in speech) because we can analyse the situation in any game without having to make any reference at all to past moves or intentions: 'In order to describe the position on the board, it is quite useless to refer to what happened ten seconds ago. All this applies equally to a language, and confirms the radical distinction between diachronic and

synchronic' *Course in General Linguistics*, p. 103. From the process view this is mistaken because it abstracts from the intensive aspects of the game, such as time pressures, and because it assumes we can abstract structure from its underlying condition in multiple intensive processes in the sign.

10. Gilles Deleuze, *Logique du sens*, Paris: Minuit, 1969, p. 92 (all translations mine). Gilles Deleuze, *The Logic of Sense*, trans. Mark Lester and Charles Stivale, New York: Columbia, 1990.

11. Miguel de Beistegui gives a deep account of genesis through intensity in relation to extensity: 'Intensity is thus inseparable from extensity ... they are two sides of the real, the complete picture of the movement of being as genesis.' See Miguel de Beistegui, *Truth and Genesis*, Bloomington: Indiana University Press, p. 310. Beistegui takes this research further in *Immanence: Deleuze and Philosophy* with a connection to some ideas developed here in relation to the event as neither stable nor unstable. In my view, his reading underplays the role of process in Deleuze, so where Beistegui uses the term metastable for the event I would rather refer to processes of stabilisation and destabilisation. See Miguel de Beistegui, *Immanence: Deleuze and Philosophy*, Edinburgh: Edinburgh University Press, 2010, p. 96. As a counter to this materialist approach to intensity, see Daniel Smith's study of the sign, sensibility and intensity in a transcendental post-Kantian vein: '[Intensive forces] can only be sensed from the point of view of the transcendental sensibility that apprehends it immediately in the encounter as the limit of sensibility itself.' Daniel W. Smith, *Essays on Deleuze*, Edinburgh: Edinburgh University Press, 2012, p. 95.

12. Jeffrey Bell gives a very helpful account of force and paradox, in the Deleuzian sense, in a scientific context. He uses the term 'paradoxa' in a similar way to my use of process sign as a point of instability within a system. See Jeffrey A. Bell, *Philosophy at the Edge of Chaos: Gilles Deleuze and the Philosophy of Difference*, Toronto: University of Toronto Press, 2006, pp. 203–4.

13. Deleuze, *Logique du sens*, p. 92.

14. Tamar Frankel has done enlightening research on the reasons for the recurrence of Ponzi schemes in relation to dishonesty and regulation: 'Here lies our greatest danger. A society that accepts a little dishonesty as a way of life is headed towards deception and abuse of trust on a grand scale.' Tamar Frankel, *The Ponzi Scheme Puzzle: A History and Analysis of Con Artists and Victims*, Oxford: Oxford University Press, 2012, p. 189.

15. For a very good explanation of sensibility as the condition for language and thought see Levi Bryant's *Difference and Givenness: Deleuze's Transcendental Empiricism and the Ontology of Immanence*, Chicago: Northwestern University Press, 2008: '*The Logic of Sense* is concerned with the conditions under which language is possible' (p. 96).

16. Deleuze, *Logique du sens*, 95.

17. See, for instance, Deleuze's discussion of Laurel and Hardy and the Marx brothers in *Cinéma 1: L'image movement*, Paris: Minuit, 1983, pp. 268–9, or his contrast of humour and irony in *Différence et répétition*, Paris: PUF, 1968, pp. 12–20.

18. Deleuze, *Logique du sens*, 95.

19. Sean Bowden has done very helpful work on time and event in Deleuze's *Logic of Sense*; for how this relates to structure see Sean Bowden, *The Priority of Events: Deleuze's Logic of Sense*, Edinburgh: Edinburgh University Press, 2011, pp. 173–80.

20. Anne Sauvagnargues, *Deleuze et l'art*, Paris: Presses Universitaires de France, p. 62.

21. Alfred North Whitehead, *Process and Reality*, ed. David Ray Griffin and Donald W. Sherburne, New York: The Free Press, 1978, p. 3.

22. Isabelle Stengers explains this novel account of continuity by contrasting the continuity of scientific laws and the discontinuity of actual occasions in relation to that continuity. I have preferred to make the contrast between continuity as process and lawful continuity, in order to avoid the idea that process is discontinuous in the sense of validly divisible: 'Whitehead is not claiming thereby that physics is wrong when it explains change in terms of physical entities continuously interacting with each other, and he is not asking us to avoid any interpretation of ourselves as living, intentional continuities. The role of actual occasions entails restraining the authority of explanations that take for granted any continuous endurance.' Isabelle Stengers, 'A Constructivist Reading of *Process and Reality*', in Nicholas Gaskill and A. J. Nocek (eds), *The Lure of Whitehead*, Minneapolis: University of Minnesota Press, 2014, pp. 43–64, esp. 58.

23. Whitehead, *Process and Reality*, p. 129.

24. Ibid., p. 215.

25. Discussions of Whitehead and signs are rare, but there is a deep discussion of signs and wonder by Isabelle Stengers where she seeks to generalise the wonder of expressive signs through Whitehead's actual occasions. See Stengers, 'A Constructivist Reading of *Process and Reality*', pp. 52–8. Stengers describes the role these occasions play

as 'fantastic metaphysical existents' and as 'speculative abstractions' (p. 57). There is a sense in which I want the process sign to draw on this constructivist definition of speculation and the power of its creations in 'the transformation of emphasis that they must be able to produce with regard to the powerful and pragmatically justified abstractions that lure and sometimes dominate our experience' (p. 57). My aim is to define the process sign with a function of alarm and creative alternative to the lure of abstractions defined as stipulations over the sign. I have discussed this kind of wonder as the stage of romance in Whitehead's philosophy of education in 'Whitehead's Curse', in Gaskill and Nocek (eds), *The Lure of Whitehead*, pp. 249–66.

26. Whitehead, *Process and Reality*, p. 88.

27. For a rewarding and original reading of Whitehead's idea of the subject as superject, see Didier Debaise, 'Possessive Subjects: A Speculative Interpretation of Nonhumans', in Gaskill and Nocek (eds), *The Lure of Whitehead*, pp. 299–311, esp. 305–9. Debaise's idea of the speculative and Keith Robinson's work on the creative in Whitehead's account of the event were influential in my work on the idea of a speculative definition of the sign as process. See Keith Robinson, 'The Event and the Occasion: Deleuze, Whitehead and Creativity', in Gaskill and Nocek (eds), *The Lure of Whitehead*, pp. 207–31.

28. Whitehead, *Process and Reality*, p. 3.

29. Ibid., p. 4.

30. Ibid., p. 4.

31. My position on Whitehead is therefore consistent with recent scholarship, for instance in agreeing with Leemon B. McHenry and his powerful study of Whitehead's process philosophy as produced by a revisionary approach to event ontology rather than a descriptive metaphysics: 'an event ontology has advantages over the traditional substance theory in so far as it affords greater empirical adequacy, explanatory power and unification within the context of modern theoretical physics.' Leemon B. McHenry, *The Event Universe: The Revisionary Metaphysics of Alfred North Whitehead*, Edinburgh: Edinburgh University Press, 2015, p. 127. My difference with this research is that I do not think that the speculative philosophy of signs should be revisionary in this way due to the restrictions brought about by the demands for adequacy, explanatory power and unification in relation to modern physics. This restricts the ability of speculative philosophy to develop critical and creative tools through a more open definition of its terms.

CHAPTER 8

1. For a good explanation of this visceral aspect of process philosophy as leading to action, see Brian Massumi's work on affect and event: 'Ultimately, the thinking of speculative pragmatism that is activist philosophy belongs to nature. Its aesthetico-politics compose a nature philosophy.' Brian Massumi, *Semblance and Event: Activist Philosophy and the Occurrent Arts*, Cambridge, MA: MIT, 2011, p. 28. See also John Protevi's important work on political physiology after Deleuze: *Political Affect: Connecting the Social and the Somatic*, Minneapolis: University of Minnesota Press, 2009.
2. Jean-François Lyotard, *Le Différend*, Paris: Minuit, 1983, p. 200 (my translation).

Index